THE SEAL OF THE UNITY OF THE THREE

By the same author:

Great Clarity: Daoism and Alchemy in Early Medieval China (Stanford University Press, 2006)

The Encyclopedia of Taoism, editor (Routledge, 2008)

Awakening to Reality: The "Regulated Verses" of the Wuzhen pian, *a Taoist Classic of Internal Alchemy* (Golden Elixir Press, 2009)

Fabrizio Pregadio

The Seal of the Unity of the Three

A Study and Translation of the *Cantong qi*,
the Source of the Taoist Way of the Golden Elixir

Golden Elixir Press

Golden Elixir Press, Mountain View, CA
www.goldenelixir.com
press@goldenelixir.com

ISBN 978-0-9843082-7-9 (cloth)

ISBN 978-0-9843082-8-6 (paperback)

Typeset in Sabon. Text area proportioned in the Golden Section.

Cover: Liu Haichan, a Taoist Immortal. Painting by Yan Hui, ca. 1300
(detail).

To Yoshiko

Contents

Preface

This book contains a complete translation and a study of the *Zhouyi cantong qi* (The Seal of the Unity of the Three, in Accordance with the *Book of Changes*), the text that most lineages of Taoist alchemy place at the origins of their traditions.

My work on the *Cantong qi* began in the autumn of 1990, when I translated parts of Peng Xiao's text found in the Taoist Canon (*Daozang*). As my work progressed, I became aware of the remarkably large textual tradition of the *Cantong qi*, and began to acquire reproductions of editions found in libraries in China, Japan, and elsewhere. A major turning point occurred in 2001, when I happened to find the apparently single extant exemplar of the earliest edition of Chen Zhixu's commentary, published in 1484 and now preserved at the Shanghai Library. I still remember the smile of the librarian when she realized that I had made a complete photocopy of the text with my own hands, but allowed me to keep it. That exemplar is at the basis of the translation found in the present book.

Eventually, the Shanghai text became one of several editions that I used to compare and collate the text of the *Cantong qi* found in different commentaries: the two extant Tang-dynasty commentaries (both dating from ca. 700) and the commentaries by Peng Xiao (947), Zhu Xi (1197), Yu Yan (1284), and Chen Zhixu (ca. 1330). In addition to revealing a synopsis of the textual history of the *Cantong qi*, the collation clarified several points, two of which are especially important with regard to this translation.

First, the collation showed to me that the "true" form of a work of this nature is not to be found at the purely textual level. Not only is the *Cantong qi*, in the first place, the work of an anonymous "collective entity" (see my Introduction, § 3), and therefore cannot be tied to the intent of an individual author; but to varying extents, the authors of the different commentaries have shaped the text in the variant forms in which we know it today, by introducing new readings, emending errors found in earlier editions, polishing supposed imperfections, establishing sections of different length, moving certain poems from one part of the text to another, normalizing the four- or five- character verses, improving the rhymes, and so forth. Like the major scriptures of all traditions, however, the "original" *Cantong qi* is not found in any of its particular redactions or editions.

Second, having resolved that my work would not be based on a reconstructed text, the collation served to identify the edition that I have used to translate the *Cantong qi*. Whether or not this may also deemed to be true of his commentary, Chen Zhixu's redaction is likely to contain the best version of the *Cantong qi* among those composed before the Ming period (i.e., until the mid-fourteenth century). The two Tang redactions present a fascinating, but "raw" state of the text; Peng Xiao's redaction, despite its renown, is not authentic, having undergone contamination in the early thirteenth century with dozens of readings drawn from Zhu Xi's redaction; Zhu Xi's redaction in its turn introduces many peculiar variants; and Yu Yan's redaction, while being quite elegant and accompanied by a learned commentary, sometimes makes bold choices among different possible readings. Although Chen Zhixu's text presents its own issues (about four dozen readings are not documented in earlier extant sources, but most of them are of little or no consequence), it contains a mature and reliable state of the text before the Ming- and Qing-dynasty commentaries—most of which, incidentally, are entirely or partly based on this redaction.

As a result of the collation, I decided therefore that my translation would be based on the 1484 edition of Chen Zhixu's text, edited and newly subdivided into sections according to the criteria documented elsewhere in the present book. I re-translated the portions that I had already rendered into English, and continued to work on those that I had not yet translated.

In due course, another issue that I had become aware of, but had decided to leave for as long as possible unanswered in order to focus on the translation, confronted me directly. Since the beginning, I had intended to provide, in addition to the translation, short explications of the subject of each section, and notes on individual verses.

Influenced by the later tradition of Neidan (Internal Alchemy), almost all commentators and a large majority of adepts and scholars have read the *Cantong qi* as the earliest Neidan text, maintaining that the whole work pertains to alchemy and was composed by a single author, Wei Boyang, during the Later Han dynasty (according to tradition, around 150 CE). In this perspective, virtually every statement of the text is understood as being originally written with reference to Neidan. To give only one example, the descriptions of the three main cosmological cycles—the day, the month, and the year—are read as veiled accounts of the alchemical "fire times" (*huohou*), although it should be clear that here, as in many other cases, the *Cantong qi* expounds doctrines that later traditions have used to devise their practices. Moreover, the earliest sources that document what we now call Neidan and draw on the *Cantong qi* were written no less than six hundred years after its reputed date. Should I, nevertheless, present the *Cantong qi* as a Neidan text—and if so, on the basis of which particular commentary?

At the same time, while I was consulting several traditional commentaries in order to translate the text, I had begun to notice that, in addition to the mainstream Neidan interpretation, there has also been a different, less well-known way of reading the *Cantong qi* within the Taoist tradition. In this view, alchemy is one of the three major subjects dealt with in the text, and referred to in its title; the other two are a cosmology that explicates how the world is related to the Dao, and a description of the highest state of realization, which is defined as the Taoist "non-doing," or *wuwei*. Seen in this perspective, alchemy is—in the very words of the *Cantong qi*—the "lower" gradual path that, once accomplished, opens the gates to the "higher" state, which is instantaneously realized and involves going beyond alchemy (see my Introduction, § 7). It should be noted that this view does not refute the Neidan readings of the *Cantong qi*, but broadens the definition of Way of the Golden Elixir (*jindan zhi dao*) to include not only the Neidan practices, but also their doctrinal foundations, while retaining the necessary distinctions between doctrines and practices. It also has an effect on a significant point: The *Cantong qi* is not the first Neidan text, but the first text of Neidan.

As I note in my Introduction, this perspective clarifies several aspects of the *Cantong qi*, including not only the import of its poems, but also its dating and its influence on the history of Chinese alchemy. It also sheds light on one of the many puzzling aspects of this text, namely the sequence of its poems: each of the two main Books of the *Cantong qi* is made of three parallel parts, respectively concerned with the three subjects mentioned above—a feature that is hardly possible to notice if the whole text is read from the perspective of Neidan in the strict sense.

I began therefore, at first tentatively, then more confidently, to rewrite my earlier notes by taking account of this way of reading the text. I also decided to present my work in a first version, found in the present book, that omits most of the historical, textual, and bibliographic details, and focuses almost exclusively on the translation and the annotations. Other parts of my work will be published at a later time.

I express here all my gratitude to Noreen Khawaja for the advice and guidance that she has given in improving my translation. When, in the early summer of 2011, we revised the last verse of the last poem, it seemed impossible to believe that we had worked together for four years. Her knowledge of Classical Chinese, her immediate understanding of the meaning of verses of the *Cantong qi*, and her elegant English have surprised (and confounded) me many times. Any reader who enjoys the translation of the *Cantong qi* found in this book should remember that Noreen shares at least a substantial part of the merit, and usually more than just a part. I alone bear full responsibility for any errors found in the translation and in other parts of the book.

Several friends have shared, at one or another stage, my work on this book. First, let me thank Carla Bonò, formerly librarian at the Fondazione Giorgio Cini in Venice. In her name I also express my gratitude to her colleagues who, in different parts of the world, have assisted me in finding, consulting, and reproducing a substantial number of editions of the *Cantong qi*. I am deeply grateful to Benjamin Brose, George Clonos, Franco Gatti, Laura Mariano, Jason Avi Protass, Donatella Rossi, Alessandra Sisti, Dominic Steavu, Su Xiaoqin, Elena Valussi, and Yang Zhaohua. All of them have helped to clarify not only my understanding of the text, but also the purpose of my work, and therefore have contributed to shape this book. My only regret is that Monica Esposito, who left us sooner than expected, could not see this book, after all the conversations that she and I had on the *Cantong qi*, in Kyoto and elsewhere, and her constant encouragement to complete and publish my translation.

Fabrizio Pregadio
Summer 2011

Introduction

"The *Cantong qi* is the forefather of the scriptures on the Elixir of all times. Its words are ancient and profound, arcane and subtle. No one can fathom their meaning." Thus begins a preface found in one of the commentaries to the *Zhouyi cantong qi* (The Seal of the Unity of the Three, in Accordance with the *Book of Changes*). These words express several significant features of the work translated in the present book: the charm of its verses, the depth of its discourse, its enigmatic language, and its intimate relation to the Taoist alchemical traditions.[1]

Many earlier and later authors and commentators have written similar words to describe this work. Under an allusive poetical language and thick layers of images and symbols, the *Cantong qi* (as the text is often called) hides the exposition of a doctrine that inspired a large number of commentaries and other works, and attracted the attention not only of Taoist masters and adepts, but also of philosophers, cosmologists, poets, literati, calligraphers, philologists, and bibliophiles. At least thirty-eight commentaries to the *Cantong qi* written through the end of the nineteenth century are extant, and dozens of texts found in the Taoist Canon (*Daozang*) and elsewhere are related to it. The two main Tang poets, Li Bai (Li Po) and Bai Juyi, wrote poems about this work, and a short text by the same title was composed by Shitou Xiqian (700–91), the reputed forefather of the Caodong lineage of Chan Buddhism (better known in the West under its Japanese name, Sōtō Zen). Except for the *Daode jing* and the *Zhuangzi*, few other Taoist works have enjoyed a similarly vast and diversified exegetical tradition.

Despite this textual profusion, several circumstances have contributed to persisting issues in understanding this work: its obscure language, the wide range of interpretations offered in the commen-

---

[1] The passage quoted above is found in Ruan Dengbing's preface to Yu Yan's *Zhouyi cantong qi fahui*, 1a, composed in 1284.

taries, the contrasting views on its nature and history, and, not least, the multiple possible meanings of several terms and verses. These issues have been augmented—and, in part, inevitably caused—by the fact that the main tradition on which the *Cantong qi* has exerted its influence, and by which it has been read and interpreted, is Taoist alchemy, in both of its branches: Waidan, or External Alchemy, and Neidan, or Internal Alchemy.[2]

In particular, Neidan is the legacy that has contributed to shape the dominant image and understanding of the *Cantong qi* in China, by placing this work at the origins of its teachings and practices, and by offering explications that differ in many details among different authors, but have one point in common: the *Cantong qi* contains a complete illustration of the principles and methods of Internal Alchemy. According to this view, the *Cantong qi* is an alchemical text, and in particular, is the first Neidan text. In addition to this one, there has been, within the Taoist tradition, a second, less well-known way of reading the text. This reading takes account of a point that is reflected in the title of the *Cantong qi*, is stated more than once in its verses, and is often discussed by its commentators, including some of those associated with Neidan: the *Cantong qi* is concerned not with one, but with three major subjects, and joins them to one another in a single doctrine, of which alchemy is one aspect. To introduce our discussion of this point, we shall look at one of the most visible, but also most complex, aspects of the *Cantong qi*, namely, its title.

§ 1. THE TITLE OF THE *CANTONG QI*

In its complete form, the title of the *Cantong qi* is made of two main parts. The first part, *Zhouyi* 周易 (Changes of the Zhou), is another name of the *Yijing*, or *Book of Changes*, whose cosmological system plays a fundamental role in the *Cantong qi*.[3] Placing the name of one

---

[2] External Alchemy is based on the refining of minerals and metals, which are heated in a vessel in order to extract their pure essences and compound them into different elixirs. In Internal Alchemy, the ingredients of the Elixir are the prime components of the cosmos and the human being, and the entire process takes place within the practitioner. External Alchemy is documented from the second century BCE, and Internal Alchemy from the eighth century CE.

[3] The Zhou (1045–246 BCE) is the dynasty during which, probably as

of the Classics before the actual title of a work reflects the usage of the "weft texts" (*weishu*, commonly referred to as the "apocrypha" among Western scholars), an early textual corpus whose cosmology is rooted in the *Book of Changes*.

The relation of the *Cantong qi* to this corpus will be examined below; as we shall see, it is not entirely clear whether the relation has textual grounds, or only lies in the background that the *Cantong qi* shares with the cosmological traditions. The last word in the second part of the title of the *Cantong qi*, nevertheless, also suggests an association with the "weft texts." *Qi* 契, literally meaning "token, pledge, seal" or "contract," belongs to a series of closely related words that appear in the titles of several apocryphal texts, and later also became important in Taoism. These words—which include *you* 郵 (mark), *qian* 鈐 (seal, badge), and especially *fu* 符 (*symbolon*, sign, token, tally)—refer to two significant aspects of the apocrypha and of the Taoist writings that share similar perspectives. A text belonging to this genre is a manifest sign of a divine revelation; at the same time, it represents its legitimate possessor's intangible but unbreakable bonds to the source of the revelation, and grants access to it.[4]

Concerning the expression *cantong* 參同, commentators and other authors have offered two main interpretations. According to the first view, *can* 參 means "merging, being one," and *tong* 同 means "unity." Since *qi* 契 also indicates the idea of "joining into one" (in this case, the possessor of the text and the source of its doctrine), all three words in the title of the *Cantong qi*, according to this view, refer to the ideas of union and oneness. On the basis of this reading, the title of the *Cantong qi* should be translated, for example, as *Joining as One with Unity*. This interpretation was first stated in the anonymous

early as the ninth or the eighth century BCE, the divinatory portions of the *Book of Changes* were composed. Most of the cosmological portions date, instead, from the third-second centuries BCE. These portions include the *Xici* or *Appended Statements*, from which the *Cantong qi* draws several sentences. According to another view, *zhouyi* means, approximately, "cyclical change." A synthetic but highly reliable survey of the composition and the dating of the *Book of Changes* is found in Shaughnessy, "I ching (Chou i)."

[4] These features of the apocrypha were clearly stated in a masterly study by Anna Seidel: ". . . a typical apocryphal title always indicates that its text, besides telling of divine revelation, is in itself a certificate testifying to the owner's favor with Heaven" ("Imperial Treasures and Taoist Sacraments," 309).

Waidan commentary (ca. 700), and later in the commentaries by Peng Xiao (947) and Zhu Xi (1197). The *Cantong qi* itself uses the word *can* with this meaning in one of its verses (43:12).

According to the second view, *can* 參 means, or rather stands for, *san* 三, "three." In this view, the title of the *Cantong qi* alludes to its property of being a *seal* that testifies to the *unity* of *three* components and, for that reason, enables its possessor to comprehend their unity. This reading of the word *can* was first explicitly suggested in the commentary by Yu Yan (1284), and was later accepted by several other commentators and authors.[5]

Which of the two interpretations is correct is not a meaningful question, since whoever chose the title *Cantong qi* was certainly aware of its dual sense. It is, instead, worthy of note that those who favor the second reading often support it by quoting passages found in the final portions of the *Cantong qi* (sections 84 and 87). These passages state that the *Cantong qi* is concerned with "three ways," which stem from, and lead to, the same source. The three ways are defined as the system of the *Book of Changes*, Taoism (Huang-Lao, so called from the names of the Yellow Emperor and Laozi), and alchemy ("the work with the fire of the furnace").

The order in which the three subjects are mentioned is significant—so significant that, to my knowledge, all authors and commentators who mention the three subjects refer to them in the same order, even when they refer to them with different Chinese terms.[6] The reason of this arrangement can be understood in light of the *Cantong qi*'s own doctrines. "Cosmology" in the *Cantong qi* is not only an explication of the functioning of the cosmos, but in first place an

---

[5] It should be noted that, although the anonymous Waidan commentary explains *can* as meaning "to merge" (*za* 雜), it mentions the merging of "*three things*" (*sanwu* 三物), identifying them in alchemical terms as Water, Soil, and Metal. See *Zhouyi cantong qi zhu*, 1.1a.

[6] Several commentators, for example, refer to the "three ways" as those of "government" (*yuzheng*), "nourishing one's Nature" (*yangxing*), and "preserving and ingesting" (*fushi*). The use of the term "government" is explained by the fact that at the center of the Chinese cosmological system stands, in both a symbolic and a literal way, the ruler, who is, in the human realm, the supreme guarantor of the balance among Heaven, Earth, and Man. In accordance with this view, the ruler is often mentioned in the cosmological portions of the *Cantong qi*. On the term *fushi* see the textual note to verse 27:3, page 236.

exposition of the relation of the cosmos to the Dao, and of man's position in relation to both. Based on this fundamental view, the *Cantong qi* presents two ways of realization. The first is what it calls Taoism ("Huang-Lao"), which for the *Cantong qi* is the way of "non-doing," canonized in the *Daode jing*. The second is alchemy—in the form canonized by the *Cantong qi* itself—which is the way of "doing." Borrowing two terms from the *Daode jing*, the *Cantong qi* defines these two ways as those of "superior virtue" and "inferior virtue," respectively (see section 20).

When this understanding of the purport of the *Cantong qi* is taken into account, certain important aspects of the text are clarified. First, it is not difficult to identify, within the mystifying, but certainly not haphazard, sequence of poems in the first two Books, several contiguous portions that are devoted to each of the three main subjects:

Book 1: sections 1–17, Cosmology; 18–27, Taoism; 28–42, Alchemy
Book 2: sections 43–52, Cosmology; 53–61, Taoism; 62–74, Alchemy

As suggested below (pp. 29 ff.), the final Book 3 is made of later, miscellaneous materials.[7] Second, this understanding of the purport of the *Cantong qi* helps to make sense of other issues, such as the different traditional views on its authorship, and the dating of its alchemical portions.

The next three sections of this Introduction (§ 2–4) are concerned with these and other related questions. They are followed by a short presentation of the main commentaries to the *Cantong qi* (§ 5), and by an overview of its three main subjects (§ 6–8). The concluding section (§ 9) looks at the pivotal role played by this work in the shift from External to Internal Alchemy.

§ 2. A SINGLE AUTHOR, OR MULTIPLE AUTHORS?

For about a millennium, the authorship of the *Cantong qi* has been attributed to Wei Boyang, a character with distinctly legendary

---

[7] Sections 22–25 contain a general description of the principles of alchemy as the way of "inferior virtue," and thus pertain to the "Taoist" portions. The subdivisions suggested above are close to those that Liu Yiming adopts in his version of the "Ancient Text" of the *Cantong qi* (1799). The main differences are that, in Liu Yiming's text, sections 37–38 concern cosmology; 39–40, Taoism; 61, alchemy; and 70–71 and 74, Taoism. On the "Ancient Text" see below, pp. 31 ff.

features said to be an alchemist, and to come from the Shangyu district of Kuaiji, in the southeastern region of Jiangnan.[8] According to the most recurrent account, Wei Boyang first transmitted his work to Xu Congshi, a native of Qingzhou in the present-day northern province of Shandong, who wrote a commentary on it. At the time of Emperor Huan of the Later Han (r. 146–167), Wei Boyang again transmitted the *Cantong qi* to Chunyu Shutong, who also came from Shangyu and began to circulate the text.

While Wei Boyang was a southern alchemist, Xu Congshi and Chunyu Shutong were representatives of the Han-dynasty cosmological legacies of northern China. One of the questions raised by the account summarized above is the following: Why does an alchemist transmit his work to two cosmologists? To answer this question, we must first look closer at the identities of the three masters who, according to tradition, were involved in the creation and the early transmission of the *Cantong qi*.

Wei Boyang

The best-known account of Wei Boyang is found in the *Shenxian zhuan* (Biographies of the Divine Immortals), a work attributed to Ge Hong (283–243). According to this record (translated below, p. 263), Wei Boyang was a native of Wu (present-day Jiangsu, and parts of Anhui and Zhejiang) and was "the son of a high-ranking family." The story tells that Wei Boyang and three disciples retired to a mountain and compounded an elixir. When they tested it on a dog, the dog died. Despite this, Wei Boyang and one of his disciples decided to ingest the compound, and they also died. After the two other disciples had left, Wei Boyang came to life again. He poured some of the elixir into the mouths of the dead disciple and the dog, and they also revived. Thus Wei Boyang and his faithful disciple, "whose surname was Yu," attained immortality. With an abrupt change in tone and language, the account ends with a final paragraph, which mentions Wei Boyang's

---

[8] In the second century CE, when Wei Boyang is deemed to have composed the *Cantong qi*, Kuaiji was a large commandery corresponding to present-day eastern Jiangsu and western Zhejiang. Its territory partially overlapped the region south of the lower Yangzi River known as Jiangnan. Wei Boyang's birthplace is said to correspond to present-day Fenghui in Shangyu, about 80 km east of Hangzhou.

authorship of the *Cantong qi* and of another work entitled *The Five Categories* (*Wu xianglei*), and criticizes those who read the *Cantong qi* as a work concerned with cosmology instead of alchemy. As we shall see, this is the first of several hints about the different views between these two traditions with regard to the *Cantong qi*.

Several centuries later, Peng Xiao (?–955) gives an entirely different portrait of Wei Boyang in his well-known commentary, dating from 947 CE (see the translation below, p. 264). The alchemist who retires on a mountain with his disciples, tests his elixir on a dog, and is reborn after death becomes, in Peng Xiao's account, a learned master who is competent in prose and poetry, is versed in the esoteric texts, cultivates the Dao "in secret and silence," and nourishes himself "in Empty Non-being." In another passage of his work, moreover, Peng Xiao reveals an important detail about the authorship of the three Books of the *Cantong qi*, which differs from the account found in the *Shenxian zhuan*:

> Some texts on the Dao say that the *Cantong qi* is in three Books, and that Master Wei [Boyang], Xu Congshi, and Chunyu Shutong each wrote one Book. However, the Master also wrote *The Five Categories*, where he says, "I now write again to fill the lacunae."[9] Clearly [the whole *Cantong qi*] was written only by the Master. (*Zhouyi cantong qi fenzhang tong zhenyi*, commentary to *zhang* 83)

As shown by this passage, in Peng Xiao's time a different view existed that attributed each of the three Books of the text to Wei Boyang, Xu Congshi, and Chunyu Shutong, respectively. Peng Xiao rejects this view and states that Wei Boyang wrote the entire *Cantong qi*.

Xu Congshi and Chunyu Shutong

The variant accounts in the *Shenxian zhuan* and in Peng Xiao's commentary reflect differences in the traditional views on the authorship and, especially, the nature of the *Cantong qi*. Before we consider these differences, we should look at the identities of the two other masters.

Very few details, even hagiographic, are available about Xu Congshi. From Peng Xiao we only learn that he was deemed a native of Qingzhou, in the present-day northern region of Shandong; other

---

[9] This sentence is found in the present text of the *Cantong qi*, 83:7–8.

sources suggest that he was an attendant at the Qingzhou local court
(as also shown by his personal name, *congshi*, which means
"retainer"). Details about the tradition represented by Xu Congshi
emerge, nevertheless, in relation to Chunyu Shutong, the third master
mentioned by Peng Xiao in his account. The most elaborate narrative
about him is found in Tao Hongjing's (456–536) *Zhengao* (True
Revelations), where he appears in a section devoted to the administration of the otherworld. His charge in that context is to examine those
who have attained the Dao.[10]

Tao Hongjing's account deserves attention. First, he reports that
Chunyu came from Shangyu—the same birthplace of Wei Boyang—
and was proficient in the "arts of the numbers" (*shushu*), i.e., cosmology, prognostication, and the related sciences. At the time of Emperor
Huan (r. 146–167) he was a District Magistrate in Xuzhou (present-
day southern Shandong and northern Jiangsu). Later he returned to
the Wu region in the south, where he received an alchemical text from
an immortal named Huiche zi. Emperor Ling (r. 168–189) intended to
summon Chunyu to the capital, but he declined the offer. Tao
Hongjing then quotes a passage on Chunyu's life as coming from the
Cantong qi, which is not found in its present-day text. Here he is
indicated as a disciple of Xu Congshi, and his activities are described
in more detail:

> At the time of Emperor Huan, Chunyu Shutong, who was a native
> of Shangyu, received the arts [of the numbers] from Xu Congshi,
> who was a native of Qingzhou. Looking above and observing the
> signs of Heaven, he was able to deal with calamities and unusual
> events. There were several confirmations [of his predictions].
> Because of his knowledge of those arts, he was appointed "master
> of the methods" (*fangshi*). (*Zhengao*, 12.8a-b)

Other sources confirm that Chunyu Shutong was an expert in the
Book of Changes and the "weft texts" (i.e., the apocrypha), and
recount his divinatory feats. The main feature of the passage quoted
above, however, is the mention of the *fangshi*, or "masters of the
methods," a general designation of practitioners whose homeland—in

---

[10] The *Zhengao* (a title also translated as *Revelations of the Perfected*) is a
major Taoist work of the late Six Dynasties, where Tao Hongjing reports and
codifies the story and the contents of the revelations at the basis of the
Shangqing (Highest Clarity) tradition of Taoism, which occurred in 364–70.

an actual or emblematic sense—was Shandong. These practitioners were admitted to court by several emperors and local rulers, especially during the Han dynasty, to give advice on governance and other subjects. Their expertise included numerology, astrology, divination, and other sciences that share the same background as the cosmological portions of the *Cantong qi*.[11]

Two Views on the Authorship of the Cantong qi

It is hardly possible to overlook the absence of the alchemist Wei Boyang from both accounts reported by Tao Hongjing—who was himself a southerner, a practitioner of alchemy, and a very learned authority on the Taoist local traditions of Jiangnan. Even when Tao Hongjing depicts Chunyu Shutong as a student of alchemy, his master is not Wei Boyang. As we shall see, this is not the only detail suggesting that, while in Tao Hongjing's time Wei Boyang was known as an alchemist, he was not yet known as the author of the *Cantong qi*.[12]

In the next section of his Introduction, we shall look at the broader context of these issues, which directly affect the dating of the text. Here we only need to note that sources dating from the Tang period (seventh-ninth centuries) show that, at that time, there were two main views regarding the authorship and the early transmission of the *Cantong qi*. Both views relate the composition of the *Cantong qi* to the *Longhu jing* (Book of the Dragon and Tiger), an earlier, enigmatic work on which we shall return shortly (pp. 12 ff.).

According to the first view, the primary creator of the *Cantong qi* is Xu Congshi, the master of the "arts of the numbers" who came from Shandong. His disciple, Chunyu Shutong, is a *fangshi* expert in the same field and in the science of prediction. These skills show that those who maintained that the *Cantong qi* originated with Xu Congshi saw the text as a product of the northern *fangshi* milieux based in

[11] On the *fangshi* see Ngo Van Xuyet, *Divination, magie et politique dans la Chine ancienne*, and the biographies translated in DeWoskin, *Doctors, Diviners, and Magicians of Ancient China*.

[12] It should be added that, in another work in which Tao Hongjing ranks a large number of deities and immortals according to the heavens that they inhabit, he cites again Chunyu Shutong (under one of his additional names, Chunyu Zhen), but makes no mention of Wei Boyang. See *Dongxuan lingbao zhenling weiye tu*, 21a and 22a.

Shandong, and as a work belonging in the first place to the cosmological and the esoteric traditions of the Han dynasty. According to this view, Wei Boyang is a disciple of either Xu Congshi or Chunyu Shutong. In more detail, there are three different accounts of the relations among the reputed authors of the *Cantong qi*.[13] (1) Xu Congshi receives the *Longhu jing* from an immortal, and transmits it to his disciple Chunyu Shutong, who writes the second chapter; Wei Boyang's role merely consists in changing the title of this work to *Cantong qi*. (2) Xu Congshi writes the *Longhu jing*; Wei Boyang writes the *Wu xianglei* (The Five Categories) and re-entitles the whole work *Cantong qi*; Chunyu Shutong writes an additional chapter. (3) Xu Congshi writes the first chapter of the *Cantong qi* using the *Longhu jing* as his model; Wei Boyang writes the second chapter; Chunyu Shutong writes the third chapter.[14]

According to the second view, it is Wei Boyang, the master of the alchemical arts, who writes the whole *Cantong qi* on the basis of the *Longhu jing*. As we have seen, Wei Boyang's biography in the *Shenxian zhuan* depicts him as a recluse adept from Jiangnan, who withdraws on a mountain with his disciples in order to compound an elixir that bestows life free from death. The traditions that attributed the authorship of the *Cantong qi* to Wei Boyang deemed the text to be a creation of the alchemical lineages of southeastern China.

These two views coexisted during the Tang period. In the mid-eighth century, Liu Zhigu—who belongs to the alchemical tradition—

[13] These views are documented by Liu Zhigu's *Riyue xuanshu lun* (Essay on the Mysterious Pivot of the Sun and the Moon), in *Daoshu* (Pivot of the Dao), 26.1a-1b; and by the prefaces to the two Tang-dynasty commentaries to the *Cantong qi*, on which see below, § 5. Liu Zhigu's work, dating from ca. 750, is the first extant essay on the *Cantong qi*.

[14] To quote one example of these views, the anonymous Waidan commentary to the *Cantong qi*, dating from ca. 700, is quite explicit about the roles played by Xu Congshi, Chunyu Shutong, and Wei Boyang in the creation of the text: "Xu Congshi transmitted it to Master Chunyu Shutong . . . who wrote another part entitled *The Five Categories* (*Wu xianglei*). . . . Chunyu was the first to transmit the whole text to Master Wei Boyang" (*Zhouyi cantong qi zhu*, Preface, 1a-2a). Elsewhere, this commentary ascribes the *Cantong qi* to Xu Congshi alone. For example, the notes on the verse, "He contemplates on high the manifest signs of Heaven" (11:8), state: "The True Man Xu Congshi looked above and contemplated the images of the trigrams; thus he determined Yin and Yang." Analogous statements are found in the notes to sentences 14:47–49, 37:19–20, and 42:15–16.

reports the second and the third accounts of the creation of the *Cantong qi* cited above; he concludes, however, that Wei Boyang is actually the author of the whole text. Two centuries later, another alchemist, Peng Xiao, also refers to accounts of a shared authorship, but cites and praises Liu Zhigu's discussion, and becomes the first major author to promote the same view.[15] Peng Xiao's narrative, moreover, transforms Wei Boyang into an alchemist who was also a specialist of the "weft texts," precisely the lore in which Xu Congshi and Chunyu Shutong were also expert. With the development of the Neidan traditions, this view became established. Since then, there has been virtually unanimous consent that the *Cantong qi* was not only transmitted, but also entirely composed, within the context of the alchemical tradition—at least until the early sixteenth century, when the "Ancient Text" of the *Cantong qi* was created, and the two other masters were again assigned a role in its composition (see below, pp. 31 ff.).

The question asked earlier—why an alchemist should hand down his work to two cosmologists—can now be answered, and the answer is plain. When the views of the authorship of the *Cantong qi* changed, the roles of the three characters were inverted. The alchemist is no more a disciple of cosmologists: Wei Boyang is now the master of Xu Congshi and Chunyu Shutong.

§ 3. THE DATING RIDDLE

The two possible ways of reading of the *Cantong qi* defined at the beginning of this Introduction should be taken into account with regard to any attempt to discuss and establish the date of the text. According to the first reading, the *Cantong qi* has provided the alchemical traditions with an integral description of the principles at the basis of their practices. In agreement with their perspectives, these traditions have called the *Cantong qi* an "alchemical text" and have interpreted all its verses as related to alchemy—including those found in portions concerned with cosmology, with actual or symbolic astronomical phenomena (for example, the joining of the Sun and the Moon at the end of a time cycle), with the True Man and the sage ruler (both seen, in this light, as metaphors of the alchemist), and

---

[15] See Liu Zhigu's *Riyue xuanshu lun*, 26.1b; and Peng Xiao's commentary to *zhang* 83, quoted above.

with virtually any other subject. This reading has certainly been the most widespread, and has led to the view that the *Cantong qi* has a single author (Wei Boyang), a single date (the Han period), and a single subject (alchemy).

In the second reading, alchemy constitutes, with Taoism (in the sense defined above) and cosmology, one of the three main subjects of the *Cantong qi*, and each subject forms one of three main textual components. The three subjects are integrated with one another into a unique presentation of a doctrine that includes a metaphysics, a cosmology, a description of the highest realized state, and a canonical form of practice. From this perspective, it should be sufficiently clear that those who wove the fabric of this presentation cannot have been either the cosmologists or the alchemists, but only the anonymous authors of the Taoist portions, which describe the state of complete realization by drawing concepts, terms, and images from the *Daode jing* and the *Zhuangzi* (see especially section 18). Being possessed of this state is called in the *Cantong qi* the way of "superior virtue." Alchemy, the only form of practice that the *Cantong qi* upholds, is the complementary, and preparatory, way of "inferior virtue."

The first perspective reflects a traditional truth that can hardly be disputed, and is in all respects inalienable and virtually impervious to historical analysis. The second one, instead, allows a broader scope to inquiries into the origins of the three subjects and the respective textual components. This perspective also clears the complex issue of dating the *Cantong qi* of some of its burden: the received text is the product of a composition process that involved representatives of different traditions, and was completed in several stages. This, in turn, helps to clarify certain controversial aspects of the text and its history.

The Cantong qi *and the* Longhu jing

One of the first questions to address concerns the supposed origins of the *Cantong qi* in an earlier scripture. Several commentaries and other works maintain that Wei Boyang wrote his *Cantong qi* by taking as a model the *Longhu jing*, or *Scripture of the Dragon and Tiger*, a work whose title immediately evokes the alchemical arts.[16] This claim is

---

[16] Dragon and Tiger are, usually, emblems of Yang and Yin, respectively. In alchemy, their roles are inverted: the Dragon is an emblem of True Yin (True

widespread, but is perplexing, since no material or even bibliographic trace of a text called *Longhu jing* exists during the whole first millennium of our era.

The history of the *Longhu jing* is complex, but runs parallel to the traditions about the authorship of the *Cantong qi* that we have outlined above. In the earliest sources, as we have seen, the master associated with the *Longhu jing* is not Wei Boyang, the alchemist, but Xu Congshi, the cosmologist, who is depicted as the original recipient—or even as the author—of this text. In light of the controversies about the authorship of the *Cantong qi*, it seems clear that the accounts associating the *Longhu jing* with Xu Congshi served to answer an important question: How could someone known as a cosmologist and a diviner create a text like the *Cantong qi*, which is substantially (if not entirely, according to the prevalent view) devoted to alchemy? The reply was straightforward: Xu Congshi could write a work on alchemy because he had received—or even, according to some, written—an earlier alchemical text, the *Longhu jing*.

During the Tang period, when different views on the authorship of the *Cantong qi* were still current, a work entitled *Jinbi jing* (Scripture on Gold and Jade) was composed on the basis of the *Cantong qi*.[17] This work is a shorter paraphrase of the *Cantong qi*, approximately corresponding to the first half of Book 1 (sections 1–25 in the present translation). The paraphrase replaces the imagery of the *Cantong qi* with the language of alchemy, and does so with such consistency and persistence that one might call the *Jinbi jing* an alchemical version of the initial portions of the *Cantong qi*, which do not concern alchemy, but cosmology and the Taoist way of "superior virtue."[18] During the

Mercury), and the Tiger is an emblem of True Yang (True Lead).

[17] The present version of this work, entitled *Jindan jinbi qiantong jue* (Instructions on Gold and Jade for Comprehending the Unseen by the Golden Elixir), is found in the *Yunji qiqian*, 73.7b-11b. While the present version is anonymous, bibliographic sources attribute this work to Yang Canwei (or Sanwei), adding that it was based on an even earlier work written by Liu Yan during the Six Dynasties. (The presence of the graph *can* 參, or *san* 三, in the author's name is certainly not due to chance.) On this work see Wang Ming, "*Zhouyi cantong qi* kaozheng," 279–83.

[18] To give one example of the textual correspondences, the initial verses of the *Cantong qi* (1:1–2) read: "Qian and Kun are the door and the gate of change, the father and the mother of all hexagrams." In the *Jinbi jing*, they read: "The Divine Chamber (i.e., the crucible) is the axis and the hinge of the

Song dynasty, the *Jinbi jing* was chosen to represent the "ancient" (i.e., "authentic") text of the *Longhu jing*, and was reentitled *Guwen longhu jing* (Ancient Text of the Scripture of the Dragon and Tiger). Two editions of this work are contained in the Taoist Canon; their text is the same as the *Jinbi jing*.

When the issues of authorship were settled, and Wei Boyang was elected the only author of the *Cantong qi*, most commentators and other authors continued to claim that the *Cantong qi* derives from the *Longhu jing*, but made Wei Boyang, instead of Xu Congshi, the original recipient of this text (for one example, see Peng Xiao's account, translated on p. 265). Other authors, however, were aware that the *Longhu jing* that existed in their times—in other words, the text that earlier was entitled *Jinbi jing*—was nothing but an alchemical rendition of the *Cantong qi*. For example, Yu Yan wrote in his commentary:

> Essentially, when Master Wei [Boyang] wrote the *Cantong qi*, he borrowed the images of the *Book of Changes* to illustrate the secrets of compounding the Elixir; he did not develop the discourses of the *Longhu jing*. Had he truly developed the discourses of the *Longhu jing*, he would have called his work "The Seal of the Unity of the Three in Accordance with the Dragon and the Tiger," and not "The Seal of the Unity of the Three in Accordance with the *Book of Changes*." (*Zhouyi cantong qi shiyi*, 3a-4a)[19]

The Cantong qi *and the* "Studies of the Book of Changes"

The roots of the cosmological discourse of the *Cantong qi* lie in the tradition usually designated in China as *Yixue*, or "Studies of the *Book of Changes*," whose essential elements were elaborated during the Han period (202 BCE-220 CE). This tradition, as its name implies, expands the views of the *Changes* into multiple directions, with emphasis on numerology and prognostication. To some extent, the *Cantong qi* is one example of these developments. Exactly for this reason, the parts of the text concerned with cosmology are those that

---

Elixir, the father and the mother of all minerals." The whole text continues along similar lines.

[19] Yu Yan's words reflect an earlier, similar statement by Zhu Xi, found in his *Zhouyi cantong qi [kaoyi]*, 1.4b-5a.

present the most obscure issues with regard to their date, as they involve their possible origins—not only in a conceptual sense, but also in a hypothetical earlier textual form—within that tradition.

While many analogies are apparent, but not sufficient to shed full light on these issues, several scholars have suggested that the association between the *Cantong qi* and the "Studies of the *Book of Changes*" is manifest in the work of Yu Fan (164–233), the last great cosmologist of the Han period. In this connection, attention has been drawn to what could be the only piece of textual evidence concerning the Han date of the *Cantong qi*, or at least of its cosmological portions. A seventh-century lexicon of classical texts ascribes Yu Fan with a commentary to the *Cantong qi*, and cites a passage from that work that appears to refer to the sentence "Sun and Moon make change," found in the present-day *Cantong qi* (7:3). The passage reads:

> Yu Fan's commentary to the *Cantong qi* says: The graph *yi* 易 ("change") is formed by a "sun" 日 with a "moon" 月 below it. (*Jingdian shiwen*, 2.1a)[20]

This sentence would seem to show that a text entitled *Cantong qi* existed by about 200 CE, and that Yu Fan wrote a now-lost commentary on it. Whether the evidence is conclusive, however, is dubious. It seems impossible to disregard the fact that, if this evidence is accepted, the Han date of the *Cantong qi* is validated by a single sentence, quoted for the first time five centuries after its supposed original date not from the *Cantong qi* itself, but from a related work that is now lost.

The short passage translated above, however, raises other questions that indirectly help to throw light on the history of the text. The sentence apparently referred to by Yu Fan ("Sun and Moon make change") is attributed, by a major Han-dynasty source, to one or more "secret writings" (*bishu*), an expression that is usually deemed to refer to the apocryphal texts.[21] Did Yu Fan, therefore, write a

---

[20] The Chinese text of this passage can also be punctuated in a different way, which yields a quite different translation: "According to Yu Fan's commentary [to the *Book of Changes*], the *Cantong qi* says that this graph (namely, yi 易, "change") is formed by a "sun" with a "moon" below it." The first punctuation, however, fits the pattern of quotations in the *Jingdian shiwen*, and appears to be more accurate than the second one.

[21] See *Shuowen jiezi* (Elucidations on the Signs and Explications of the

commentary to the *Cantong qi*, or was he ascribed with it by his lineage? If he did write a commentary, was that *Cantong qi* the same as the present-day text, or was it perhaps one of the apocrypha? If an "apocryphal" *Cantong qi* has ever existed, how would it be related to the present-day text? None of these questions can be answered on the basis of direct evidence. Certain bibliographic and textual details, however, clarify some of the issues.

First, Yu Fan is also ascribed with a lost commentary to a work by Jing Fang (77–37 BCE), an earlier cosmologist who had belonged to his own lineage. The title of this work—which is also lost—is *Cantong qi Lüli zhi* (possibly meaning "Monograph on the Pitch-pipes and the Calendar According to the *Cantong qi*").[22] Was this is the work on which Yu Fan wrote the commentary quoted in the seventh-century lexicon? This cannot be known, but is not the point at issue. The point, rather, is that at least one work appears to have existed under the title *Cantong qi*, even before the traditional date in which Wei Boyang is believed to have written the present-day work that bears this title. It is also worthy of note that one of the cosmological portions in the present-day *Cantong qi* contains the expression *lüli* ("pitch-pipes and calendar"; see verse 2:8). Whether Jing Fang's work, or any other lost Han-dynasty text, was a precursor of the current *Cantong qi*, however, is impossible to ascertain.

A second detail is of greater consequence. As we shall see (below, p. 42), the *Cantong qi* represents the cycle of the lunar month by means of the cosmological pattern known as Matching Stems (*najia*). The version of this pattern used in the *Cantong qi* is attributed to Yu Fan. A fragment of his lost commentary to the *Book of Changes* contains this description:

> On the evening of the third day, [the Moon] is an image of Zhen
> ☳ and comes forth at *geng* 庚. On the eighth day, it is an image of
> Dui ☱ and appears at *ding* 丁. On the fifteenth day, it is an image
> of Qian ☰ and is full at *jia* 甲. At the dawn of the sixteenth day, it
> is an image of Xun ☴ and withdraws at *xin* 辛. On the twenty-
> third day, it is an image of Gen ☶ and disappears at *bing* 丙. On

Graphs), 9B.18a, and the discussion in Wang Ming, "*Zhouyi cantong qi kaozheng*," 242–48. See also note 23 below.

[22] What the title *Cantong qi* may have meant in the first century BCE is an issue in itself. It is simply unimaginable that the "three," at that time, may have been cosmology, Taoism, and alchemy.

the thirtieth day, it is an image of Kun ☷ and is extinguished at *yi*
乙. (*Zhouyi jijie*, 14.350)

The wording of this passage is notably similar to section 13 of the
Cantong qi. Moreover, Yu Fan's commentary also contains a description of the conjunction of Sun and Moon at the end of each month
(see the translation below, p. 43), a symbolic event that the *Cantong
qi* describes, in its turn, in sections 10 and 48. Scholars who uphold
Wei Boyang's authorship of the *Cantong qi* (in ca. 150 CE) have
suggested that Yu Fan drew these descriptions directly from the
Cantong qi. The reverse is more likely to be true: the *Cantong qi*
presents a poetical rendition of Yu Fan's passages. If this suggestion is
correct, not only Yu Fan could not write a commentary to the
present-day *Cantong qi*, but the composition of these portions would
be postdated by at least one century.

The Cantong qi *and the Apocrypha*

To answer the third question asked above—whether an "apocryphal"
Cantong qi has ever existed—we should first look in some detail at its
context. The tradition of the "Studies of the *Book of Changes*" is also
associated with the "weft texts" (*weishu*), i.e., the so-called
apocrypha. This body of writings was composed during the Han
period with two main purposes, closely related to one another: the
esoteric explication of the Classics (*jing*, a word whose primary
meaning is "warp") and the legitimation of imperial authority, assert-
ed by means of predictions that were supposedly concealed in the text
of the Classics, and that the apocrypha finally disclosed by way of
Heaven's revelations. In addition, as we saw at the beginning of this
Introduction, these texts were proof of, and key to, access to the very
source of those revelations. From this point of view, the *Cantong qi*
would be a text that explains, or develops, certain concealed aspects of
the *Book of Changes*. The apocrypha once formed a textual corpus of
remarkable size. Due to their strong political overtones, however, they
were often banned or destroyed in the course of Chinese history, and are
now almost exclusively preserved in the form of short quotations in
other works.

The association between the *Cantong qi* and the apocrypha has
been suggested by several commentators and many modern scholars.

Doubtlessly, several details point to a relation to this body of literature. The most visible indicator, as we saw above, is the three-character title (*Cantong qi*) placed after the name of the correlated Classic
(*Zhouyi*, or *Book of Changes*). The *Cantong qi* shares this feature
with most apocrypha. For their ideas, imagery, and language, moreover, certain parts of the text seem to reflect the vision of the apocrypha; sections 15–17 may be the clearest example in this regard. The
same is true of a few individual verses. The sentence "Sun and Moon
make change" (7:3), already cited above in relation to Yu Fan, is said
to reflect the views of the apocrypha, which emphasize the idea of the
analogic function of forms, including the characters of the written
language, and in this perspective develop symbolic etymologies for
certain words (this is also the subject of section 6 of the *Cantong qi*).[23]
The description of the state of transcendence found in section 27
concludes by saying that the adept will "obtain the Register and
receive the Chart," one of similar expressions that in the apocrypha
designate the mandate granted by Heaven to a sovereign.[24] The sentence "sesame extends the length of your life" (33:1) is also found, in
exactly the same form, among the fragments of one of the best-
known apocrypha.[25]

   Despite this, there is no precise indication that the *Cantong qi* has
ever been a "weft text" in the precise sense of this term at any time of
its history. Its title has never been included in the lists of apocryphal
works found in the dynastic histories, and none of its verses is quoted
in the preserved fragments of those works. While the analogies between the *Cantong qi* and the apocrypha are not in doubt, they
appear to derive, in the first place, from the grounds that its cosmological portions share with the "Studies of the *Book of Changes*."

   To summarize this part of our discussion, the cosmological portions of the *Cantong qi* are obviously related to both the "Studies of
the *Book of Changes*" and the apocrypha. There is, however, no trace

---

[23] For example, one of the surviving "weft texts" associated with the *Book
of Changes*, the *Qian zuodu* (Opening the Way to the Understanding of Qian
☰), states that the main meaning of the word *yi* ("change") is "the Sun and
the Moon holding one another." See *Isho shūsei*, 1A: 48.
   [24] See Seidel, "Imperial Treasures," 308–9.
   [25] *Yuanshen qi* (Seal of the Verification of Spirit), in *Isho shūsei*, V:50.
Other passages of the *Cantong qi* that may be related to the apocrypha are
quoted in Yang Xiaolei, "*Zhouyi cantong qi* yanjiu," 559.

of any direct textual precursor belonging to either tradition; the relation is likely to be one of shared perspectives, language, and imagery, rather than one of direct textual filiation. As for Yu Fan's gloss on the character *yi* ("change"), it does not seem to be sufficiently reliable to date the *Cantong qi* to the Han dynasty. More substantial evidence concerning Yu Fan suggests, on the contrary, that the cosmological portions of the *Cantong qi* were written, or at least completed, after the end of the Han period.

Relation to Alchemy

Whether the alchemical portions of the *Cantong qi* are concerned with Waidan or with other forms of alchemy is an important question that will be addressed later in the present Introduction. For our present purposes, it suffices to consider how the alchemical model of the *Cantong qi* compares to the model of alchemical texts that share its traditional date.

Among the large number of Chinese scholars who have expressed their views about the date of the *Cantong qi*, the opinions of Chen Guofu (1914–2000) are especially worthy of attention. While not all those who have discussed this subject have been familiar with the alchemical sources—in particular, with the sources of Waidan, the only form in which alchemy is documented during the Han period— Chen Guofu was for several decades the main Chinese expert in this field, and could not fail to notice a major detail: no extant alchemical work dating from the Han period is based on the doctrinal principles of the *Cantong qi*, or uses its cosmological model and its language.[26]

The importance of this remark cannot be underestimated. As we have seen, the portions of the *Cantong qi* concerned with cosmology are rooted in the Han-dynasty traditions centered on the *Book of Changes*, and share the perspectives and language of those traditions. The portions concerned with alchemy, instead, are remarkably different from the methods described in the earliest Waidan texts. In fact, the scope of Chen Guofu's remark may be broadened to include two further points. First, neither the *Cantong qi* nor its cosmological and alchemical models play any visible influence on extant Waidan texts dating not only from the Han period, but also from the whole Six

---

[26] See Chen Guofu, "*Zhouyi cantong qi*," 352–54.

Dynasties (i.e., until the sixth century inclusive). These texts are based on an alchemical model that is quite different from the one illustrated in the *Cantong qi* (see below, § 8). Second, the same can be said with even more confidence about Neidan, since no text belonging to this branch of Chinese alchemy has existed—or has left traces of its existence—until the eighth century.

Ge Hong, *the* Baopu zi, *and the* Shenxian zhuan

One of the texts that do not display any influence of the *Cantong qi* and its alchemical views is Ge Hong's major work, the *Baopu zi* (Book of the Master Who Embraces Spontaneous Nature), which was composed around 320 and contains two chapters entirely devoted to alchemy. Even so, the question of whether Ge Hong knew Wei Boyang and the *Cantong qi* requires attention, because Ge Hong is also the reputed author of the *Shenxian zhuan*, the work that contains Wei Boyang's earliest hagiographic account. Since the evidence in this regard is ambiguous, if not contradictory, I will first outline the main points.

First, in his *Baopu zi*, Ge Hong cites a *Wei Boyang neijing*, or *Inner Scripture of Wei Boyang*, among the texts that belonged to his master.[27] While this work, according to some scholars, can only be the *Cantong qi*, its contents are unknown, and even its title is not recorded elsewhere. Whether the *Wei Boyang neijing* was the *Cantong qi*, or was somehow related to it, is therefore impossible either to demonstrate or to refute. However, Ge Hong's citation provides a first undeniable hint that Ge Hong knew of a Wei Boyang, who gave his name to a text possibly dealing with alchemy.[28]

Second, three distinct passages of the *Baopu zi* mention a court archivist named Boyang, whose son served as a general in the kingdom

[27] *Baopu zi neipian*, 19.334. In titles of Taoist texts, *nei* ("inner") usually denotes works that, at least in principle, were not intended for open circulation.
[28] The only clue about the possible alchemical nature of this work is the fact that Ge Hong lists its title immediately after those of two alchemical texts, the *Danhu jing* (Scripture of the Cinnabar Pot, or Scripture of the Elixir's Pot) and the *Minshan jing* (Scripture of Mount Min). While the first text is otherwise unknown, an alchemical method found in the second one is quoted in *Baopu zi neipian*, 4.78 (Ware, *Alchemy, Medicine and Religion*, 83–84).

of Wei, and whose advice was sought by Confucius.[29] These passages do not refer to Wei Boyang, but to Laozi: one of Laozi's names was Boyang—a significant detail to which we shall return later—and his accounts recorded in many sources include all three details mentioned above.[30] Elsewhere in the *Baopu zi*, instead, Boyang is depicted as the model sage of those who retire on a mountain to pursue self-cultivation:

> ... And when those who peer at life through a pipe, forming personal opinions and expounding mindless speeches, hear that there is someone dwelling in mountains and forests who takes the doings of Boyang as his ideal, they slander and poke fun at him saying, "That is a minor path, not worth bothering with." (*Baopu zi neipian*, 10.185)[31]

It is unlikely that the Boyang mentioned in this passage is Laozi, whose hagiography does not mention his "dwelling in mountains and forests." He might, instead, be Wei Boyang who, as we have seen, retired on a mountain with his disciples in order to compound an elixir.[32]

The third, and main, possible piece of evidence on Ge Hong's knowledge of the *Cantong qi* is the tale of Wei Boyang in the *Shenxian zhuan* (Biographies of the Divine Immortals; translated on p. 263). This account, already discussed above, has been cited in several later works and many modern studies to confirm the traditional attribution of the *Cantong qi* to Wei Boyang. The nature and history of the

---

[29] "Boyang was an archivist. . . . Among those who have obtained the Dao, no one is higher than Boyang. He had a son named Zong, who became a general in [the kingdom of] Wei. . . . After paying his respects to Boyang, Confucius wanted to compare himself with Pengzu." *Baopu zi neipian*, 8.148, 3.52, and 7.138; see Ware, 137, 64, and 129, respectively. Pengzu is one of the paragons of the Taoist immortal sage.

[30] On Boyang as a name of Laozi see Kaltenmark, *Le Lie-sien tchouan*, 60–62, and Seidel, *La divinisation de Lao Tseu*, 29- 30 and passim.

[31] See Ware, 167.

[32] It should be added that the passage quoted above bears some similarities with these verses of the *Cantong qi*, which criticize those who practice incorrect alchemical methods: "Relying on *opinion* and *written words* (lit., written speeches), / they *foolishly* act as they like . . . / As if *peering through a pipe*, unable to see broadly, / they can hardly assess what impends" (36:5–6 and 25–26). I am unable to say whether the correspondence is due to chance alone, or the *Cantong qi* verses were composed on the basis of written lore concerning Wei Boyang.

Shenxian zhuan—a collection of short tales surviving only in quotations or reconstructed editions, both of which are much later than its supposed date—are not the only factors that raise doubts on the value of this evidence. Taking for granted that Ge Hong did write that anecdote (the first source to report it in full dates only from the year 978), there are good reasons to question the authenticity of the final paragraph that names Wei Boyang the author of the *Cantong qi*: except for this passage, nothing in the tale of the *Shenxian zhuan* would suggest that its subject is the author of the *Cantong qi*.[33]

We shall return to the last point presently. For the moment, it suffices to summarize the evidence seen above. Ge Hong knew of a Wei Boyang, whom he mentions in his *Baopu zi* first as the author of a *Wei Boyang neijing*, a text that may have been concerned with alchemy, and possibly again as a sage who lived secluded among the mountains. Wei Boyang is also the subject of one of the hagiographies found in the *Shenxian zhuan*, another work attributed to Ge Hong. This tale depicts him as an alchemist, and contains a final passage that mentions his authorship of the *Cantong qi*. On the other hand, it is unlikely—at the very least—that Ge Hong knew of a *Cantong qi* written by Wei Boyang. His *Baopu zi*, in fact, does not yield any testimony to the fact that Ge Hong knew the *Cantong qi* at all.

Since Ge Hong knew Wei Boyang, why does he ignore a text of such importance as the *Cantong qi* in the *Baopu zi*? One answer could be that the *Wei Boyang neijing* is the *Cantong qi*; Ge Hong knew of its existence, but did not receive it from his master. This would imply, however, that the *Cantong qi* and its alchemical model originated in the Han period, and were disregarded by the Chinese alchemical tradition for a half millennium. In light of what we have seen about the authorship of the *Cantong qi*, there is another way to find coherence in the apparently inconsistent evidence summarized above. Just like Tao Hongjing, two centuries later, cites the *Cantong qi* without mentioning Wei Boyang, the Wei Boyang known to Ge Hong was not yet acknowledged as the author of the *Cantong qi*. This, however, leaves one question unanswered: Why does Ge Hong cites Wei Boyang as the author of the *Cantong qi* in the *Shenxian zhuan*?

---

[33] The *Shenxian zhuan* account of Wei Boyang is first found in the *Taiping guangji* (Extended Collection of Records of the Taiping xingguo Reign Period; 978), 2.11–12. Earlier, Liu Zhigu had cited only the final passage in his *Riyue xuanshu lun*, 26.1a.

The Cantong qi *in Jiangnan*

The last important point to clarify with regard to Ge Hong concerns the final paragraph of Wei Boyang's biography in the *Shenxian zhuan*. This paragraph not only attributes the *Cantong qi* to Wei Boyang, but also criticizes the "scholars" (*ru*) who read the text as a work concerned with cosmology. Since this criticism is expressed in the biography of an alchemist, it should be appraised, once again, in light of the different views about the authorship of the *Cantong qi*.

The first unequivocal mentions of the *Cantong qi* date from around 500 CE. Writing at the very end of the fifth century, Tao Hongjing (456–536) refers, as we saw above, to the *Cantong qi* in connection with Chunyu Shutong. Around the same years, his older contemporary Jiang Yan (444–505) mentions the *Cantong qi* in a poem devoted to an immortal named Qin Gao. The relevant lines of this poem read, in Arthur Waley's translation:[34]

> He proved the truth of the *Cantong qi*;
> in a golden furnace he melted the Holy Drug.
> (*Jiang Wentong jihui zhu*, 3.111)

About one century later, Yan Zhitui (531–91) reports the cryptogram found in one of the final sections the *Cantong qi*.[35]

Although the citations of the *Cantong qi* during the Six Dynasties are few and are dispersed in sources of diverse nature, they provide important details on the history of the text in this period. Jiang Yan was from Jiankang (present-day Nanjing); Tao Hongjing was born and lived in the same area; and Yan Zhitui came from Shandong in the north, but spent part of his life at the court of the southern Liang dynasty in Jiankang. All those who mention the *Cantong qi* during the Six Dynasties were closely related to Jiangnan, showing that the *Cantong qi*, at that time, was transmitted in southeastern China. Jiang Yan's poem attests, moreover, that the *Cantong qi* was used in association with alchemy by the end of the fifth century.

[34] See Waley, "Notes on Chinese Alchemy," 8.

[35] *Yanshi jiaxun* (Family Instructions for the Yan Clan), 2.20a; trans. Teng Ssu-yü, *Family Instructions for the Yan Clan*, 185. On the cryptogram, see the textual notes on section 88, p. 244. Note that Yan Zhitui reports only the combination of characters that form the word *zao* ("composed by"), and not those that form the name "Wei Boyang."

In the common sense of the term, the history of the *Cantong qi* begins with these citations. The events that followed are best described individually, even though they occurred in parallel to one another. The first point to consider is that the transmission of the *Cantong qi* in Jiangnan is likely to have originated with the milieux that handed down the Han-dynasty "Studies of the *Book of Changes*" and the lore of the apocryphal texts. These milieux included the lineage represented by Yu Fan, who not only came from Jiangnan, but was himself a native of Shangyu, like Wei Boyang and apparently Chunyu Shutong. It is by no means certain that Yu Fan's lineage was directly involved in the transmission of the *Cantong qi*, but several hints seen above—in the first place, his being ascribed with a commentary to the *Cantong qi*—allow this assumption. Whether this and other lineages transmitted a Han-dynasty *Cantong qi*, or a slightly later *Cantong qi* written on the basis of one or more unidentified Han-dynasty writings, is only marginally important. The main point is that these lineages, which were related to the *Book of Changes*, attributed the composition of the *Cantong qi* to representatives of cosmological tradition, namely Xu Congshi and Chunyu Shutong.

In the early fourth century, Ge Hong (a native of Jiangnan) was familiar with lore about an earlier alchemist named Wei Boyang, but does not seem to have known the *Cantong qi* in any of its forms. About two hundred years later, Tao Hongjing (who came from the same area) cites a *Cantong qi*, but does not mention Wei Boyang as its author. His account, instead, refers to the *Cantong qi* as a source on Chunyu Shutong, and testifies to Chunyu's integration into the southern traditions. The diviner who had learned the "arts of the numbers" from a master in Shandong is said to be a native of Shangyu, like Wei Boyang; he is turned into an alchemist, having received a text on the elixirs from an immortal; and he is appointed as an officer of the otherworldly bureaucracy, in the shape that by that time had been constructed by the Taoist traditions of Jiangnan.

When we try to consider the details seen above in relation to one another, they suggest that the alchemical portions of the *Cantong qi* were composed in Jiangnan after Ge Hong's time. The representatives of the southern alchemical lineages created a new alchemical model that was directly based on the doctrines of the *Book of Changes* and its cosmology, and differed in this and other essential respects from the one documented by the earlier and contemporary

Waidan texts, and by the alchemical chapters in Ge Hong's *Baopu zi*. As we learn from Jiang Yan's poem, this process was essentially achieved by the end of the fifth century, when the *Cantong qi* was used in association with alchemy. We have no evidence that the alchemical portions of the text were already written at that time. Nevertheless, it was certainly as part of these events that Wei Boyang, an exemplary master of the southeastern alchemical traditions, began to be named as the author of the entire *Cantong qi*. As we have seen, several centuries would elapse before this role became widely accepted; in fact, other lineages—not only cosmological, but also alchemical—continued to ascribe the *Cantong qi* to Xu Congshi and Chunyu Shutong even during the Tang dynasty.[36] Wei Boyang was fully accredited with the authorship of the whole *Cantong qi* only around the turn of the first millennium.

Seen under this light, the purpose of the additional final paragraph in the *Shenxian zhuan* biography of Wei Boyang becomes clear: the representatives of the alchemical lineages intended to show that the *Cantong qi* describes the foundations of their own doctrines and practices. This explains why that paragraph not only mentions the alchemist Wei Boyang, but also denounces the "scholars" who, "knowing nothing about the divine Elixir . . . have written several commentaries based on Yin and Yang." Clearly the allusion here is to those who interpreted the *Cantong qi* as a work on cosmology.[37] Under the same light, it is almost impossible to escape the assumption that Wei Boyang's putative disciple "whose surname was Yu," quite oddly mentioned in the *Shenxian zhuan* without his first name, is none other than Yu Fan, the cosmologist, who is now portrayed as a faithful follower of Wei Boyang, the alchemist. Whether or not this assumption is correct, it is hardly conceivable that the final paragraph of the *Shenxian zhuan* biography of Wei Boyang was written by Ge Hong.

[36] We have seen a clear example of this in note 14 above, where the Waidan commentary attributes the *Cantong qi* to Chunyu Shutong.

[37] And not, as is assumed in Schipper and Verellen, *The Taoist Canon: A Historical Companion to the Daozang*, 324, to those who interpreted the text "in sexual terms," who would hardly be called "scholars" (*ru*) in a work like the *Shenxian zhuan*.

Taoism and the "Unity of the Three"

We shall now approach the last and most important historical question that surround the *Cantong qi*: Who wrote the text in its present form? Leaving aside the fact that whoever wrote the *Cantong qi* mastered the art of poetry, any answer to this question can only proceed from consideration of its doctrines. It should also be clear, by now, that the answer cannot consist in naming an author, but a tradition whose representatives are, by definition, anonymous.[38]

One remark is essential but sufficient to answer this question. The distinction between the paths of "superior virtue" and "inferior virtue"—the paths of non-doing (*wuwei*) and of alchemy, respectively—is drawn from the perspective of the former path, and conforms to principles set forth in the *Daode jing* and elaborated on in the *Zhuangzi* (see § 7). From this perspective, the practice of alchemy—performed in accordance with the principles formulated in the *Cantong qi*—represents the preparatory, gradual practice that, if entirely accomplished, grants access to the highest realized state (see *Cantong qi*, section 20, and its notes). This perspective lies at the core of the Taoist portions of the *Cantong qi*, but invests the whole text and gives unity to its three main subjects. If this point is taken into account, it is evident that those who gave the *Cantong qi* its present shape could only be the nameless representatives of the Taoist traditions of Jiangnan, who had essential ties to the doctrines of the *Daode jing* and the *Zhuangzi*.

One final point deserves attention. The Taoist portions of the *Cantong qi* contain passages that criticize practices different from the alchemical ones, including the Taoist methods of meditation on the inner deities (see below, § 7 and § 8). Despite this, the *Cantong qi* draws some of its terminology from texts pertaining to Taoist meditation, and in particular from the "Inner" version of the *Scripture of the Yellow Court* (*Huangting jing*), a work belonging to the Shangqing revelations of 364–70.[39] Since the shared terms are evenly distributed among the

---

[38] By "present form" I mean a shape substantially similar to the present one, with the likely exception of Book 3 which, as we shall see, is later than the other two Books. I do not mean, in any case, the redaction of the *Cantong qi* that is at the basis of the present translation.

[39] For one of the main examples, see the note to sentence 24:11. See also Pregadio, *Great Clarity*, p. 230 note 31.

different parts of the *Cantong qi*, one hand—the anonymous, collective "hand" of the southern Taoist traditions—revised the text, probably after the end of the fourth century.

Conclusion

This survey has by no means answered all questions concerning the date of the *Cantong qi*: as we shall see, the different prosodic forms of the text, the tradition that it contains a "Canon" and a "Commentary," and the virtually certain later date of Book 3 raise further issues. We may, nevertheless, briefly summarize the main results of our inquiry.

One or more texts entitled *Cantong qi* may have existed during the Han period, but if any such text did exist, it was certainly not the present one. With regard to the individual components of the present-day *Cantong qi*, its cosmological portions definitely reflect a Han background. However, they were almost certainly composed, or at least completed (possibly on the basis of one or more Han-dynasty texts), after the end of the Han period by lineages that transmitted the "Studies of the *Book of Changes*" and the apocrypha in Jiangnan. Yu Fan's lineage was almost certainly one of those involved. The alchemical portions also cannot date from the Han period. Their precise time of composition remains unknown; we do know that the *Cantong qi*, in one or another of its forms, was used in association with alchemy by the end of the fifth century, but its alchemical model began to affect the history of Chinese alchemy only from the seventh century for Waidan, and from the eighth century for Neidan. As for the Taoist portions, it is virtually certain that they were not composed before the end of the fourth century.

We may conclude, therefore, by saying that the *Cantong qi* was composed in different stages, perhaps from the Han period onward, and did not reach a form substantially similar to the present one before ca. 450, and possibly one or even two centuries later.

More important than any attempt to establish a precise date, however, is the fact that, in light of what we have seen, Wei Boyang is much more than a semi-legendary alchemist who lived in the mid-second century. Just like the Boyang who preceded him is for the *Daode jing*, Wei Boyang is the symbolic representative of a nameless "collective entity": the tradition that integrated the different components of the *Cantong qi* with one another, and created with this work the main exposition of the Way of the Golden Elixir.

§ 4. THE THREE BOOKS AND THE "ANCIENT TEXT"

The textual form of the *Cantong qi* is defined by two main features:

(1) In all redactions until the one produced by Chen Zhixu in ca. 1330, and in most of the later ones, the *Cantong qi* is divided into three main parts, or "Books" (*pian*).

(2) The last part, or Book 3, contains three distinct compositions, which in certain redactions are followed by an additional "postface."

Speculations about the authorship of the three main parts abound in both commentaries and modern studies, where they are variously attributed to Wei Boyang, Xu Congshi, or Chunyu Shutong. Whoever stands behind these names, it may be safely assumed that the text found in Books 1 and 2 (corresponding to sections 1–42 and 43–74 in the present translation) and the additional compositions found in Book 3 (sections 75–88) originated separately from one another.

Books 1 and 2: The Main Text

Except for a few passages in prose, Books 1 and 2 are made of rhymed verses in four or five characters. Sections written in either prosodic form follow one another without any order or regularity; the only noticeable feature in this regard is that the five-character verses prevail in Book 1, while Book 2 is almost entirely made of four-character verses. This is unrelated to any prevalence of subjects, which are written in one or the other format and, as we have seen, are equally treated in both Books. Several commentators and scholars have suggested that the two meters are related to the tradition—developed on the basis of early accounts on the creation of the text—that the *Cantong qi* contains a main text, or "Canon" ("Jing"), and a "Commentary" ("Zhu"). There is no agreement, however, on which portions might constitute the "Canon" and the "Commentary."

On the other hand, one of the most evident, but also most enigmatic, features of Books 1 and 2 is the fact that several sections written in different meters mirror one another. Some of the main correspondences include those between sections 1 and 43, on the representation of change by trigrams and hexagrams; 3 and 45, on the sixty-hexagram cycle; 10 and 48, on the joining of the Sun and Moon;

13 and 49, on the cycle of trigrams; and 39–40 and 62, on the alchemical conjunction of Lead and Mercury. Several scholars have drawn attention to this feature and have discussed the possible historical priorities among these portions of the text. One point, however, does not seem to have been considered. The *Cantong qi* describes three main cosmological cycles: those of the sixty hexagrams during the days, of the eight trigrams during the month, and of the twelve "sovereign hexagrams" (*bigua*) during the year (see below, pp. 41 ff.). The first cycle is described once in four-character verses and once in five-character verses (sections 45 and 3, respectively); the second cycle also is described once in four-character verses and once in five-character verses (sections 49 and 13); but the third cycle is described only in four-character verses (section 51). In the extent to which the twelve-hexagram cycle is integral to the doctrines of the *Cantong qi*, its description may be deemed to be part of the original core of the text; and as long as this assumption is correct, the original core would consist of the portions in four-character verses. Whether and how this may be related to the view that the *Cantong qi* includes a "Canon" and a "Commentary" remains unclear. Nevertheless, the mirrored sections suggest that, in addition to the separate composition of the portions on cosmology, Taoism, and alchemy, the individual sections that form Books 1 and 2 were written in different times.

Book 3: Additional Writings

Book 3 contains three distinct additional compositions:

(1) "Epilogue" ("Luanci," sections 75–81), mostly written according to the *saoti* prosody, so called after the *Lisao* (Encountering Sorrow) piece in the *Songs of Chu* (*Chuci*).[40]

(2) "Song of the Tripod" ("Dingqi ge," section 82), a poem in three-character verses, another prosodic form not found in the first two Books.

(3) "Filling Lacunae" ("Busai yituo," sections 83–88), consisting in a statement that the teachings of the *Cantong qi* are based on the *Book of Changes*, Taoism, and alchemy; a poem on the instant

---

[40] In some of the *Songs of Chu*, the "Epilogue" is the portion appended to a poem in order to summarize its essential points.

between the end of a time cycle and the beginning of the next one; and a final portion in which the author describes himself and his work. The final portion contains the sentence, "The name of my book is *The Seal of the Unity of the Three*," showing that it concerns the entire text, and not only "Filling Lacunae."[41]

Several commentators have suggested that either the whole Book 3, or only "Filling Lacunae," corresponds to *The Five Categories*, the second work attributed to Wei Boyang in the *Shenxian zhuan*. In certain redactions, moreover, Book 3 is concluded by an anonymous postface entitled "Eulogium" ("Zanxu," not included in the present translation).[42]

The best-known and most important composition of Book 3 is the "Song of the Tripod." This poem can be read a synopsis of the alchemical content of the *Cantong qi*, but one detail shows that its views do not fully match those of Books 1 and 2. Section 51 of the *Cantong qi* describes the cycle of the Sun during the year, saying that the Yang principle rises during the first six months, and declines during the last six months. This cycle, and its description, became the main models for the practice of the "fire times" (*huohou*) in both Waidan and Neidan. According to the "Song," instead, the fire should be strong at the beginning of the heating, mild at the middle, and then again strong at the end; these three stages respectively should last 70,

---

[41] This section is entitled "Filling Lacunae" by Peng Xiao; "The Five Categories" ("Wu xianglei") by Zhu Xi; and "Postface" ("Xu") by Yu Yan. Chen Zhixu divides it into two parts, respectively entitled "Filling Lacunae" ("Busai yituo," sections 83–85) and "Author's Postface: My Bequest" ("Zixu qihou," sections 86–88).

[42] Yu Yan does not refer to the "Postface" as consisting of "The Five Categories," but of "The Three Categories" ("San xianglei"). In his view, this title refers to the three main subjects of the *Cantong qi*. Several later commentators, including those of the "Ancient Text," have followed Yu Yan's view and have adopted the title "Three Categories" instead of "Five Categories" for the final portion of the text. Yu Yan also suggests that, as a title, "Three Categories" is synonymous with "Seal of the Unity of the Three": *can* 參 corresponds to *san* 三 (both words mean "three"); *tong* 同 ("to join") corresponds to *xiang* 相 ("reciprocal, mutual"); and *qi* 契 (here understood as "token, tally") corresponds to *lei* 類 ('category," but as a verb also meaning "to agree with, to match," like the two parts of a tally). According to this explanation, the title "San xianglei" should be translated "The Mutual Correspondences of the Three." See *Zhouyi cantong qi fahui*, 10.13b-14a, and *Zhouyi cantong qi shiyi*, 23b-24a.

260, and 30 days. With other details, this shows that the "Song" was composed separately from Books 1 and 2.[43]

The "Ancient Text"

In the early sixteenth century, a new version of the *Cantong qi*, anachronistically called *Guwen cantong qi*, or *Ancient Text of the Cantong qi*, was created on the basis of a complete rearrangement of the scripture. This version divides the sections in verses of four characters from those in verses of five characters, following a suggestion that was first given by Yu Yan in 1284. Its origins can be traced back to Du Yicheng, who came from Suzhou (like Yu Yan) and wrote a now-lost commentary on it in 1517.[44]

Several authors of commentaries to the standard version of the *Cantong qi* have regarded the Ancient Text as spurious, and similar criticism has also been voiced by Chinese scholars from the Qing period onward. This view has been partly influenced by the controversial personality of Yang Shen (1488–1559), who, about three decades after Du Yicheng, claimed to have found the Ancient Text in a stone casket, and published it under his own name. Nevertheless, the prestige enjoyed by the Ancient Text within Ming, Qing, and present-day lineages of Neidan suggests that the verdict of non-authenticity is inaccurate. Not only does the text, despite the different arrangement, include the whole *Cantong qi*, without any addition and with the omission of only a few verses; but no one without a solid

---

[43] Meng Naichang, *Zhouyi cantong qi kaobian*, 47–48, has suggested that the "Song" was included in the *Cantong qi* on the basis of an early record of a different version, entitled "Song of Lord Lao" ("Laojun ge"), which is now included in the biography of Laozi's disciple, Yin Xi, found in *Lishi zhenxian tidao tongjian*, 8.5b-6a.

[44] Yu Yan's remarks on this subject are found at the very end of his commentary (*Zhouyi cantong qi fahui*, 9.19b-21a). He refers to this as a sudden realization that he had after he finished to write his work: "Suddenly one evening, while I was in complete quietude, I heard something like a whisper saying: 'Wei Boyang wrote the *Cantong qi*, and Xu Congshi made a commentary. The sequence of the bamboo slips was disrupted; this is why the portions in four-character verses, those in five-character verses, and those in prose are in disorder.' . . . I wish I could subdivide the text into three parts, respectively made of four-character verses, five-character verses, and prose, so that text and commentary are not confused, in order to facilitate the inquiries of future students. However, my book is complete, and I cannot change it."

knowledge of the standard version of the *Cantong qi*, and of its doctrinal principles, could have fabricated a work of this nature. In the arrangement of the Ancient Text, the four- and five-character verses are not reproduced in the same sequence as in the standard version; and in the new arrangement, the discourse of *Cantong qi* reveals a much clearer pattern.

The account of the composition of the Ancient Text includes all three authors traditionally deemed to have been involved in the creation of the standard version—and this is the main reason why several commentators, for whom Wei Boyang could only be the single author of the whole *Cantong qi*, rejected the Ancient Text altogether.[45] According to the new version, Wei Boyang wrote the "Canon" in verses of four characters; Xu Congshi (whom the Ancient Text exegetes regularly identify as Xu Jingxiu) contributed a "Commentary" in verses of five characters; and Chunyu Shutong added a final section, entitled "The Three Categories." In the Ancient Text, both the "Canon" and the "Commentary" are divided into three chapters, respectively devoted to cosmology, Taoism, and alchemy.

The Ancient Text exists, in its turn, in versions that differ in significant or minor ways from one another in the sequence of their sections. Two of them deserve note, for opposite reasons. One of the best-known versions was edited and commented by Qiu Zhao'ao (1704). Disagreeing with the view that "Canon" and "Commentary" are divided into three main parts respectively devoted to cosmology, Taoism, and alchemy, this commentator reads the whole *Cantong qi* as a Neidan text; and since the arrangement into three parts is irrelevant to his views, he merely subdivides both the "Canon" and the "Commentary" into 18 sections, essentially disrupting the very *raison d'être* of the Ancient Text.[46] On the other hand, the equally well-known commentary written by Liu Yiming in 1799 (entitled *Cantong zhizhi*, or *Straightforward Directions on the Cantong qi*) represents a major revision of the Ancient Text based on its own principles. In this version, the individual portions within the "Canon" and the "Com-

---

[45] Despite their criticism, the Ancient Text inspired the new, inventive formats of the standard version of the *Cantong qi* contained in the commentaries by Xu Wei (ca. 1570), Li Guangdi (ca. 1700), and Li Shixu (1823). The views of Zhu Yuanyu (1669) and Dong Dening (1787) on the three main subjects of the *Cantong qi* are also clearly inspired by those of the Ancient Text.

[46] See *Guben Zhouyi cantong qi jizhu*, "Liyan ershi tiao," 10a-12a.

mentary" are rearranged according to their subjects—cosmology, Taoism, and alchemy—in such a way that they follow corresponding sequences. This enables Liu Yiming to precisely point out for each portion of the "Commentary" a corresponding portion of the "Canon." Regardless of whether the *Cantong qi* actually does contain a "Canon" and a "Commentary," Liu Yiming's work is the one that best brings to light certain correspondences that exist among different portions of the *Cantong qi*, but are not easily discerned in the standard text.

§ 5. MAIN COMMENTARIES

At least thirty-eight traditional commentaries to the *Cantong qi* are extant, written between ca. 700 and the final years of the Qing dynasty. Different sources—in particular, bibliographies and premodern library catalogues—yield information on about twice as many lost commentaries and closely related works.[47]

Commentaries in the Taoist Canon

The Taoist Canon (*Daozang*) of 1445 contains the following commentaries to the standard text:

(1) *Zhouyi cantong qi zhu* (Commentary to the *Cantong qi*). Anonymous, dating from ca. 700, containing the only surviving explication of the *Cantong qi* as a work concerned with Waidan. Only the portion corresponding to Book 1 is extant.[48]

(2) *Zhouyi cantong qi*. Attributed to a venerable Taoist immortal, Yin Changsheng, also dating from ca. 700.

(3) *Zhouyi cantong qi fenzhang tong zhenyi* (True Meaning of the *Cantong qi*, with a Subdivision into Sections). Peng Xiao (?–955), dating from 947. The portion entitled *Zhouyi cantong qi dingqi ge mingjing tu* (The "Song of the Tripod" and the "Chart of the

---

[47] On these works, see my *The Seal of the Unity of the Three*, vol. 2: *Bibliographic Studies on the Cantong qi* (forthcoming).

[48] The preface describes the work as consisting of three parts. Moreover, the commentary refers twice (1.19b and 1.20a) to passages that should be found in the missing part of the text. This shows that the work originally included the entire *Cantong qi*.

Bright Mirror" of the *Cantong qi*) is printed as a separate work in
the Taoist Canon.[49]

(4) *Zhouyi cantong qi kaoyi* (Investigation of Discrepancies in the
Cantong qi). Zhu Xi (1130–1200), dating from 1197.

(5) *Zhouyi cantong qi*. Chu Yong (also known as Chu Huagu, fl. ca.
1230), dating from ca. 1230.

(6) *Zhouyi cantong qi jie* (Explication of the *Cantong qi*). Chen
Xianwei (?–after 1254), dating from 1234.

(7) *Zhouyi cantong qi fahui* (Elucidation of the *Cantong qi*). Yu Yan
(1258–1314), dating from 1284. The portion entitled *Shiyi* (Explication of Doubtful Points) is printed as a separate work in the
Taoist Canon.

(8) *Zhouyi cantong qi zhu* (Commentary to the *Cantong qi*). Anonymous Neidan commentary, dating from after 1208.

Four of these commentaries—those by Peng Xiao, Zhu Xi, Chen
Xianwei, and Yu Yan—are also extant in several other editions.

The first two commentaries present a somewhat unrefined state of
the text, not divided into sections, with several sentences not yet
normalized into four- or five-character verses, and—a significant
detail—with more explicit allusions to Waidan compared to the later
redactions (where certain sentences appear in slightly modified
forms). In the mid-tenth century, Peng Xiao revised the text and
produced the version that is, directly or indirectly, at the basis of most
later commentaries. His work, which is divided into 90 sections, has
not reached us in its original form; there is clear evidence that it was
altered in the early thirteenth century with the incorporation of
several dozen readings drawn from Zhu Xi's text. The revised version
of Peng Xiao's text is faithfully followed by the anonymous Neidan
commentary. The first text to be based on a comparison of earlier
editions was established by Zhu Xi, but his work was deprived of
most of its critical notes by the mid-fourteenth century. Zhu Xi's text
in turn served as a model to Chu Yong. The two remaining commentaries in the Taoist Canon are those by Chen Xianwei, whose text
derives from Peng Xiao; and by Yu Yan, who based his work on Zhu
Xi's text, but eliminated many of the archaisms and the peculiar

---

[49] The "Chart" is Peng Xiao's own work. It illustrates several sets of
cosmological emblems used in the *Cantong qi*, with explanatory notes.

readings that had been introduced by Zhu Xi. Yu Yan's learned commentary contains quotations from about one hundred different texts, and is accompanied by philological notes on variants found in earlier editions.

Later Commentaries

The Neidan commentary by Chen Zhixu (1290–ca. 1368) is entitled *Zhouyi cantong qi zhujie* (Commentary and Explication of the *Cantong qi*) and dates from ca. 1330. Like Peng Xiao had done before him, Chen Zhixu proposes a new arrangement of the *Cantong qi*. In addition to the customary three Books, he subdivides the text into thirty-five chapters (*zhang*). His text is ultimately based on Peng Xiao's redaction, but contains about four dozen readings that are not documented in earlier extant works. It became well known—albeit anonymously—to a large number of literati through its inclusion in the *Han Wei congshu* (Collected Works of the Han and the Wei Dynasties), a highly regarded and well-distributed compilation that contains the text found in Zhang Wenlong's commentary of 1566, which is based in turn on Chen Zhixu's redaction.

With the exception of Zhu Xi's work, all extant commentaries to the *Cantong qi* written through the Yuan period (1279–1368) are related to the Taoist alchemical traditions. During the Ming (1368–1644) and the Qing (1644–1912) dynasties, the *Cantong qi* continued to exert its prestige on Neidan, but its influence also extended to other fields. Zhu Xi's commentary, in particular, inspired many literati to read the text and write about it. The commentaries by Xu Wei (ca. 1570) and Wang Wenlu (1582) during the Ming period, and those by Li Guangdi (ca. 1700), Wang Fu (ca. 1750), and Li Shixu (1823) during the Qing period, are representative of this trend. The redaction by Chen Zhixu was, either on its own or in a substantial way, at the basis of the commentaries by Xu Wei, Wang Wenlu, Li Guangdi, and Wang Fu, as well as those by Zhang Wenlong (1566), Zhen Shu (1636), and Dong Dening (1787). Other commentators, including Lu Xixing (1569, revised in 1573) and Zhu Yuanyu (1669), based their texts on other redactions.[50]

---

[50] These details are provided on the basis of major textual variants found in different redactions of the *Cantong qi*, which can serve as main indicators of textual filiation. See my work cited in note 47 above.

During the Ming period, as we saw above, Du Yicheng created the "Ancient Text" ("Guwen") version of the *Cantong qi*. Ten commentaries to this version are extant, including those by Wang Jiachun (1591?), Peng Haogu (1599), Qiu Zhao'ao (1704), and Liu Yiming (1799), whose authors were affiliated with different Ming and Qing lineages of Neidan.

§ 6. DAO, COSMOS, AND MAN

The main purpose of the cosmological portions of the *Cantong qi* is to define the relation of the cosmos to the Dao. This relation is described by means of emblems that represent the modes taken on by the Dao in its self-manifestation, and the corresponding main features of Being. On the basis of this definition, a set of principles is derived that serve to establish the cosmological science of alchemy, described elsewhere in the *Cantong qi*.

The cosmological portions of the *Cantong qi* give prominence to the role and functions of the ruler. The king, being placed at the symbolic center of the human realm—his kingdom, and more specifically his court—should guarantee the reciprocal agreement of Heaven, Earth, and mankind. Trigrams and hexagrams of the *Book of Changes*, and other related emblems, enable him to comprehend the patterns of Heaven and Earth, and to model his governance on those patterns. These portions of the text could be read literally as advice given to the ruler, or metaphorically as instructions addressed to the alchemist. It should not be forgotten, however, that in a work like the *Cantong qi*, the ruler in his relation to the kingdom is, in the first place, a subordinate counterpart of the sage in his relation to the whole of Being (in accordance with the principles of the *Daode jing*).

The main subjects of the cosmological portions of the *Cantong qi* are the following (references are to the numbers of sections):

1. Qian and Kun, Kan and Li: 1, 4–5, 43
2. Sun and Moon: 7, 8, 10, 48
3. Day (60 hexagrams): 3, 45
4. Month (8 trigrams): 13, 49

5. Year (12 hexagrams): 51–52
6. Ruler and governance: 2, 14, 15, 17, 44, 47

Qian, Kun, Kan, Li

Although the names Qian, Kun, Kan, and Li belong to the vocabulary
of the *Book of Changes*, it would be impossible to understand the
functions that they play in a work like the *Cantong qi* as long as they
are seen as no more than trigrams or hexagrams. From the perspective
of the *Cantong qi*, Qian, Kun, Kan, and Li are formless principles
that serve to explicate how the Dao generates the relative domain and
manifests itself in it. The corresponding trigrams and hexagrams are
symbolic forms (*xiang*) used to represent those principles.

Qian and Kun are the two primary modes taken on by the Dao in
generating the world:

> Great indeed is Qian, the Origin! The ten thousand things owe
> their beginning to him . . . Perfect indeed is Kun, the Origin! The
> ten thousand things owe their birth to her. (*Book of Changes*,
> "Commentary on the Judgement" on the hexagrams Qian ☰ and
> Kun ☷)

Qian is the active ("creative") principle, essence, Yang, and Heaven;
Kun is the passive ("receptive") principle, substance, Yin, and Earth.
Being permanently joined to one another in the precosmic domain,
Qian entrusts its creative power to Kun, and Kun brings creation to
accomplishment.

In the everlasting instant in which Qian and Kun give birth to the
cosmos, the Yang of Qian moves into Kun, and, in response, the Yin of
Kun moves into Qian. In the symbolic representation by the corresponding trigrams, Qian ☰ entrusts its essence to Kun and becomes Li
☲; Kun ☷ receives that essence from Qian and becomes Kan ☵.

Kan and Li, therefore, replace Qian and Kun in the cosmic domain.
Since they harbor the Yang of Qian and the Yin of Kun, respectively, as
their own inner essences, they enable the Yin and Yang of the precosmic domain to operate in the cosmic domain. For this reason, Kan and
Li are said to be the "functions" (*yong*, a word also meaning "operation") of Qian and Kun, while Qian and Kun are the "substantive
basis" (*ti*) of Kan and Li (see section 4). The main images of Qian and
Kun are Heaven and Earth, which are immutably joined to one

another. The main images of Kan and Li are the Moon and the Sun, which alternate in their growth and decline during the longer or shorter time cycles. This alternation (day and night, seasons, etc.) is the main visible sign of the operation of Qian and Kun in the cosmos.

This vision pertains to the relative world in which we live, and is meaningful only within its boundaries. Qian, Kun, Kan, and Li fundamentally reside within the Dao, undifferentiated from one another (43:13–14). By analogy, they also reside within the spaceless and timeless point at the center of the cosmos, namely, the Heart of Heaven (*tianxin*), at the core of multiplicity and change (12:1). Their differentiation occurs only within the relative domain, where they serve to explicate the relation of the Dao to the world, and its constant presence throughout space and time.

The Five Agents

The five agents are Wood, Fire, Soil, Metal, and Water (see tables 1 and 2). They carry the Original Breath issued from the Dao into the cosmos, and represent its differentiation in the world of multiplicity. In a different but related function, moreover, the five agents make it possible to classify items belonging to different sets—directions of space, segments of time cycles, numbers, colors, planets, minerals, and organs of the human body, to mention only the sets used in the *Cantong qi*—into five emblematic categories, in order to show the relations that occur among items belonging to the same category and among those that belong to different categories. For example, with regard to the first type of relation, the agent Wood associates the east, the spring, the numbers 3 and 8, the color green, the planet Jupiter, and the organ liver with one another. With regard to the second type of relation, spring and summer, respectively associated with Wood and Fire, exemplify two different states of the Yang principle (the same it true, therefore, of Jupiter and Mars, the liver and the heart, and so forth).

The agents are generated in the first place by the division of original Unity into Yin and Yang, and by the further subdivision of Yin and Yang into four states. These four states are defined by two distinct series of terms. The first series emphasizes stages of cyclical change, respectively called "minor Yang" (Wood), "great Yang" (Fire), "minor Yin" (Metal), and "great Yin" (Water). The second series, instead, emphasizes the different states of the two polar principles. Here Water and Fire are Yin and Yang, and Wood and Metal are True Yin and True Yang (*zhenyin* and *zhenyang*), respectively. The second series is especially important in alchemy.

Soil, the fifth agent, is positioned at the center and has both a Yang and a Yin aspect, respectively represented by the celestial stems *wu* 戊 and *ji* 己. Being at the center, Soil stands for the source from which the other four agents derive. It partakes of all of them, and therefore guarantees the conjunction of the world of multiplicity to the original state of Unity (see section 7).

The five agents can be arranged into different sequences. The *Cantong qi* refers to four of these sequences:

(1) The "cosmogonic" sequence is the order in which the agents are generated as part of the cosmogonic process. The sequence is Water 水 → Fire 火 → Wood 木 → Metal 金 → Soil 土. The *Cantong qi* refers to this sequence, in particular, in verses 22:5–6 ("Water is the axis of the Dao: its number is 1") and 72:14 ("the son is at the origin of the five agents," where Water is the first "child" of the One, or Unity).

(2) The "generation" sequence (*xiangsheng*) is the order in which the agents give birth to one another. The sequence is Wood 木 → Fire 火 → Soil 土 → Metal 金 → Water 水 (at the end of the cycle, Water generates Wood). In the *Cantong qi*, whose alchemical model is based on the "conquest" and the "inversion" sequences (see below), the "generation" sequence is virtually ignored. It is incidentally mentioned only in sections 32 and 71 to point out that Soil (which is generated by Fire and generates Metal) conquers Water (which is generated by Metal and generates Wood).

(3) The "conquest" sequence (*xiangke*) is the order in which the agents overcome or displace one another. The sequence is Water 水 → Fire 火 → Metal 金 → Wood 木 → Soil 土 (to be read as "Water conquers Fire; Fire conquers Metal," etc.; at the end of the cycle, Soil conquers Water). This is one of the two main sequences referred to in the *Cantong qi* and in the alchemical traditions based on its doctrines. To give one example of several possible configurations, the two ingredients of the Elixir correspond to Water and Fire; first Water (containing True Lead) conquers Fire (containing True Mercury); then Soil (the agent representing the

Elixir) conquers Water (see, e.g., 32:13–14: "When Water flourish-es, Fire is extinguished, and both die, together returning to gener-ous Soil").

(4) The "inversion" sequence consists in the inversion of the "genera-tion" sequence. This is the second main arrangement of the agents referred to in the alchemical portions of the *Cantong qi*. The inversion concerns two pairs of agents. While in the "generation" sequence Wood generates Fire, and Metal generates Water, in the alchemical process it is Fire (native cinnabar) that generates Wood (True Mercury), and Water (black lead) that generates Metal (True Lead). In other words, Yang generates True Yin, and Yin generates True Yang. This pattern is explicitly mentioned, e.g., in verses 23:1–2 ("Metal is the mother of Water — [but] the mother is hidden in the embryo of her son") and 72:1–4 ("When the Wooden essence of cinnabar finds Metal, they pair with each other: Metal and Water dwell in conjunction, Wood and Fire are companions").

Other Emblems

The other main sets of cosmological emblems used in the *Cantong qi* are the following:

Celestial Stems (tiangan) *and Earthly Branches* (dizhi). These two series of emblems, respectively made of ten and twelve items, serve to mark directions of space as well as units of time. Each series is associ-ated with the five agents and, through them, with all other sets of entities and phenomena categorized according to the quinary pattern (see tables 12 and 13). In the *Cantong qi*, the two main stems are *wu* 戊 and *ji* 己; they associated with the agent Soil and represent the Yang and Yin aspects of Unity, respectively (see sections 7, 32, and 72). The branches are mainly used to represent the individual segments of temporal cycles based on the duodenary pattern, namely the day with its twelve "double hours" and the year with its twelve months (see especially sections 3, 45, and 51).

Pitch-pipes (lü), *or "Bells and Pitch-pipes"* (zhonglü). This series of twelve emblems (see table 11) performs a function virtually identical to the twelve earthly branches (see especially section 51).

Lunar Lodges (xiu). The twenty-eight lodges (see table 16) are constellations that the Sun crosses in its apparent journey through the sky during the year. Like the two previous sets, their function in the *Cantong qi* is purely emblematic: being divided into four groups of seven, they represent the four quarters of space, and therefore are associated with the four external agents (see sections 49 and 73).

Time Cycles

As was mentioned above, the cosmological portions of the *Cantong qi* give emphasis to three emblematic time cycles: the day, the month, and the year. These cycles manifest the presence of the One Breath of the Dao in the cosmos. All of them—but especially the third one—became models of the "fire times" (*huohou*) in alchemy, which determine the process needed to heat the Elixir.

Sixty Hexagrams: The Diurnal Cycle. The first pattern concerns the thirty days of the lunar month (see sections 3 and 45). During each day, the Yang, active principle prevails at daytime, from dawn to dusk, and the Yin, passive principle prevails at nighttime, from dusk to dawn. The two parts of the day are ruled by a pair of hexagrams: a Yang hexagram presides over the first, "outward" half, and a Yin hexagram presides over the second, "inward" half.

Accordingly, sixty of the sixty-four hexagrams are distributed among the thirty days of the month (see table 7). The remaining four hexagrams, namely Qian ☰, Kun ☷, Kan ☵, and Li ☲, reside at the Center; they enable the time cycles to occur, but are not part of their operation. The sixty hexagrams follow one another in the order in which they are arranged in the *Book of Changes* and are described in its appendix entitled "Hexagrams in Sequence." In this appendix, the hexagrams are sorted into pairs, formed either by inverting the solid and broken lines of the first hexagram (e.g., Qian ☰ is followed by Kun ☷) or by turning the first hexagram upside down (e.g., Zhun ䷂ is followed by Meng ䷃). Zhun ䷂ and Meng ䷃, the first and second hexagrams after Qian and Kun, respectively correspond to daytime and nighttime of the month's first day. Jiji ䷾ and Weiji ䷿, the next-to-last and last hexagrams, respectively correspond to daytime and nighttime of the month's last day.

Therefore the rise and decline of Yin and Yang during the day is marked and measured by the twelve individual lines of the ruling pair of hexagrams. Each line is associated with one of the twelve "double hours." The twelve lines, moreover, are related to the twelve earthly branches (see fig. 4): the rise of the Yang principle along the six lines of the first hexagram is represented by the first six branches (*zi* 子, *chou* 丑, *yin* 寅, *mao* 卯, *chen* 辰, and *si* 巳), and the rise of the Yin principle along the six lines of the second hexagram is represented by the last six branches (*wu* 午, *wei* 未, *shen* 申, *you* 酉, *xu* 戌, and *hai* 亥). (Section 45 uses a different, more complex set of associations with the branches; see the note to table 8.)

"Matching Stems": The Monthly Cycle. The second main cosmological cycle described in the *Cantong qi* concerns the thirty days of the lunar month. This cycle, described by the device known as *najia*, or Matching Stems, is the subject of sections 13 and 49.[51]

As we saw above, the version of the *najia* device used in the *Cantong qi* is ascribed to Yu Fan. In this version, the month is divided into six parts of five days each: 1–5, 6–10, 11–15, 16–20, 21–25, and 26–30 (compare *Cantong qi*, 3:1: "In one month there are six nodes of five days"). Six trigrams, namely, Zhen ☳, Dui ☱, Qian ☰, Xun ☴, Gen ☶, and Kun ☷, are matched, with the corresponding stems, to nodal days in the waxing and waning of the Moon (see table 10): the 3rd (middle day of the first node), the 8th (middle day of the second node), the 15th (last day of the third node), the 16th (first day of the fourth node), the 23rd (middle day of the fifth node), and the 30th (last day of the sixth node). The six trigrams represent the growth and the decline of the Yang principle (the solid line ▬), from its birth at the beginning of the month to its complete obscuration at the end of the month.

The most significant aspect of the Matching Stems is the event that happens between the end of a lunar cycle and the beginning of the next one. Yu Fan describes this event saying that, during the night of the thirtieth day, the Moon "flows to *wu* 戊," the Yang celestial stem that is associated with Soil and the Center and represents the Moon's own inner brilliance (True Yang within Yin). There the Moon joins with the Sun, whose inner light is represented by *ji* 己, the Yin stem associated with Soil and the Center (True Yin within Yang):

----

[51] In the name *najia*, the term *jia* literally denotes the first celestial stem, but refers by extension to all ten stems, which are matched with (*na*, lit. "received by") the trigrams or the hexagrams.

Between the night of the month's last day and the dawn of next month's first day, the Moon flows to *wu* 戊. The center of the Sun is Li ☲; being an image of Li, the Sun accords with *ji* 己. *Wu* and *ji* are the positions of the agent Soil: their images appear in the Center. (*Zhouyi jijie*, 14.350)

This event is the subject of sections 10 and 48 of the *Cantong qi*. The monthly conjunction of the Sun (日) and the Moon (月) regenerates the light (明) after the darkness of the month's last night. At the end of the month, Kun ☷, pure Yin, stands for the complete obscuration of the Yang principle, and now dominates over the entire cosmos. However, being the mother, Kun gives birth to her first son, Zhen ☳, the initial trigram in the new lunar cycle, whose lower Yang line represents the rebirth of light. After an instant of suspension, time again begins to flow, and the next month begins.

"Twelve-Stage Ebb and Flow": The Yearly Cycle. The third main cosmological cycle, known as Twelve-stage Ebb and Flow (*shi'er xiaoxi*), represents cyclical change by the twelve so-called "sovereign hexagrams" (*bigua*). In a way similar to the Matching Stems pattern, here too the solid and broken lines flow first upwards and then downwards; however, while the Matching Stems device takes the month as a time unit, the "sovereign hexagrams" reproduce the rise and fall of Yin and Yang during the year (see table 11).

This cycle is the subject of section 51 of the *Cantong qi*. Beginning with Fu ䷗, which represents the first stage of the growth of Yang, each hexagram represents one lunar month. The twelve-stage sequence makes it possible to establish correspondences with other duodenary series: the earthly branches, the pitch-pipes, and the watches of the day (*shi*, often referred to as "double hours"). More details on this pattern will be found in the notes to section 51.

The Artisan and the Charioteer

One of the initial passages of the *Cantong qi* establishes a similitude between "the Way of Yin and Yang" and the crafts of the artisan and the charioteer, who "level the marking-cord and the plumb-line, hold the bit and the bridle, align the compass and the square, and follow the tracks and the ruts" (2:3–6). These images should be given much more attention than they can receive here. I will point out a few of their main values and associations.

Compass, square, plumb-line, and marking-cord. These tools stand—in this order—for Heaven and Earth (respectively said in the Chinese tradition to be "round" and "square"), the vertical axis and the horizontal plane (respectively pertaining, in their turn, to Heaven and Earth). The symbolic functions of these tools are to fathom the patterns of Heaven and Earth, and to reproduce those patterns in different microcosmic settings: the kingdom, the alchemical laboratory, the human being.

The four tools, as well as other implements that perform analogous functions (the level,[52] the scale, and the weight) are mentioned together in several early Chinese texts belonging to different traditions or schools of thought. At the center of these descriptions is the king. In this context, the artisan's tools refer to the principles that serve as a basis for governance; they signify, in particular, the laws and ordinances issued by the sage ruler in accordance with the patterns of Heaven and Earth, and the "rites" (*li,* i.e., the fundamental social institutions and traditions), which should comply with the same patterns. One of many relevant passages found in those texts states:

> Laws and ordinances are the compass, the square, the marking-cord, and the plumb-line to administer the people. If the square is not aligned, it cannot make things squared; if the marking-cord is not reliable, it cannot make things straight. The laws are established jointly by the lord and his ministers; the power is held only by the ruler. (*Guanzi,* 17.1/123/27)[53]

The most significant point to note is that these tools are often cited in the *Zhuangzi,* where their image, however, becomes unquestionably negative. In this work we read, for example:

> Huizi said to Zhuangzi: "I have a big tree of the kind men call *shu.* Its trunk is too gnarled and bumpy to apply a marking-cord or a plumb-line to, its branches too bent and twisty to match up to a compass or square." . . . Zhuangzi said: "Axes will never shorten

---

[52] Note that the word "level," *zhun,* is used as a verb in the *Cantong qi* passage quoted above.

[53] See Rickett, *Guanzi,* 2:210.

its life, nothing can ever harm it. If there's no use for it, how can it come to grief or pain?" (*Zhuangzi*, 1.39)[54]

The same negative view is expressed in this passage::

> The potter says, "I'm good at handling clay! To round it, I apply the compass; to square it, I apply the square." The carpenter says, "I'm good at handling wood! To arc it, I apply the curve; to make it straight, I apply the marking-cord." But as far as inborn nature is concerned, the clay and the wood surely have no wish to be subjected to compass and square, curve and plumb-line. (*Zhuangzi*, 9.330)[55]

These passages might appear to expose a major conflict between the views of the *Zhuangzi* and those of the *Cantong qi*. It is not difficult, however, to note that the artisan's tools perform their essential functions in the context of the cosmological sciences (the art of government, the alchemical arts), which correspond to what the *Cantong qi* calls the way of "inferior virtue." Both passages of the *Zhuangzi* quoted above contrast the use of those tools to the operation of nondoing (the *shu* tree, which preserves itself by its being "useless" and therefore "not used") and to the cultivation of the "inborn nature," which correspond to what the *Cantong qi* calls the way of "superior virtue."

Bit, bridle, tracks, and ruts. The other terms mentioned in the passage of the *Cantong qi* quoted above evoke the art of charioteering. The images of the chariot and its parts are among the most recurrent ones in the *Cantong qi*.[56] They pertain to three main contexts, each of which is related to the others.

The first context is the Taoist vision of the cosmos: the chariot, and particularly its wheels, is a metaphor of the cosmos' constitution and functioning. The wheel represents the circular compass of space and the cyclical movement of time; the hub that is placed at its center—an image of the emptiness that gives birth to existence—holds

---

[54] Trans. Watson, *The Complete Works of Chuang Tzu*, 35, slightly modified.

[55] Trans. Watson, 104, slightly modified.

[56] For references, see the Index of Main Subjects at the end of this book, under the entries "chariot"; "bit and bridle"; "hub and axle"; and "wheel and spokes."

the axle, which is made by Qian and Kun joined to one another (see *Cantong qi*, section 1).

The second context is the art of rulership—an association immediately shown by the word *yu* 御, whose meanings include "driving a chariot," "mastering a subject," and "governing a country." On high, the chariot of the supreme Emperor of Heaven is the Northern Dipper, which is placed at the center of the cosmos and rules on the sectors of space and the sequences of the time (see the notes to section 15). Below, analogously, the human ruler drives a chariot that is led by a dragon and a mare (two traditional images of Qian and Kun), and bears the emblems of the *Book of Changes* that represent the different states of the unfolding of space and time (see section 43).

Third, and most important, the art of charioteering is a traditional analogy for the operation of the Taoist saint, as described, for example, in this passage of the *Liezi*:

> If you respond with the bridle to what you feel in the bit, with the hand to what you feel in the bridle, with the mind to what you feel in the hand, then you will see without eyes and urge without a goad; relaxed in mind and straight in posture, holding six bridles without confusing them, you will place the twenty-four hooves exactly where you want them, and swing around, advance and withdraw with perfect precision. (*Liezi*, 5.185–86)[57]

All three contexts and functions described above are unified in one of the passages that describe the saintly man in the *Huainan zi*:

> The great man is tranquil and has no thoughts. Heaven is his canopy, Earth is his chariot, the four seasons are his steeds, and Yin and Yang are his charioteers. By riding the clouds and traveling in the mist, he is one with the creation and transformation of things. . . . Because Heaven is his canopy, there is nothing that he does not encompass; because the Earth is his chariot, there is nothing that he does not carry; because the four seasons are his steeds, there is nothing that he does not lead; because Yin and

---

[57] Trans. Graham, *The Book of Lieh-tzu*, 114. A passage immediately preceding this one is translated below in the note to verse 58:5. — Considering the symbology of the chariot, it is impossible to disregard the analogy between the six horses of the *Liezi* and the six dragons that represent the stages of the lunar cycle. See the notes to section 49 of the *Cantong qi*.

Yang are his charioteers, there is nothing that he does manage. (*Huainan zi*, 1.18, 22)[58]

§ 7. THE WAY OF "NON-DOING"

Either as a direct reflection of its historical origins, or to assert in an explicit way its roots in Han-dynasty legacies, the *Cantong qi* refers to Taoism as "Huang-Lao" (26:27, 84:3, and 87:10), one of the names by which the Taoist tradition was known during the Han period.[59] By this term, however, the *Cantong qi* means the foundational principles expressed in the *Daode jing* and the *Zhuangzi*, two works that are repeatedly quoted in the Taoist portions of the text.[60] The foremost of these principles, for the *Cantong qi*, is "non-doing" (*wuwei*), which defines the operation of the Taoist saint in the world. In relation to this theme, the *Cantong qi* also defines the scope of the only form of practice that it upholds—the alchemical conjunction of Lead and Mercury—and sharply criticizes other methods or pursuits.

The main subjects of the Taoist portions of the *Cantong qi* are the following:

1. Distinction between "superior virtue" and "inferior virtue": 20–21
2. "Superior virtue": 18–19, 58–60
3. "Inferior virtue": 22–25
4. The origins of existence: 53–56
5. The natural course of things: 57
6. Criticism of other practices: 26–27

[58] See Le Blanc and Mathieu, *Huainan zi*, 18.

[59] The term "Huang-Lao" derives from the names of the Yellow Emperor (Huangdi) and Laozi. From a historical point of view, the contours of this branch of Taoism are not entirely clear; it seems to have been based on the teachings of the *Daode jing* combined with the techniques of the *fangshi* (the above-mentioned "masters of the methods"), and to have placed emphasis on the application of those teachings and techniques to the art of government. The Yellow Emperor, one of the mythical sovereigns and founders of the Chinese civilization, was the patron deity of the *fangshi*, an early recipient of alchemical revelations, and—most important—the model ruler who applies Laozi's teachings to his governance.

[60] I have used above, and will continue to use in the rest of this book, the word "Taoism" to refer to these portions and themes of the *Cantong qi*. The present section clarifies how this term is relevant to the *Cantong qi*.

Superior Virtue, Inferior Virtue

Section 20 of the *Cantong qi* states:

> "Superior virtue has no doing":
> it does not use examining and seeking.
> "Inferior virtue does":
> its operation does not rest.

These verses are directly based on a passage of the *Daode jing*:

> Superior virtue has no doing:
> there is nothing whereby it does.
> Inferior virtue does:
> there is something whereby it does.
>   (*Daode jing*, 38)

In both the *Daode jing* and the *Cantong qi*, the subject of these verses is the distinction between non-doing (*wuwei*) and doing (*youwei*), referred to as the ways of "superior virtue" (*shangde*) and "inferior virtue" (*xiade*), respectively. This point, which is essential to understand the doctrinal perspectives of the *Cantong qi*, will be discussed here mainly by means of quotations from the commentaries by Chen Zhixu and Liu Yiming.

To explicate the way of superior virtue, Chen Zhixu refers to another well-known statement of the *Daode jing*, which describes the operation of non-doing saying: "Decrease and then again decrease until there is no doing: there is no doing, but nothing is not done" (*Daode jing*, 48). Chen Zhixu writes:

> Superior virtue refers to the one who embodies complete virtue, to the person for whom "nothing is not done." . . . This is the transformation operated by the saintly man who performs non-doing, the function of the great man who achieves non-doing. . . . In superior virtue "there is no doing, but nothing is not done." . . . Therefore the *Cantong qi* says, "it does not use examining and seeking."

Chen Zhixu then continues by describing the way of inferior virtue:

> Inferior virtue refers to the one who "steals the creation and transformation [of things]," to the person who "thieves the ten

thousand things." . . . This is the way of the saintly man who "is in accordance with his inner nature," the function of the man of spirit who "does." . . . In inferior virtue there is doing and something whereby it does. . . . Therefore the *Cantong qi* says, "its operation does not rest." (*Zhouyi cantong qi zhujie*, commentary to *zhang* 7)[61]

According to Chen Zhixu, therefore, in the way of superior virtue the state prior to the separation of the One into the two is spontaneously attained. The distinction between "one" and "two" does not even arise, and the unity of the precelestial and the postcelestial domains is immediately realized. There is no need to seek the One Breath, and therefore no support (no "whereby," *yi* 以) is necessary to find it. Inferior virtue, instead, focuses on seeking; its unceasing search of the One Breath needs supports, and the postcelestial domain is "used" (*yi* 以) to find the precelestial state hidden within it.

The explanation given by Liu Yiming is analogous, but more elaborate. First, Liu Yiming says that, in the way of superior virtue, "one embraces the Origin and guards Unity, and performs the way of non-doing; thus one can exhaust all pursuits." In the way of inferior virtue, instead, "one begins from effort and ends with stability, and performs the way of doing; then one is able to revert to the Origin." Next, Liu Yiming gives a clear explanation of the differences between the two paths:

The reason why superior virtue "does not use examining and seeking" is that in the person of superior virtue, Celestial Reality has never been damaged and extraneous breaths have never en-

---

[61] The phrases "stealing the creation and transformation" and "thieving the ten thousand things" allude to the man who seeks and finds the secret of Nature, the One Breath underlying and giving birth to multiplicity. Both expressions derive from texts that played a major influence within the Neidan tradition. The *Yinfu jing* (Scripture of the Hidden Response) says: "Heaven and Earth are the thieves of the ten thousand things, the ten thousand things are the thieves of man, and man is the thief of the ten thousand things." The *Ruyao jing* (Mirror for Compounding the Medicine) says: "Thieve Heaven and Earth, seize creation and transformation!" "Being in accordance with one's inner nature" derives, instead, from the opening sentences of the *Zhongyong* (The Middle Course), a Confucian work sometimes quoted by Neidan authors: "What Heaven has conferred is the inner nature; being in accordance with inner nature is the Way; cultivating the Way is the teaching."

tered. Since one immediately awakens to one's fundamental
nature, there is nothing to cultivate and nothing to verify. One
goes directly to the "other shore" (*bi'an, nirvāṇa*), and the function of examining and seeking does not operate.

The reason why the operation of inferior virtue "does not rest"
is that Celestial Reality is lacking, and cognition has begun.
Although one could immediately awaken to one's fundamental
nature, one cannot follow it as it is. One must use the way of
gradual cultivation and the function of "augmenting and decreasing": by augmenting and then again augmenting, by decreasing
and then again decreasing, one comes to what cannot be augmented or decreased. When Righteousness is pure and Humanity is
ripe, one reaches the point of cessation. This is why the unceasing
use [of inferior virtue] is valuable.

In its literal meaning, "augmenting and decreasing" (*zengjian*) is a
Neidan term that refers to "augmenting Mercury" and "decreasing
Lead" when, after the Elixir has been compounded, one should
terminate "doing" and enter the state of "non-doing." At that time,
Lead, which represents the One Breath—and the very search of the
One Breath—decreases, and Mercury, which represents one's own
fundamentally pure consciousness, free from any flaws, increases.

Despite the significant differences between superior and inferior
virtue, Liu Yiming emphasizes that the two paths lead to same goal:

> Superior virtue and inferior virtue are different and are not the
> same. Therefore their uses are dissimilar. However, when inferior
> virtue comes to the state in which Righteousness is pure and
> Humanity is ripe, it leads to the same goal as superior virtue.[62]

Liu Yiming concludes his explication by saying:

> To tentatively illustrate the meaning of "its operation does not
> rest" with regard to inferior virtue, it consists in the way of revert-

---

[62] "Righteousness is pure and Humanity is ripe" is a Neo-Confucian
expression. To understand the use that Liu Yiming makes of this expression,
it should be remembered that the *Daode jing* passage (section 38) quoted
above continues by describing the rise of Humanity (*ren*) and Righteousness
(*yi*)—the two main "Confucian" virtues—as due to the loss of the Dao and of
"superior virtue." "Righteousness is pure and Humanity is ripe" describes, in
Liu Yiming's usage, the state in which these virtues return to their perfect
condition, so that they also become expressions of "superior virtue."

ing to the state prior to Heaven within the state posterior to Heaven. Reverting to the state prior to Heaven within the state posterior to Heaven is the way of "knowing the white and keeping to the black." (*Cantong zhizhi*, "Jingwen," "Zhongpian")

The verse "Know the white, keep to the black" (derived from the *Daode jing*, 28) introduces the description of the main principles of alchemy in the *Cantong qi* (see section 22). In other words, as Liu Yiming points out, the way of "inferior virtue" is the way of alchemy. Performing a practice—either "internal" or "external"—is a form of "doing": the alchemical process is conducted in order to (*yi* 以) attain the realized state; its purpose is to prepare one to enter the state of "non doing," and is fulfilled only when this happens. This process— which is gradual, and differs in this respect from immediate realization, the prerogative of superior virtue—is at the core of alchemy, in all of its forms. Later Neidan texts will continue to express the same view in similar terms.[63]

At the same time, the distinction between "superior virtue" and "inferior virtue" refers to the difference between the doctrine and its application to a particular cosmological science—in this case, alchemy.[64] This distinction is analogous to the one made in the Western esoteric tradition between the "great mysteries" and the "small mysteries." With regard to this point, the *Cantong qi* presents a general exposition of the doctrine, defines the difference between the two related types of realization, and describes the main features of both.

---

[63] To give one example, *Awakening to Reality* (*Wuzhen pian*), the text at the basis of several Neidan traditions, states: "It begins with *doing*, and hardly can one see a thing, / when it comes to *non-doing*, all begin to understand. / But if you only see *non-doing* as the essential marvel, / how can you know that *doing* is the foundation?" ("Jueju," poem 42).

[64] The three main cosmological sciences in the Chinese tradition are the "art of government," which seeks the balance of Heaven, Earth, and Man, in order to guarantee their conformity and alignment to the Dao; ritual, which is performed for larger or smaller communities, in order to renew their "alliance with the Dao"; and alchemy, which is performed by the individual in order to "return to the Dao." The first of these sciences is discussed in the *Daode jing* itself; the second and the third ones were developed within the Taoist tradition.

The True Man

The realized being is called True Man (*zhenren*) in the *Cantong qi* (33:18, 58:3, 82:58).[65] There is no need to spend too many words in order to define his inner condition. Suffice it to remark that its descriptions in the *Cantong qi* are based on passages of the *Daode jing* and the *Zhuangzi*, the two main texts that define the state of complete realization according to the principles and the discourse of Taoism (see especially the notes to section 18).

As much care as possible should be taken to avoid reading these portions of the *Cantong qi* as descriptions of "alchemical" or other practices. This applies, for example, to section 60, which is concerned with the breathing of the realized person. Breath, says this passage, "will stream from the head to the toes; on reaching the end, it will rise once again" (60:5–6). Just like the True Man in the *Zhuangzi*, who "breathes through his heels," the form of breathing described in the *Cantong qi* occurs spontaneously to those who operate in the world taking the Dao as their model.[66]

Criticism of Other Practices

The *Cantong qi* devotes much attention to practices deemed to be inadequate for true realization. These practices are of two kinds. The first consists of non-alchemical practices, including breathing, meditation on the inner gods, sexual practices, and worship of spirits and minor deities (see especially section 26). All these practices and methods were current during the Han period and the Six Dynasties. The *Cantong qi* follows here a trend that had begun in earlier Taoist works, the first of which is the *Zhuangzi* with its disapproval of breathing methods and *daoyin* ("guiding and pulling," a practice based on sets of bodily postures).[67] Similar warnings about the perfor-

---

[65] *Zhenren* is also translated as Perfected and in other ways. My use of the word "man" here and elsewhere in this book is conventional. Note that *ren* in Chinese means "person," and the premodern sense of "man" is "human being."

[66] For the sentence referred to above cf. *Zhuangzi*, 6.228: "The True Man breathes through the heels, the common man breathes through the throat." See Watson, 78.

[67] "Inspiring and expiring while emitting the sounds *chui* and *xu*, exhaling the old and inhaling the new [breath], hanging like a bear and stretching like a

mance of incorrect practices, or the incorrect interpretation of certain notions and terms, will continue in later traditions related to the *Cantong qi*, often becoming even more radical.

The second kind of criticism is addressed to alchemical practices that are not based on the principle of "being of the same kind" (or "category," *tonglei*), a principle that receives one of its first enunciations in the *Zhuangzi*.[68] Section 36 of the *Cantong qi* reproves several Waidan methods. It is enough to read that section with attention to notice that the criticism is not addressed to Waidan per se, but to the Waidan methods that are not based on the conjunction of lead and mercury. Only lead and mercury, according to the *Cantong qi*, are of the "same kind" as Qian and Kun, and can represent and enable their conjunction.

§ 8. ALCHEMY IN THE *CANTONG QI*

For its own nature, the alchemical language lends itself to two main functions. The first is the description of alchemical ideas and practices in the strict sense. The second is the illustration of metaphysical and cosmological doctrines, many of whose features can be expressed by means of alchemical symbolism and vocabulary. When the symbolic usage of the language prevails over the literal one (as it does in the *Cantong qi*), the alchemical terms connote in the first place formless principles, and the material entities or phenomena literally denoted by those terms are seen as instances of those principles. A particular alchemical term, in this way, essentially becomes another name of the principle that it connotes; as such, it can also be used to refer to any entity or phenomenon that, in the alchemical discourse, is seen as an instance of that principle. To give one example, the alchemical term

---

bird—these are only methods for longevity. Masters of *daoyin*, people who 'nourish their form' (the physical body), and those who pursue a longevity like Pengzu's are fond of this. However . . . being longevous without practicing *daoyin* means forgetting everything but possessing everything. Calmly residing in the Ultimateless, where all good things come to attend—this is the Way of Heaven and Earth, and is the virtue of the sage" (*Zhuangzi*, 15.237–38; see Watson, pp. 167–68).

[68] See below the note to sentence 35:9. The *Zhuangzi* passage is found in one of the later portions of this work, which seem to date from the third century BCE.

"true lead" denotes refined lead, but connotes the principle of True Yang. "True Lead" thus becomes another name of True Yang, and in this function refers not only to refined lead, but also to other instances of the same principle. Analogously, any other term or image that literally denotes an instance of True Yang can connote "true lead": for instance, Metal, the White Tiger, the color white, Kan ☵, the earthly branches *geng* 庚 and *xin* 辛, and so forth.

It is essentially for this reason that, although the alchemical portions of the *Cantong qi* refer to Waidan methods, they can be read as descriptions of Neidan practices. This possibility is not only entirely coherent with the nature of the alchemical language, but is also implied in it: the alchemical language is based on the notion of analogy. Although this should be sufficiently clear, it may be useful to add that Neidan is by no means equivalent to the "symbolic" aspects of Taoist alchemy: as a practice, its position compared to the plane of the doctrines is largely equivalent to the position of Waidan. The doctrines of the *Cantong qi*, in other words, do not belong to either Waidan or Neidan: they pertain to both.

Under this light, it seems clear that the *Cantong qi* provides an alchemical model that can be applied to both Waidan and Neidan; but it uses the language of Waidan to describe the compounding of the Elixir for the simple reason that Waidan was the form in which alchemy existed when the text was composed. In other words, it is not the task of the *Cantong qi* to describe Neidan under the guise of Waidan. Leaving aside the historical questions that it would raise, this view would be reductive for a work of this scope. The task of the *Cantong qi* is not to describe alchemical practices, as many other texts do, but to show how the practice of alchemy can comply with the principles of metaphysics and cosmology.

The main subjects dealt with in the alchemical portions of the *Cantong qi* are the following:

1. Lead and Mercury: 28–29, 68
2. Description of the method: 39–40, 62, 78
3. The five agents and the Elixir: 32–33, 41, 63, 72, 79
4. The principle of "belonging to the same kind": 34–35, 69, 74, 80
5. The principle of "inversion": 64, 73
6. The tripod: 82
7. Erroneous alchemical methods: 36, 65

To point out the main differences between the alchemical model of the *Cantong qi* and the earlier Waidan model, this section will be introduced by a brief description of the main features of early alchemy.

Main Features of Early Alchemy

The first identifiable tradition in the history of Chinese alchemy, known as Taiqing (Great Clarity), developed between the third and the sixth centuries in Jiangnan, not far from Wei Boyang's putative birthplace. In this tradition, compounding the elixirs constitutes the central part of a larger process that consists of several stages, each of which is marked by the performance of rites. Receiving the scriptures and the oral instructions, building the laboratory, kindling the fire, and ingesting the elixirs require offering pledges to one's master and to the gods, observing rules on seclusion and purification, performing ceremonies to delimit and protect the ritual area, and making invocations to the highest deities asking that they favor the success of the alchemical work.

Within this ritual framework, the cosmological and alchemical model used in the *Cantong qi* plays no role. Not only are the emblems of the *Book of Changes*, which represent sequences of cosmological configurations and become fundamental in the later tradition, entirely ignored; but more importantly, no attempt is made to reproduce those sequences by means of the elixir ingredients.

In this respect, one of the most relevant features of the Taiqing and other early alchemical texts is the subordinate role attributed to lead and mercury, which are never used together as the only ingredients of any elixir. A lead-mercury compound is sometimes used as the lower and higher layers in the tripod, with the main ingredients of the elixirs; its function is to symbolically incorporate Heaven and Earth into the vessel. The compound, however, is not an elixir in itself.[69] The *Cantong qi*, instead, proposes a model of alchemical doctrine and practice in which the two metals are given prominence. This model came to influence virtually the entire later history of Chinese alchemy.[70]

---

[69] See Pregadio, *Great Clarity*, pp. 75–76.

[70] On the influence of the cosmological model of the *Cantong qi* on Waidan, see Sivin, "The Theoretical Background of Elixir Alchemy." There are no studies on the historical origins of Neidan; for some relevant issues, see Pregadio, "Early Daoist Meditation and the Origins of Inner Alchemy."

The Alchemical Model of the Cantong qi

The alchemical discourse of the *Cantong qi* revolves around Lead and Mercury. Its basic principles are simple and straightforward, and proceed directly from its views on the relation between the Dao and the "ten thousand things" (*wanwu*). As in the whole of Taoism, this relation is explained by means of a sequence of stages. The absolute principle establishes itself as Unity, which divides itself into the active and the passive principles—namely, Qian and Kun, respectively equivalent to original Yang and Yin, or True Yang and True Yin. The re-conjunction of these principles gives birth to all entities and phenomena in the world. All these "stages" occur simultaneously.

From its own perspective, dominated by duality, the cosmos is a reflection of the absolute principle; and like all reflections, it is an inverted image of that principle. In the cosmos, True Yang is concealed within Yin, and True Yin is concealed within Yang. Each Yang entity, therefore, harbors True Yin, and vice versa. In the terminology of the *Book of Changes*, the Yang and Yin prior to the generation of the world correspond to Qian and Kun, and the Yin and Yang posterior to the generation of the cosmos correspond to Kan and Li, respectively. The trigrams of the *Book of Changes* clearly represent this configuration: Qian ☰ (True Yang) is the solid line within Kan ☵ (Yin), and Kun ☷ (True Yin) is the broken line within Li ☲ (Yang).[71]

First and foremost among the entities that reflect the absolute principle is the cosmos itself. The world is Yin in relation to the Dao, but conceals its One Breath, which is True Yang. The alchemical process, therefore, consists in tracing the stages of the generative process of the cosmos in a reverse sequence, in order to recover the hidden One Breath and return to it. In alchemical language, True Lead (☰) and True Mercury (☷) respectively represent True Yang and True Yin. The Yin and Yang entities that respectively contain these authentic principles are represented by "black lead" (i.e., native lead ☵) and cinnabar (☲). In the strict sense of the term, alchemy consists in

---

[71] True Yin is also called "Yin within Yang," and True Yang, "Yang within Yin." Kan ☵ and Li ☲ are equivalent to the black and white halves of the well-known Yin-Yang emblem: the black half contains a white dot (equal to the inner line within Kan ☵, "Yang within Yin"), and the white half contains a black dot (equal to the inner line within Li ☲, "Yin within Yang").

extracting True Lead from "black lead" and True Mercury from cinnabar, and in joining them to one another.

A crucial point to consider, which directly derives from the principles outlined above, is that True Yang is the counterpart of True Yin, but—being the One Breath of the Dao—it is also the state of Unity prior to its subdivision into Yin and Yang (this aspect of True Yang is often referred to as Pure Yang, *chunyang*). This explains the priority given to True Yang in the alchemical process.[72] As a consequence, "Lead" has three meanings in alchemy. From the higher to the lower one, these meanings are: (1) The state of Unity before its separation into Yin and Yang; (2) The True Yang of the precelestial state (True Lead), which is a counterpart of True Yin (True Mercury); (3) The Yin of the postcelestial state ("black lead"), which is a counterpart of postcelestial Yang (cinnabar).

When the five agents (*wuxing*) are used to represent the alchemical process, the basic configuration is equivalent to the one seen above. "Black lead" and cinnabar are Water and Fire, and True Lead and True Mercury are Metal and Wood. As we saw earlier, in the inverted sequence of the five agents, which is one of those active in the alchemical process, Water ("black lead") generates Metal (True Lead), and Fire (cinnabar) generates Wood (True Mercury).

Soil, the fifth agent, allows the entire alchemical process to unfold, and also represent its completion. Positioned at the center of the other agents, Soil is emblematic of Unity containing True Yin and True Yang. Its Yang half corresponds to the inner line of Kan ☵ (True Lead), and is typically represented by the celestial stem *wu* 戊. Its Yin half corresponds to the inner line of Li ☲ (True Mercury), and is represented by the celestial stem *ji* 己. Being found within both ingredients of the Elixir, Soil stands for their fundamental unity, and enables them to conjoin.

---

[72] This, too, ultimately reflects the perspectives of the relative domain, which is the starting point of alchemy. As long as it may be named, the pure, absolute, undifferentiated state of Non-Being is Pure Yin. Alchemically, this state is Mercury; but few authors of alchemical texts are inclined to provide details on this point. The *Wuzhen pian* (Awakening to Reality) refers to it saying: "When you use Lead, you should not use ordinary lead—but even True Lead is discarded after you have used it. These are the wondrous instructions on using Lead. Use Lead and do not use Lead: these are trustworthy words" ("Jueju," poem 9).

§ 9. FROM THE EXTERNAL ELIXIR TO THE INTERNAL ELIXIR

Whether the *Cantong qi* is read as the first Neidan text or as the text
that gave rise to Neidan, it played a pivotal function in the shift from
"external" to "internal" alchemical practices. This shift, which occurred during the Tang period (seventh-ninth centuries), has sometimes been understood as a transposition of "external" practices to an
inner plane, and has often been described as owed to the increase of
cases of elixir poisoning (which even affected the Tang imperial court:
at least two Tang emperors died after they ingested an elixir). Leaving
aside the fact that, according to this view, Chinese alchemists would
have needed several centuries to become aware that many of their
ingredients were deadly, there are clear indications that the transition
from Waidan to Neidan was a much more complex phenomenon.

Alchemical Images in Early Meditation Practices

To look at the first main element that played a role in the shift from
the External to the Internal Elixir, we should consider certain aspects
of the early Taoist meditation practices.

The influence of these practices in the transition from Waidan to
Neidan has been noted by several scholars, who in this context have
emphasized the important role played by the Shangqing (Highest
Clarity) tradition of Taoism, where meditation is the main form of
practice. In this respect, however, Shangqing did not innovate, but
rather developed and re-codified earlier traditions. In fact, the first
clear instances of the use of images and vocabulary that would later
be inherited by Neidan are found in the two main early texts on Taoist
meditation, the *Central Scripture of Laozi* (*Laozi zhongjing*) and the
Scripture of the Yellow Court (*Huangting jing*). Both works are
concerned with meditation on the inner gods, and both antedate the
Shangqing revelations of 364–70 by about one and half centuries.

The images of the "embryo" and the "infant" found in these
works are the direct precursors of the "embryo" and the "infant" that
Neidan adepts generate and nourish by means of their practices. I will
give here only the main example. In the *Central Scripture*, the Red
Child (Chizi) is the innermost deity of the human being, and is said to
represents one's own "true self" (*zhenwu*):

He resides exactly in the ducts of the stomach. He sits facing due south on a couch of jade and pearls, and a flowery canopy of yellow clouds covers him. He is clothed in garments with pearls of five hues. His mother resides above on his right, embracing and nourishing him, and his father resides above on his left, instructing and defending him. . . . He feeds on the Yellow Essence and the Red Breath, drinking and ingesting the Fount of Nectar. (*Laozi zhongjing*, section 12)

To ensure that this and the other inner gods are maintained in their residences, adepts should provide nourishment to them and their dwellings. Accordingly, meditation practices involve the visualization of nutritive essences and breaths delivered to the gods that inhabit one's body. In particular, as shown by the passage just quoted, the *Central Scripture* instructs adepts to circulate a "yellow essence" (*huangjing*) and a "red breath" (*chiqi*) within their bodies, which respectively represent the Moon and the Sun. The following description concerns the provisions supplied to the Red Child:

Constantly think that below your nipples are the Sun and the Moon. Within the Sun and the Moon are a Yellow Essence and a Red Breath that enter the Crimson Palace (the heart). Then again they enter the Yellow Court (the spleen) and the Purple Chamber (the gallbladder). [Finally] the Yellow Essence and the Red Breath thoroughly fill the Great Granary (the stomach). The Red Child is within the ducts of the stomach. (*Laozi zhongjing*, section 11)

There are clear analogies between the essences and the breaths of the Sun and the Moon that are mentioned in this passage, and the Yin and Yang essences and breaths by which, centuries later, Neidan adepts would generate and nourish their own inner "embryos." These associations become explicit in another passage of the *Central Scripture*:

The heart is the Sun, the kidneys are the Moon, the spleen is the Dipper. The breath of the heart descends, the breath of the kidneys rises. They join and become one, and are unceasingly distributed to the four limbs. (*Laozi zhongjing*, sec. 51)

An analogous practice is performed by Neidan adepts when they join the Fire of the heart and the Water of the kidneys with one another.[73]

---

[73] On the corresponding Neidan practice, see Despeux, *Taoïsme et corps humain*, pp. 152–58.

Two other features of the *Central Scripture* require attention. First, besides the inner essences and breaths, another source of nourishment of the gods is the practitioner's own salivary juices. These juices have the function of "irrigating" (*guan*) the inner organs in which the gods reside. In addition to Fount of Nectar (*liquan*), mentioned in the first passage quoted above, the *Central Scripture* and the *Yellow Court* define the salivary juices with terms derived from Waidan or having alchemical connotations, including Mysterious Pearl (*xuanzhu*), Jade Sap (*yujiang*), Jade Blossom (*yuying*), Jade Pond (*yuchi*), Jade Liquor (*yuye*), Golden Nectar (*jinli*), and even Golden Liquor (*jinye*). Second, the meditation practices of the *Central Scripture* include invocations addressed to the inner gods, in which the practitioner asks the gods to dispense him an elixir. If the term "internal elixir" was not already charged with other meanings, it could be an appropriate definition for the nourishment that the inner gods are invited to provide.

The other main text on early Taoist meditation, the *Scripture of the Yellow Court*, contains a brief mention of the "inner embryo," one of the most distinctive notions of Neidan:

> By coagulating the essence and nurturing the womb,
> you will generate a living being (*shen*);
> preserve the embryo, stop the flow of the essence,
> and you will live a long life.
>
> (*Huangting neijing jing*, sec. 20)

Whereas this example is isolated in the *Yellow Court*, the creation of an immortal body, or an immortal self, by means of a return to a self-generated inner embryo is repeatedly mentioned in the Shangqing sources. With a remarkable use of alchemical imagery, one of these sources applies a classical Waidan term, Nine Elixirs (*jiudan*), to the breaths of the Nine Heavens received by the human being during its embryonic development. In the Shangqing view, however, gestation also accounts for the creation of "knots" and "nodes" that serve to support the five viscera, but ultimately are responsible for one's death. To "untie the knots" (*jiejie*), an adept is instructed to re-experience his embryonic development in meditation. Beginning on the anniversary of his conception, he receives again the Nine Elixirs from month to month, and each time, one of his inner organs is turned into gold or jade. In the remaining three months, he visualizes the Original Father within his upper Cinnabar Field, and the Original Mother within his lower Cinnabar

Field. They issue a green and a yellow breath, respectively, that join in the middle Cinnabar Field and generate an immortal infant.[74]

These examples, chosen among several others, show that certain fundamental ideas, images, and practices that characterize Neidan existed several centuries before the beginning of its documented history. One essential feature of the Neidan practice, however, is missing in the *Central Scripture* and the *Yellow Court*: the use of a cosmology that serves to explain the generative process of the cosmos from the Dao, and to frame a practice that reverses that process and leads to the generation of the Elixir or the "embryo."

Two Alchemical Models

This cosmology and the related alchemical model—the second main element that influenced the shift from the External to the Internal Elixir—are expounded in *Cantong qi*. Among the alchemical methods that are criticized in the *Cantong qi* is the one based on cinnabar and mercury (see 36:11–12, and the note on these verses). This detail is significant. Although lead and mercury are the two emblematic substances at the heart of the *Cantong qi*, they are not the only pair of ingredients employed in Chinese alchemy. Another major representation, typical of Waidan, is centered on cinnabar and mercury. In some respects, the two pairs of substances perform analogous functions. The cyclical extraction of mercury (Yin) from cinnabar (Yang) and its addition to sulphur (Yang), which is typically repeated nine times, yields an essence that is deemed to represent Pure Yang (*chunyang*). The conjunction of True Mercury (Yin) and True Lead (Yang) produces an Elixir endowed with the same properties: Pure Yang denotes the state prior to the separation of the One into the Two.

The analogies between these two processes should not conceal a key event in the development of alchemy in China. From the early Tang period (seventh/eighth centuries) onward, lead and mercury become the main substances in Waidan, both as ingredients of the Elixir and as emblems of cosmological principles. Several Tang-dynasty works provide evidence of this shift through their advocacy of lead and mercury and their explicit rejection of cinnabar, with the usual rationale that Yang (cinnabar) alone cannot produce the Elixir.[75] In the new,

---

[74] On this practice see Robinet, *Taoist Meditation*, pp. 139–43.
[75] For some examples, see Pregadio, *Great Clarity*, 220–23.

ultimately successful model, cinnabar is retained only as the substance that incorporates True Mercury, or as an emblem of Yang containing True Yin. The corresponding ingredient that represents Yin containing True Yang is native lead, which holds True Lead.

These works document the stage in the history of Chinese alchemy in which an earlier dominant model, based on the extraction of mercury from cinnabar, was being replaced with a new model based on the conjunction of lead and mercury—the model described in the *Cantong qi*. The shift was crucial in the history of Chinese alchemy for two reasons. First, the Waidan alchemists began to use a symbolic system that affords a clear way to describe a metaphysics (the non-duality of Dao and cosmos), a cosmogony (the birth of the cosmos from the Dao), and a cosmology (the functioning of the cosmos as the operation of the Absolute in the relative) by means of Yin and Yang, the five agents, the trigrams and hexagrams of the *Book of Changes*, and other sets of emblems. Correlating the Waidan process to this system was impossible for methods based on cinnabar and mercury (let alone for those based on other ingredients). Second, the adoption of this system paved the way for the emergence of Neidan, which adopts the same views, and emphasizes their relevance to the human being. True Lead and True Mercury are retained as emblems of True Yang and True Yin, respectively, but become purely symbolic terms that define the prime constituents—both physical and non-physical— of the human being at the basis of the Neidan practices.

New Forms of Practice

The primary purport of the *Cantong qi* is to explicate the bond that exists between the Dao and the cosmos, the Absolute and the relative: change is the operation of the constant and formless Dao in the world of form. Alchemy comes into play when the *Cantong qi* expounds its way to "return to the Dao." But although the *Cantong qi* allusively describes a Waidan process (sections 39–40, 62, 78) and clarifies many of its facets (22–25, 32–35, 41, 63–64, etc.), the task of providing details on the alchemical practices is left to commentaries and other works, which focus on the application of its doctrines to the com-pounding of the External or the Internal Elixir.

In this context, the multiple deities of the external and the internal pantheons serve no more: the only "deity" mentioned in the *Cantong qi* is God Himself, the Great One (Taiyi), the Oneness of Being, without whom cosmogony could not occur and the whole edifice of cosmology could not be built (19:5, 27:11). It is important to note that, with regard to this point, the same process invests both the earlier Waidan traditions and the meditation practices: the gods who were addressed by means of invocations and pleaded to favor the compounding of the elixirs—or to provide an elixir "internally" to the practitioner of meditation—play no role in the Waidan and Neidan traditions based on the *Cantong qi*. This does not mean that the ritual features of the external or the internal practices are entirely removed: as a practice, alchemy itself is a "cosmological ritual." In their intermediary function between the domains of Formlessness and form, however, the deities of the external and the internal pantheons are replaced by other images: the emblems of cosmology and the alchemical symbols proper.

It does not surprise, therefore, that the *Cantong qi* explicitly advises against meditation on the inner gods (26:1–2). Certain clusters of terms that recur in the *Cantong qi* show that the focus is a different one. Now the adept examines, investigates, searches, inquires, quests, and inspects; he gauges and measures; he reflects, ponders, infers, and assesses.[76] This is not mere intellectual activity in the modern sense of the term: it relies on the intellect as the knowing faculty of Spirit, and takes place through "contemplation" (*guan*; 11:8, 14:5) and the cessation of the flow of thoughts (59:4).

With the changes mentioned above, the whole outlook is transformed. The shift from Waidan to Neidan occurs first at the doctrinal level; the new practices result from the grafting of earlier methods onto a different doctrine. The change is first clearly visible in Waidan, where the conversion of earlier practices to different doctrinal foundations resulted in a new way of compounding the Elixir. With another analogous, decisive shift, the earlier meditation methods were replaced by Neidan.

In other words, the same unchangeable doctrine inspired changes within both "external" and "internal" forms of practice. The *Cantong qi* expounds this doctrine.

---

[76] All terms mentioned above (*cha* 察, *kao* 考, *tan* 探, *ji* 稽, *xun* 尋, *shen* 審, *cun* 忖, *du* 度, *si* 思, *lü* 慮, *tui* 推, *kui* 揆) are found in different sections the *Cantong qi*.

Translation

This translation is based on the text found in Chen Zhixu's *Zhouyi cantong qi zhujie* (Commentary and Explication of the *Cantong qi*), composed in ca. 1330. For details on this text, see pp. 266 ff. The edited text is transcribed on pp. 269 ff.

At an early stage of my work, I have subdivided the text into sections. These subdivisions are based on the following criteria, listed in order of importance: (a) Changes in the number of characters in rhymed lines; (b) Major changes of rhyme patterns; (c) Major changes of subject matter. Beyond these criteria, I have not followed any particular model to determine the extent of each section.

For ease of reference, and in order to provide a pointer to their main subjects, I have assigned titles to the individual sections. (Sections dealing with the same subjects bear identical titles.) These titles are not found in Chen Zhixu's text, and neither correspond to, nor are inspired by, those found in the other redactions of the *Cantong qi* that I have seen. The subdivision of each section into stanzas is based on the rhyme patterns and usually follows the basic quatrain framework, which, however, the *Cantong qi* does not use consistently.

Verses are numbered consecutively within each section. A reference given in the form "24:11" means "section 24, verse 11."

Sentences that are literally or almost literally quoted from other texts are translated within quotation marks.

The earlier English translations of the *Cantong qi* by Wu Lu-ch'iang and Tenney L. Davis (1932), Zhou Shiyi (1988), and Richard Bertschinger (1994), as well as the Japanese translation by Suzuki Yoshijirō (1977), have been extremely useful. I have also consulted translations of individual passages found in works by Joseph Needham, Ho Peng Yoke, Nathan Sivin, Chan Wing-tsit, Liu Ts'un-yen, Imai Usaburō, Murakami Yoshimi, and other scholars. The present version differs from earlier translations just as much as each of them differs from all the others.

With much initial hesitancy, I have translated each verse on a separate line, instead of rendering the entire text in a looser prose form. While this has not by any means resulted into a "poetical" translation, I am ultimately pleased with this choice, as it has led me to adhere to certain formal features of the verses and to convey them, to some extent, into English. Once again, let me remind that Noreen Khawaja deserves my gratitude, and all due credit, for innumerable corrections and suggestions that have improved this translation. I bear full responsibility for any error.

My comments are in two forms: section notes and verse notes. Although I have consulted several commentaries, including those to the "Ancient Text", the section notes are not based on any specific source. I have also used modern annotated versions, especially those by Suzuki Yoshijirō, Fang Xu, and Wu Enpu. Facing different explications given by commentators and scholars—variously leaning toward Waidan, Neidan, cosmology, or other subjects, and with remarkable differences within each of these fields—I have tried to focus on the features that connect the varying interpretations to one another and that, in the first place, make them possible. Besides this, I have attempted to read, translate, and annotate the individual parts of the text from the perspective of their respective main subjects—i.e., cosmology, Taoism, or alchemy, according to the traditional understanding of the *Cantong qi* (about these subjects, see above the Introduction, § 6, § 7, and § 8).

The verse notes contain references to quotations from earlier sources; translations of closely related passages found in earlier texts; references to comparable sentences found elsewhere in the *Cantong qi*; and additional remarks on certain terms or passages. The main textual and technical notes are collected in a separate part of the book (pp. 231 ff.).

Finally, in order to avoid unnecessary complications, I often refer to Wei Boyang as the author of the *Cantong qi* in my notes, in agreement with the established tradition.

BOOK 1

1   *Qian and Kun, Kan and Li*

1–6   "Qian ☰ and Kun ☷ are the door and the gate of change,"
         the father and the mother of all hexagrams.
         Kan ☵ and Li ☲ are the inner and the outer walls,
         they spin the hub and align the axle.
         Female and male, these four trigrams
         function as a bellows and its nozzles.

2   *The artisan and the charioteer*

1–6   Enfolding and encompassing the Way of Yin and Yang
         is like being an artisan and a charioteer
         who level the marking-cord and the plumb-line,
         hold the bit and the bridle,
         align the compass and the square,
         and follow the tracks and the ruts.

7–8   Abide in the Center to control the outside:
         the numbers are found in the system of the pitch-pipes and
               the calendar.

3   *The monthly cycle of the hexagrams*

1–4   In one month there are six nodes of five days;
         warp and weft abide by the command of the Sun.
         Altogether they are sixty:
         the firm is external, the yielding internal.

5–8   At dawn of the month's first day, Zhun ䷂ is on duty;
       when sunset comes, Meng ䷃ duly takes charge.
       One hexagram for each day and each night:
       their operation follows the Sequence.

9–12   With Jiji ䷾ and Weiji ䷿ comes the clear light of the
          month's last day;
       after the end there is another beginning.
       The Sun and the Moon set periods and measures;
       movement precedes, quiescence follows.

13–16   Spring and summer accord with the inner core,
       from *zi* to *chen* and *si*;
       autumn and winter match the outer function,
       from *wu* to *xu* and *hai*.

17–20   Reward and punishment respond to spring and autumn;
       dimness and light comply with cold and heat.
       The Statements on the Lines contain humanity and righ-
          teousness,
       and issue joy or anger in accordance with the time.

21–22   Thus by responding to the four seasons,
       the five agents attain their principle.

4   *Kan and Li, the functions of Qian and Kun*

1–2   "Heaven and Earth establish their positions, and change
     occurs within them."

3–6   "Heaven and Earth" are the images of Qian ☰ and Kun
     ☷. "Establish their positions" means that they arrange
     themselves in the positions for the joining of Yin and
     Yang. "Change" means Kan ☵ and Li ☲; Kan and Li are
     the two functions of Qian and Kun.

7–10   The two functions have no fixed positions in the lines:
"flowing in cycles they go through the six empty spaces."
As their coming and going are not determinate,
so too "their ascent and descent are not constant."

5   *The emptiness within Kan and Li*

1–4   Withdrawn into obscurity, sunken and concealed,
"therein occur the transformations."
Embracing and enveloping the ten thousand things
is the guideline of the Dao.

5–8   It is from Non-Being that Being is produced:
the function of a vessel consists in its emptiness.
Therefore infer the ebb and flow,
and the nothingness within Kan ☵ and Li ☲.

6   *The Principle in words*

1–6   Words are not thoughtlessly created,
discourses are not vainly generated.
Drawing upon its evidence and seeing its attestations,
the Numinous Light is reckoned.
Graphs are joined by inferring the kinds;
they serve as signs for going back to the Principle.

7   *Sun and Moon make change*

1–4   *Wu* in Kan ☵ is the essence of the Moon,
ji in Li ☲ is the radiance of the Sun.
Sun and Moon make change,
the firm and the yielding match one another.

5–10   Soil rules over the four seasons,
       entwining beginning and end;
       green, red, black, and white
       each dwells in one direction.
       All are endowed by the Central Palace
       through the efficacy of *wu* and *ji*.

8   *The greatest images of change*

1–3   "Change consists in images," and "among the suspended
       images that send forth their light, none is greater than the
       Sun and the Moon."

4–7   "Probe the Spirit to understand the transformations":
       when Yang goes, Yin comes.
       Like a wheel that turns as its spokes converge,
       they enter and exit, unfold and contract.

9   *Change and its emblems*

1–3   In the *Changes* there are 384 lines; the signs are chosen in
       accordance with the lines. "Signs" means the sixty-four
       hexagrams.

10   *The joining of the Sun and the Moon*

1–5   Between the month's last day and dawn on next month's
       first day, Zhen ☳ comes to receive the token. At that mo-
       ment, Heaven and Earth merge their essences, and the Sun
       and the Moon reach out for one another and hold onto
       one another.

6–9   The masculine Yang spreads his mysterious emanation,
       the feminine Yin transforms her yellow wrap.

In indistinction they conjoin;
at this incipient time, the root is planted.

10–13 Steadily and orderly the seed is nourished;
from the coagulation of Spirit the corporeal frame is
formed.
This is how living beings come forth:
even the wriggling worms all proceed from this.

11   The signs of Heaven

1   Thereupon Confucius eulogized the boundless:

2–6   The virtue of Qian ☰ and Kun ☷ is cavernous and empty,
"inquiring into antiquity" we find the original sovereign,
"*guan* go the ospreys" to lay the beginnings,
the auras of the capping and the marriage ceremonies are
tied to one another,
and "in the first year" the sprouts are nurtured.

7–10 The sage is not born in vain:
he contemplates on high the manifest signs of Heaven.
The signs of Heaven advance and recede,
bending and stretching to respond to the time.

12   The hexagram Fu and the trigram Zhen

1–6   Therefore change encompasses the Heart of Heaven. The
hexagram Fu ☷ lays the initial buds; the elder son inherits
the body of his father, and sets up the foundation relying
on his mother. Ebb and flow respond to the bells and
pitch-pipes; rise and fall accord with the axis of the
Dipper.

13   *The cycle of the Moon*

1–6   On the third day, it comes forth with its clear light,
        when Zhen ☳ and *geng* match the western direction.
        On the eighth day, when Dui ☱ matches *ding*,
        the waxing quarter is level as a string.
        On the fifteenth, with the body of Qian ☰ attained,
        it is full at *jia* in the eastern direction.

7–12   The toad is with the hare and its lightless soul,
        and the Breaths of Sun and Moon shine together:
        the toad beholds the trigram nodes,
        the hare exhales the radiance of life.
        On the fifteenth, when the course is completed,
        it bends downward and declines.

13–18   When the sixteenth, in turn, acquires control,
        it appears at dawn at Xun ☴ and *xin*.
        When Gen ☶ aligns with *bing* in the south,
        it is the twenty-third, the waning quarter.
        When Kun ☷ is at *yi* on the thirtieth day,
        "forego your friends in the northeast."

19–22   When the nodes are complete, each having given way to
            another,
        they inherit the body and regenerate the dragon.
        Ren and *gui* match *jia* and *yi*,
        Qian and Kun enclose beginning and end.

23–26   As 7 and 8 make 15,
        9 and 6 correspond to them.
        These four altogether make 30:
        the Yang Breath, worn out, is extinguished and hidden.

14   *Heaven, Earth, Man*

1–2   The eight trigrams spread out among the asterisms;
          in rotating they shift, but never take leave of the Center.

3–6   Original Essence is subtle and can hardly be beheld:
          infer its rules and attest its tokens.
          "When you dwell, contemplate its images,"
          "adjust and conform to its forms and appearances."

7–10   Let the gnomon function as your norm,
          divine and forecast "to determine good and ill fortune."
          In issuing commands comply with the seasonal
              ordinances;
          never neglect the timing of the movement of the lines.

11–14   Above, examine the signs of the Chart of the River,
          below, pursue the flow of the forms of the earth,
          and between, inquire into the Heart of man.
          Combine them to investigate the Three Powers.

15–18   In movement, be in accordance with the nodes of the tri-
              grams;
          in quiescence, rely upon the Judgements and the State-
              ments.
          Only when the function of Qian ☰ and Kun ☷ is at work
          can Heaven and Earth be regulated.

15   *The essential course*

1–4   The foremost in conducting government
          is renewing the tripod and renovating the ancient.
          Be watchful in exercising control,
          and forthright in spreading the Treasure.

5–8   The essential course lies in Head and Handle:
       they are the strings to manage all transformations.
       "As lines and images move on the inside,
       good and ill fortune rise on the outside."

9–12   The five wefts intersect in their routes,
       but they move in response to the time;
       if the twenty-eight lodges opposed one another,
       they would part away from each other.

13–16 Literary Glory manages the registers,
       Terrace and Assistant inquire and adjure.
       The hundred officials are in place:
       each of them leads a department.

16   *Space and time correspond to one another*

1–4   The Sun joins with the essences of the five agents,
       the Moon matches the series of the six pitch-pipes.
       Six times five makes thirty degrees;
       when the degrees are complete, they begin once again.

17   *The ruler and the Pole Star*

1–6   "Going back to the beginning and pursuing the end"
       is the thread to understand existence and extinction.
       Sometimes the ruler is proud and self-indulgent,
       and filled with arrogance goes against the Dao.
       Sometimes a minister is evil and insincere,
       and his conduct does not follow the track.

7–10   As the quarter-moon and the full moon reach plenitude
           and recede,
       adverse events and "ill fortune" and "blame" occur.

The Upholder of the Law denounces and reproaches;
he inquires into the offenses and advises the ruler.

11–14   Just as the Pole Star holds its correct position,
and effortlessly drifts relying on what is below,
so from the Hall of Light shall you carry out governance,
and no ill ways will appear in the kingdom.

18   *Nourishing inner nature*

1–4   Innerly nourish yourself,
serene and quiescent in Empty Non-Being.
Going back to the fundament conceal your light,
and innerly illuminate your body.

5–8   "Shut the openings"
and raise and strengthen the Numinous Trunk;
as the three luminaries sink into the ground,
warmly nourish the Pearl.

9–10   "Watching, you do not see it" —
it is nearby and easy to seek.

19   *The Yellow Center*

1–2   "From the Yellow Center" it gradually "spreads through
the veining":
moistening and impregnating, it reaches the flesh and the
skin.

3–6   When the beginning is correct, the end will be flawless;
when the trunk is firm, the branches can hold.
The One, through cover and concealment,
is known by no one in the world.

20 *Superior virtue and inferior virtue*

1–4 "Superior virtue has no doing":
it does not use examining and seeking.
"Inferior virtue does":
its operation does not rest.

21 *Non-Being and Being, the "two cavities"*

1–4 Closed above, its name is Being;
closed below, its name is Non-Being.
Non-Being therefore rises above,
for above is the dwelling of the virtue of Spirit.

5–6 These are the methods of the two cavities:
Metal and Breath thus wait upon one another.

22 *The principles of alchemy*

1–2 "Know the white, keep to the black,"
and the Numinous Light will come of its own.

3–6 White is the essence of Metal,
Black the foundation of Water.
Water is the axis of the Dao:
its number is 1.

7–10 At the beginning of Yin and Yang,
Mystery holds the Yellow Sprout;
it is the ruler of the five metals,
the River Chariot of the northern direction.

11–14 That is why lead is black on the outside
but cherishes the Golden Flower within,

like the man who "wears rough-hewn clothes but cherishes
a piece of jade in his bosom,"
and outwardly behaves like a fool.

23   *Metal and Water, mother and child*

1–4   Metal is the mother of Water —
the mother is hidden in the embryo of her son.
Water is the child of Metal —
the child is stored in the womb of its mother.

24   *Born before Heaven and Earth*

1–4   The True Man is supremely wondrous:
sometimes he is, sometimes he is not.
Barely perceptible within the great abyss,
now he sinks, now he wafts.

5–8   Receding, they part and distribute themselves,
and each keeps to its sector.
When collected, it is of the white kind,
when compounded, it turns to vermilion.

9–12   To refine it make an outer protection,
so that the White lies sheltered within.
"Square and round, one inch is its diameter";
the two are indistinct, each seizes the other.

13–14   "Born before Heaven and Earth,"
it is eminent, venerable, and exalted.

25 *The Elixir in the tripod*

1–4   On its sides are ramparts and portals,
and in shape it resembles Penghu;
round and enclosed, shut and sealed off,
it is interwoven at every turn.

5–8   Guarded, defended, solid, and firm,
it reverts all misdoing and evil;
its meanders and towers are intertwined
in order "to prevent the unforeseen."

9–12   You can do this if you are free from all cares,
but hardly you can if you are toiled and distraught:
when Spirit and Breath fill the house,
no one can detain them.

13–16   Those who guard it will shine,
those who neglect it are lost.
In movement and quiescence, in rest and activity,
it constantly stays with you.

26 *Incorrect practices*

1–8   This is not the method of passing through the viscera, of inner contemplation and having a point of concentration;
of treading the Dipper and pacing the asterisms, using the six *jia* as markers of time;
of sating yourself with the nine-and-one in the Way of Yin, meddling and tampering with the original womb;
of ingesting breath till it chirps in your stomach, exhaling the pure and inhaling the evil without.

9–12   Day and night you go without slumber,
month after month, you never take rest.

From exhaustion your body daily grows weak:
you may be "vague and indistinct," but look like a fool.

13–16 Your hundred vessels stir and seethe like a cauldron,
unable to settle and clear.
Amassing soil you set up space for an altar,
and at daybreak and sunset you worship in awe.

17–20 Demonic creatures reveal their shapes,
at whose sight in your dreams you sigh with emotion.
Rejoiced in your heart, pleased in your thoughts,
you tell yourself, surely, your life will grow long.

21–24 But death, unexpected, comes ahead of its time,
and you forsake your body to rot.
Your deeds have rebounded,
for you were defiant and let slip the hinge.

25–30 The arts are so many —
for each thousand, there are ten thousand more.
Their tortuous routes run against the Yellow Emperor and
the Old Master,
their winding courses oppose the Nine Capitals.
Those who are bright comprehend the meaning of this:
in all its breadth they know where it comes from.

27 *The Great One sends forth his summons*

1–4 "Assiduously practice it"
from sunrise to nightfall, without taking rest.
For three years preserve and ingest,
and lightly will you ascend, roaming afar.

5–8 "Stepping across the fire you will not be scorched,
entering the water you will not get wet."

You will be able to retain your life or depart from this
    world,
forever content and undistraught.

9–12   With the Way completed and virtue fulfilled,
withdraw, stay concealed, and wait for your time.
The Great One will send forth his summons,
and you move your abode to the Central Land.

13–14   Your work concluded, you ascend on high
to obtain the Register and receive the Chart.

28   *White Tiger and Green Dragon*

1–2   The Records of Fire are not written in vain; look into the
Changes to comprehend them.

3–8   The supine Moon is the model of tripod and furnace,
the White Tiger is the hinge of the heating.
The mercurial Sun is the Flowing Pearl,
the Green Dragon is together with it.
Take the East and join it with the West:
hun and *po*, of their own accord, will seize one another.

29   *The "two eights"*

1–2   The waxing quarter is Dui ☱, its number is 8;
the waning quarter is Gen ☶, it is also 8.

3–6   The two quarters join their essences,
forming the bodies of Qian ☰ and Kun ☷.
Two times 8 corresponds to one pound:
the Way of the *Changes* is correct and unbiased.

30   *Constancy and change*

1–6   If gold is placed in an intense fire,
        its color is not deprived of its essential radiance;
        since the opening of Heaven and Earth,
        Sun and Moon have not decreased their light.
        Just as gold never loses its weight,
        so are the forms of the Sun and the Moon always the
            same.

31   *The true nature of Metal*

1–4   Metal at root is born from the Moon,
        when the Sun receives the token at dawn on the month's
            first day.
        Metal returns to its mother,
        when the Sun embraces the Moon in the month's last day.

5–8   Hidden within its inner and outer walls,
        sinking into the depths of cavernous Emptiness,
        Metal reverts to its ancient nature:
        the tripod glows with awesome radiance.

32   *Water and Fire return to Soil*

1–6   *Zi* and *wu* in value amount to 3,
        wu and *ji* in number are 5;
        as 3 and 5 harmonize,
        the eight minerals set the guiding thread in line.
        Exhaling and inhaling, they foster one another,
        ardently awaiting becoming husband and wife.

7–12   The yellow Soil is the father of Metal,
        the Flowing Pearl is the child of Water.
        Water treats Soil as its demon:

when soil invades, water cannot rise.
The Vermilion Sparrow is the essence of Fire:
it keeps the balance, moderating success and failure.

13–16   When Water flourishes, Fire is extinguished,
and both die, together returning to generous Soil.
Now, the three natures have joined together,
for their fundamental natures share an ancestor in common.

33   *Soil and the Elixir*

1–6   If even sesame extends the length of your life,
surely you can ingest the Reverted Elixir.
Gold by its nature does not rot or decay,
thus it is treasured among the ten thousand things;
if a master of the Art preserves and ingests it,
the span of his life will increase.

7–12   Soil roams the four seasons,
guarding the boundaries and setting the rules.
When the Golden Sand enters the five inner organs,
a mist disperses like wind and rain,
a fragrant vapor extends to the four limbs,
and one's countenance grows pleasant, moistened and fair.

13–16 All white hair turns black,
and the fallen teeth grow where they were;
an old man is again a vigorous youth,
an aged woman becomes a lovely maid.

17–18 He who transmutes his form and escapes the troubles of
the world is called a True Man.

34   *The true nature of all things*

1–4   When you throw ceruse into the fire,
         its color spoils and it reverts to lead;
         when you place ice or snow in warm water,
         it dissolves to form the Great Mystery.

5–8   As its ruler Metal takes the Sand,
         which by nature is joined with quicksilver.
         Their transformations derive from the real within them:
         end and beginning, of their own accord, depend one on
               the other.

35   *"Things of the same kind follow each other"*

1–4   To achieve transcendence by preserving and ingesting,
         you must use things of the same kind:
         grains are used for planting crops,
         eggs are employed for hatching chicks.

5–8   If you support, by its kind, its being what it is,
         a thing reaches completion and is easily moulded or smelt.
         Could a fish eye ever turn into a pearl?
         And mugwort will never make tea.

9–14   "Things of the same kind follow each other";
         if they are at odds, they cannot form the Treasure.
         Swallows and sparrows do not give birth to a phoenix,
         foxes and hares do not suckle a horse;
         water streams and does not blaze by rising up,
         fire stirs and does not wet by flowing down.

36   *Erroneous alchemical methods*

1–4   In this world there are many learned men,
        eminent, wondrous, and of excellent talent.
        Unless they suddenly have the unexpected encounter,
        they squander their fire and in vain waste their wealth.

5–8   Relying on opinion and written words,
        they foolishly act as they like:
        their principles have no foundation,
        and their attitude lacks firmness.

9–12   They pound the chalcanthite from Shao,
        and mica, and alum, and magnetite;
        they roast sulphur above camphor wood,
        and refine it with mercury made into a mud.

13–16   Blowing on the fire to melt the five minerals and copper,
        they think that this is the key for accomplishment.
        But all these things are disparate in nature and different in
            kind:
        could they ever will to be joined in one body?

17–20   With a thousand attempts they are bound to ten thousand
            failures,
        intending to be clever, becoming fools.
        Their good luck ends without achievement,
        but only the accomplished knows what this means.

21–24   From youth to the greying of hair,
        at midway they begin to waver.
        They turn their backs to the Way, and keep to delusive
            tracks;
        they leave the right path and enter the wrong.

25–26   As if peering through a pipe, unable to see broadly,
        they can hardly assess what impends.

37   *The* Book of Changes *and the* Cantong qi

1–4   As regards the greatest sages,
no one excels Fu Xi:
"he was the first to draw the eight trigrams,"
taking as models Heaven and Earth.

5–8   King Wen, the ancestor of all emperors,
joined them together and added the Statements on the
    Lines;
Confucius, outstanding among sages,
appended the Ten Wings.

9–14   These three noble lords, chosen by Heaven,
rose in turn to rule over their time.
In what they accomplished each walked at his pace,
but they did not differ in merit or virtue;
in what they produced they trod one path,
inferring the measures and inspecting the minutest details.

15–18   What has form is easy to gauge,
but the signless can hardly be envisaged.
In order that this pursuit have a model,
on behalf of the world I have composed this book.

19–22   Pure and devoid of foreknowledge and skills,
I was awakened by relying on my masters:
dazzled as if I had raised a curtain,
I opened my eyes, and climbed to a terrace on high.

38   *Wei Boyang's hesitancy*

1–6   The Records of Fire count six hundred chapters:
their import is equal, and they do not delude.
Their words contain priceless statements,
which the worldly do not earnestly consider.

Should they quest for the origin,
they would see that, at root, darkness and light dwell
         together.

7–12   How could this lowly man heedlessly dare to write down
what only the worthies discussed?
But if I tied my tongue and remained dumb,
I would cause a break in the Way and incur punishment.
And yet, should I write all the facts on bamboo and silk,
I would fear all the same to disclose the token of Heaven.

13–18   Hesitant and uncertain, sighing time after time,
I have looked upward and downward, and have written
         these trifles.
There is a method for moulding and smelting,
but I cannot thoroughly enounce it.
Concisely I will report its guidelines,
and let the branches display its luxuriance.

39   *Compounding the Elixir (First part)*

1–4   Make dikes and embankments with Metal,
so that Water may enter and effortlessly drift.
Fifteen is the measure of Metal,
the same is the number of Water.

5–10   Tend to the furnace to determine the scruples and ounces:
five parts of Water are more than enough.
In this way the two become True,
and Metal will weigh as at first.
The other three are thus not used,
but Fire, which is 2, is fastened to them.

11–16   The three things join one another:
in their transformations their shapes are divine.
The Breath of Great Yang lies underneath,

within an instant it steams and subdues.
First it liquefies, then coagulates;
it is given the name Yellow Carriage.

17–20   When its time is about to come to an end,
it wrecks its own nature and disrupts its life span.
Its form looks like ashes or soil,
its shape is like dust on a luminous window.

40   *Compounding the Elixir (Second part)*

1–4   Pound it and mix it,
and let it enter the Red-colored Gates.
Seal the joints firmly,
striving to make them as tight as you can.

5–8   A blazing fire grows below:
by day and by night its sound is unchanging and steady.
At first make it gentle so that it may be adjusted,
at the end make it fierce and let it spread out.

9–12   Watch over it with heed and caution:
inspect it attentively and regulate the amount of its
warmth.
It will rotate through twelve nodes,
and when the nodes are complete, it will again need your
care.

13–16   Now its Breath is worn out, and its life is about to be
severed;
it pauses and dies, losing its *po* and its *hun*.
Then its color changes to purple:
the Reverted Elixir, radiant and glowing, is attained.

17–18   Minutely powder it and make it into a pellet —
even one knife-point is supremely divine.

41   *Yin and Yang feed on each other*

1–4   Deducing the measures of the five agents
       is simple and uncomplicated:
       take water to drench a fire,
       and its radiant light is extinguished at once.

5–10   The Sun and the Moon always encroach upon one another
       on the month's first day and the day of full moon.
       When Water flourishes, Kan ☵ trespasses on Yang;
       when Fire decays, Li ☲ turns from daylight to dusk.
       Yin and Yang feed on each other;
       that they affect one another is the Dao as it is.

11–14 Names are used to determine the qualities,
       and cognomens to express the nature.
       When Metal goes back to its initial nature,
       then you can call it Reverted Elixir.

42   *The tradition of the* Cantong qi

1–6   Not daring to speak vainly,
       I have replicated the writings of the sages:
       the ancient records told of the Dragon and the Tiger,
       the Yellow Emperor praised the Golden Flower,
       Master Huainan refined the Autumn Stone,
       and Wang Yang commended the Yellow Sprout.

7–10   The worthies can put this in practice,
       the undeserving shall not share in it.
       The Ways of the past and the present are one:
       I have discussed and made plain what they envisage.

11–14 Students should labor and toil,
       thinking at length and reflecting in depth.

The ultimate essentials have been fully disclosed:
they gleam, and never deceive.

BOOK 2

43   *Qian and Kun, Kan and Li*

1–6   Qian ☰ the firm and Kun ☷ the yielding
        join and embrace one another;
        Yang endows, Yin receives,
        the masculine and the feminine attend one to the other.
        Attending, they create and transform,
        unfolding their Essence and Breath.

7–12   Kan ☵ and Li ☲ are at the fore:
        their radiance and glow come down and spread out.
        Mysterious and obscure, this can hardly be fathomed
        and cannot be pictured or charted.
        The sages gauged its depth;
        one with it, they set forth its foundation.

13–18   These four, in indistinction,
        are right within Empty Non-Being.
        Sixty hexagrams revolve around them,
        outspread like a chariot.
        Harnessing a dragon and a mare,
        the bright noble man holds the reins of time.

19–22   In harmony there are following and compliance:
        the path is level and begets no evil.
        Evil ways obstruct and hamper:
        they endanger the kingdom.

44   *Awaiting the time*

1–3 "The noble man dwells in his house; if he speaks his words
well, even those from more than a thousand miles away
respond to them."

4–5 This means that the ruler of a kingdom of ten thousand
chariots resides in a house surrounded by nine layers of
walls.

6–9 In issuing orders and bringing forth ordinances,
he complies with the nodes of Yin and Yang.
"Hiding his skills and awaiting the time,"
he never goes against the monthly hexagram cycle.

45   *The monthly cycle of the hexagrams*

1–6 Zhun ䷂ uses *zi* and *shen*,
Meng ䷃ employs *yin* and *xu*.
Of the remaining sixty hexagrams,
each has its own day:
let me present just these two emblems,
for here I cannot be exhaustive.

7–10 To set up righteousness, establish the punishments;
when humanity is in order, let virtue come forth.
"Those who transgress this have ill fortune;
those who comply with it have good fortune."

11–16 Thoroughly consider the laws and the ordinances,
with utter sincerity and concerted attention;
cautiously watch the markers of time,
attentively inspect the ebb and the flow.
Even with the smallest of errors,
regret and remorse would possess you.

46   *The regular phenomena of Heaven and Earth*

1–4   If the two solstices altered their measures,
         and ran twisting and turning counter to rule,
         in deep winter we would have the Great Heat,
         and in full summer, frost and snow.

5–8   If the two equinoxes inverted their routes,
         and did not agree with the water clock's notches,
         flood and drought would attack one another,
         and wind and rain would never be timely.

9–12   Locusts and worms would seethe and churn,
         and anomalies would come forth from all sides;
         strange apparitions would be seen in the skies,
         the mountains collapse and the earth fissure.

47   *Complying with the cycles of Yin and Yang*

1–4   The filial child uses his Heart,
         bringing the August Ultimate to move in response.
         What comes forth from his mouth anear
         flows to little-known regions afar.

5–10   Sometimes it provokes calamities,
         at others it brings about happiness;
         sometimes it fosters Great Peace,
         at others it engenders battles and wars.
         The origin of all these four
         lies in his own bosom.

11–14   "Movement and quiescence have constancy,"
         therefore he abides by the marking-cord and the plumb-
             line.
         Complying with the proprieties of the four seasons,
         their breaths does he receive.

15–18   "The firm and the yielding are distinguished,"
       and do not impinge upon one another;
       the five agents keep to their boundaries,
       reaching plenitude and receding without error.

19–20   The course of change flows in cycles —
       it bends and it stretches, and goes back and forth.

48   *The joining of the Sun and the Moon*

1–6   Between the month's last day and next month's first,
       they join their tallies and move to the Center.
       In the inchoate boundless,
       female and male follow one another.
       Their nurturing fluids moisten and impregnate,
       their emanations and transformations flow and spread all
          through.

7–10   The Numinous Light of Heaven and Earth
       is immeasurable.
       "Use it for benefit and to bring serenity to yourself,"
       hide yourself and remain secluded.

49   *The cycle of the Moon*

1–6   It rises in the northeast,
       the hamlet of Winnowing Basket and Dipper.
       Revolving and turning to the right,
       it brings out its disk and emits its first bud of light.
       Withdrawn in a deep pool, it lets its image appear,
       sending forth and dispersing its essence and its radiance.

7–12   Above Pleiades and Net,
       Zhen ☳ comes forth as an inkling,
       and the Yang Breath makes its start:

"Initial nine, withdrawn dragon."
Yang is set up on the third,
Yin is on par on the eighth.

13–16   On the third day Zhen ☳ moves,
on the eighth, Dui ☱ is in action.
"Nine in the second place, appearing dragon":
in harmony and equality there is light.

17–22   On the fifteenth, virtue is attained
and the body of Qian ☰ is achieved.
"Nine in the third place, at nightfall he is watchful,"
fearing that he might lose the divine token.
Flourishing and decay gradually renovate themselves,
and when they end they revert to the beginning.

23–26   When Xun ☴ takes control,
it firmly holds it in its hands.
"Nine in the fourth place, wavering flight":
advancing and receding, the course is a perilous one.

27–32   Gen ☶ rules over arrest and advance,
so that nothing contravenes the timing.
On the twenty-third day
it presides over the waning quarter.
"Nine in the fifth place, flying dragon":
sitting in the throne of Heaven, it increases its delight.

33–38   On the thirtieth, Kun ☷ inherits the charge,
binding and enclosing end and beginning.
Carrying and nourishing her children,
she is like a mother to all things in the world.
"Nine at the top, arrogant dragon,"
fighting for power in the wild.

39–44   "All nines," flutter flutter,
are the compass and square of the Dao.

The Yang numbers are now completed,
and being completed, they rise once again:
turning over their qualities, conjoining their natures,
in turn one gives way to the other.

50   The "ancestor of change"

1–6   Moving in a ring in accordance with Jade-cog and Armil,
rising and falling, ascending and descending,
it flows in cycles through the six lines,
and can hardly be beheld.
Thus it has no constant position:
it is the ancestor of change.

51   The cycle of the Sun

1–8   The dawn of the month's first day is Fu ䷗ (Return):
the Yang Breath begins to spread throughout.
"Going out and coming in without error,"
the shadow of the gnomon is tenuous but firm.
At the time of Yellow Bell, the Dipper points at *zi*:
the seedlings thrive,
a tender warmth spreads over,
and one and all regain constancy.

9–14   At Lin ䷒ (Approach), the furnace issues strips of light,
opening the way for proper radiance.
Radiance and shine gradually advance,
and daylight thus grows longer.
Great Regulator is at *chou*,
binding and aligning what is above and what is below.

15–20   Looking upward, it forms Tai ䷊ (Peace):
the firm and the yielding both come to hold sway.
As Yin and Yang conjoin,

"the small departs, the great approaches."
The spokes converge on *yin*:
they spin concurring with the time.

21–26   Gradually comes the turn of Dazhuang ䷡ (Great
            Strength),
         when the knights array themselves at the gates of *mao*.
         The elm seeds fall to the ground,
         returning to their roots.
         Punishment and virtue are opposed one to the other,
         daytime and nighttime are now unequal to each other.

27–30   At Guai ䷪ (Parting) the time has come for Yin to move
            into retreat,
         for Yang has risen and has come to the fore.
         Washing and cleansing its feathers and its quills,
         it clears away the dust of ages.

31–34   Qian ䷀ (The Creative) is strong, flourishing, and bright,
         and lays itself over the four neighborhoods.
         Yang terminates at *si*;
         residing in the Center, it has a share in everything.

35–40   At Gou ䷫ (Encounter) a new epoch comes to pass:
         for the first time "there is hoarfrost underfoot."
         "In the well there is a clear, cold spring,"
         and at Luxuriant there is *wu*.
         The guest has been subdued by Yin,
         and Yin has now become the host.

41–44   At Dun ䷠ (Withdrawal) it leaves its worldly place,
         gathering its Essence to store it up.
         Cherishing its virtue, it awaits its time,
         resting at leisure in the dark.

45–48   At Pi ䷋ (Obstruction) there are stagnation and blockade,
         and no new buds are generated.

Yin stretches and Yang bends:
the surname and forename of Yang have been erased.

49–54 Guan ☶ (Contemplation), with its equity and its balance,
examines the temper of autumn's middle month.
It nourishes the tender and the young,
the old and withered bloom again.
Shepherd's purse and wheat sprout and shoot anew,
through their bravery they are able to survive.

55–58 Bo ☶ (Splitting Apart) tears its limbs and trunk,
extinguishing its form.
The vital Breath is drained,
the supreme Spirit is forgotten and is lost.

59–62 The course comes to its end and turns around,
returning to its origin in Kun ☷ (The Receptive).
Ever complying with the patterns of the Earth,
she receives Heaven in herself, allowing it to unfold.

63–66 Mysterious and obscure! Subtle and remote!
Separate are they, and yet they are bound.
In due measure they nurture the seed
that is the origin of Yin and Yang.

67–70 Vast and broad! Vague and indistinct!
No one knows its beginnings.
"Going ahead of it brings on delusion" and you lose your
     track,
"go behind it," and you are a ruler and a lord.

52   *End and beginning*

1–4   "There is no plain that is not followed by a slope":
this is the Dao being as it is.

Transformation and change flourish and prosper,
ebb and flow depend one on the other.

5–8   It ends at Kun ☷ and then begins at Fu ☳,
as if it followed a circle or a ring.
If emperors and kings master this Way,
they will remain alive one thousand years.

53   *Non-Being and existence*

1–4   In order to nourish your nature,
prolong your life and hold off the time of death,
attentively reflect upon the end
and duly ponder what comes before.

5–8   We are endowed with a corporeal frame,
but at root our body is nothing:
as the Original Essence spreads like the clouds,
it is to Breath that we owe our beginning.

9–14 Yin and Yang set the measures,
and are the dwelling places of *hun* and *po*:
the Yang Spirit is the *hun* of the Sun,
the Yin Spirit is the *po* of the Moon.
What relates *hun* and *po* to one another
is that each is home for the other.

54   *Nature and qualities*

1–4   One's nature rules by abiding within,
implanting the seed;
one's qualities rule by engaging without,
raising enclosures and walls.

5–8   Only when the walls are whole and intact,
      can people be secure.
      At that time,
      the qualities bring Qian and Kun together.

55   *Water, the beginning*

1–4   "Qian ☰ is movement and is straight":
      Breath spreads and Essence flows.
      "Kun ☷ is quiescence and is gathered":
      it is the hut of the Dao.

5–8   The firm gives forth and then recedes,
      the yielding transmutes and thereby nurtures.
      The 9 reverts, the 7 returns,
      the 8 goes back, the 6 remains.

9–12 Man is white, woman is red;
      Metal and Fire seize one another.
      Water then stabilizes Fire:
      it is the first of the five agents.

13–18 "Superior goodness is like water"
      because it is flawless and clear.
      These are the forms and images of the Dao,
      but True Unity can hardly be charted:
      it alters itself and distributes by parting,
      and each part dwells alone, on its own.

56   *The birth of the embryo*

1–6   Similar in kind to a hen's egg,
      the white and the black tally with one another.
      But one inch in size,
      yet it is the beginning:

then the four limbs, the five viscera,
the sinews and bones join it.

7–10   When ten months have elapsed,
it exits the womb.
"Its bones are weak" and are pliant,
its flesh is as smooth as lead.

57   The Breaths of Yin and Yang

1–4   You gather fire with the *yangsui*,
which, if not for the Sun, would not produce light.
And the *fangzhu*, if not for the stars and the Moon,
could it ever collect the nectar of water?

5–8   Mysterious and remote are the two Breaths,
yet their influence pervades all things.
How much more is this so for what is near and exists in
    yourself,
proximately within your Heart?

9–10   "Yin and Yang match the Sun and the Moon,"
water and fire are their attestation.

58   The three treasures

1–4   Ears, eyes, and mouth are the three treasures:
shut them, and let nothing pass through.
The True Man withdraws in the depths of the abyss;
drifting and roaming, he keeps to the compass.

5–8   Watch and listen while wheeling around,
and opening and closing will always accord.
Take this as your lynchpin,
and movement and quiescence will never be exhausted.

9–12 The Breath of Li ☲ strengthens and guards you within,
and Kan ☵ is not employed for listening.
Dui ☱ is closed and not used for talking:
you follow the boundless with inaudible words.

59 *Achieving constancy*

1–4 When the three have been latched,
repose your body in an empty room,
and give your will to returning to Empty Non-Being;
without thoughts you attain constancy.

5–8 Going back and forth brings obstruction:
if focused, your Heart will not wander or stray.
In sleep, embrace your Spirit;
when awake, watch over existence and extinction.

9–12 Gradually your countenance will moisten
and your bones will grow solid and strong.
Having completely removed the evil of Yin,
you can establish pure Yang.

60 *The breathing of the True Man*

1–4 Cultivate this unceasingly,
and your plentiful breath will course like rain from the
  clouds,
overflowing like a marsh in the spring,
pouring forth like ice that has melted.

5–8 It will stream from the head to the toes;
on reaching the end, it will rise once again.
In its coming and going, it will spread limitless,
pervading throughout and extending all around.

9–14   Return is the attestation of the Dao,
weakness is "the handle of virtue."
When the long gathered filth is removed,
the fine and tenuous are attuned and laid forth.
The turbid is the path of the clear:
after a long dusk, the gleaming light.

61   *Incorrect practices*

1–4   The worldly people are fond of the minor arts,
and do not inspect the great depths of the Dao.
Leaving the right, they follow the evil alleys;
wanting to hurry, they meet obstruction and do not pass
   through.

5–10   It is like the blind man not leaning on a cane,
   or the deaf bent on listening to the *shang* and the *gong*;
like diving in water to catch pheasants and hares,
   or climbing a mountain to seek dragons and fish;
like sowing wheat with the aim of harvesting millet,
   or turning a compass in the attempt to draw a square.

11–14   They drain their strength and belabor their Essence and
   Spirit,
but at the end of their years they will see no result.
Should they wish to learn the method of preserving and
   ingesting,
their pursuit will be simple and uncomplicated.

62   *Compounding the Elixir*

1–6   The Flowing Pearl of Great Yang
desires ever to leave you.
When, at last, it finds the Golden Flower,
it turns about, and the two rely upon each other.

They transform into a white liquid,
coagulate and are perfectly solid.

7–12   The Golden Flower is the first to sing:
in the space of an instant
it dissolves into water —
horse-tooth and *langgan*.
The Yang is next to join it:
qualities and natures are so of themselves.

13–18   Approach it forthwith,
seize it and store it within the Forbidden Gates.
The loving mother will nurture and nourish it,
and the filial child will reward her with love;
the stern father will issue orders,
to teach and admonish his children and grandsons.

63   *The Three Fives*

1–4   The five agents rule in alternate order,
each overtaking the other in order to live.
Fire by its nature melts Metal;
when Metal cuts it, Wood blooms.

5–8   The Three Fives combine into One,
the ultimate essence of Heaven and Earth.
Oral instructions are possible;
hardly can this be transmitted in writing.

64   *Inverting the course*

1–4   From *zi* duly it turns to the right,
from *wu* it revolves to the east.
Mao and *you* are the boundaries;
the host and the guest are two.

5–10   The Dragon exhales onto the Tiger,
the Tiger inhales the Dragon's essence.
The two feed on one another
and crave one for the other;
thus they bite and they gulp,
they chew and they swallow each other.

11–15   Sparkling Wonderer keeps to the West,
Great White is across the sky.
Can anything faced by the life-taking Breath
be not overcome?

15–18   Cats capture rats,
sparrows fear hawks.
Each of them fulfills its function —
how would they dare utter a sound?

65   *Erroneous alchemical methods*

1–4   Without understanding the principles,
deceptive words are of no avail:
you will exhaust your family's possessions,
your wife and children will become hungry and poor.

5–8   From the antiquity down to the present,
millions are those who have devoted themselves to this Art,
and at the end have not found achievement:
rare have been those who have accomplished their goal.

9–10   Seeking renowned medicines far and wide
is utterly at odd with the Dao!

66   *The course of all things*

1–4   If you look into this and have the blessed encounter,
       you will behold the course of all things,
       comparing one to another according to kind,
       to assess their end and beginning.

5–8   The five agents conquer each other,
       acting, in turn, as father and mother;
       the mother bears the nurturing fluids,
       the father governs endowment.

9–12   Essence coagulates and they flow into form;
       metals and minerals do not decay.
       Thoroughly inspect this, never disclose it,
       and you will succeed in achieving the Dao.

67   *The perfect image of Heaven and Earth*

1–4   Stand a pole upon the earth and a shadow appears;
       shout into a valley and an echo comes forth.
       Is this not numinous?
       It is the perfect image of Heaven and Earth.

5–8   And yet, if you take an inch of *yege*
       or an ounce of *badou*,
       your body will stiffen as it enters the throat,
       never again able to move.

9–15   At that time,
       King Wen of the Zhou can sort out the stalks,
       Confucius can divine with the images,
       Bian Que can handle his needles,
       and Shaman Xian can beat on his drum —
       will they ever be able to revive you,
       stand you up again to walk quickly away?

68   *The Lovely Maid and the Yellow Sprout*

1–4   The Lovely Maid of the River
        is numinous and supremely divine:
        when she finds Fire she flies away,
        leaving behind not a speck of dust.

5–8   Like a demon she hides, like a dragon she conceals:
        nobody knows her whereabouts.
        If you want to control her,
        the Yellow Sprout is the root.

69   *"Heaven and Earth as they are of themselves"*

1–8   Bereft of Yin, devoid of Yang,
        creatures would go against Heaven and turn away from the
            origin.
        If a hen lays an egg on her own,
        her chick would never be formed.
        Why is this so?
        Because no joining occurred:
        the 3 and the 5 did not merge with each other,
        the firm and the yielding stayed one apart from the other.

9–16   The Essences emanated and transformed
        are Heaven and Earth as they are of themselves.
        Fire stirs and blazes by rising up,
        water streams and wets by flowing down.
        No teacher instructs them
        to behave in that way:
        "they owe their beginning to this," and are permeated and
            made good by it;
        nothing could cause them to change.

17–23   Behold the male and female
        at the time of intercourse:

the firm and the yielding are bound to each other
"and cannot be untied,"
like the two parts of a tally finding their match.
No skill and no craft is required
to be accomplished in this.

24–35   Males face downward after birth,
females lie reclined on their back:
they are endowed with these qualities while they are in the
    womb as an embryo,
and receive the first whit of Breath.
Not only at birth
can this be plainly seen:
at the time of death
we can attest it again.
It is not our father and mother
who teach us to do so:
the foundation lies in the intercourse
and is built at the start.

70   *"When Yang loses its token"*

1–2   Kan ☵ is man and is the Moon,
Li ☲ is woman and is the Sun.

3–6   Thus the Sun sends forth virtue,
the Moon unfurls radiance.
The Moon receives, the Sun gives,
and their bodies are not harmed, not depleted.

7–12   When Yang loses its token,
Yin trespasses on its light.
Between the month's last day and next month's first, it
    encroaches,
overcasting and upsetting:

Yang dissolves its form,
Yin invades, and calamity is born.

13–16   Each upon the other should man and woman wait,
inhaling, exhaling, each nourishing the other.
Feminine and masculine should mingle,
each seeking the other kind.

71   *"If man goes past the measure"*

1–4   Metal transforms into Water,
water by nature flows everywhere;
when Fire transforms into Soil,
water can proceed no further.

5–10   Man is movement and gives without,
woman is quiescence and stores within.
If man goes past the measure and exceeds his proper
        share,
he is seized by the woman;
thus the *po* latches the *hun*,
lest it be wasteful and lavish.

11–14   Neither cold nor hot,
they advance and recede in accordance with the time:
each of them attains its own harmony,
exhaling their tokens together.

72   *"The three things are one family"*

1–4   When the Wooden essence of cinnabar
finds Metal, they pair with each other:
Metal and Water dwell in conjunction,
Wood and Fire are companions.

5–8   These four, in indistinction,
      arrange themselves as Dragon and Tiger:
      the Dragon is Yang, its number is odd,
      the Tiger is Yin, its number is even.

9–12 The liver is green and is the father,
      the lungs are white and are the mother,
      the kidneys are black and are the son,
      the heart is red and is the daughter.

13–16 The spleen is yellow and is the forefather,
      and the son is at the origin of the five agents.
      The three things are one family:
      all of them return to *wu* and *ji*.

73   *Inverting the course*

1–4   The firm and the yielding rise in turn,
      going through all sectors one after the other.
      Dragon in the West, Tiger in the East,
      across the way are *mao* and *you*.

5–8   Punishment and virtue meet,
      seeing each other with delight:
      punishment rules over taking life,
      virtue rules over giving life.

9–12 In the second month, the elm seeds fall
      when Head faces *mao*;
      in the eighth month, wheat grows
      when Celestial Net accords with *you*.

13–18 *Zi* in the South, *wu* in the North,
      are each other's guiding thread.
      The numbers 1 to 9
      end and begin again:

holding the Origin at Emptiness and Rooftop,
at *zi* they spread the Essence.

74   *Using ingredients of unlike kind*

1–4   "*Guan guan* go the ospreys,
         on the islet in the river.
         The modest, retiring, virtuous, young lady:
         for our prince a good mate she."

5–10   Cocks do not live in solitude,
         nor do hens dwell on their own;
         the Dark Warrior's turtle and snake
         coil around and assist one another.
         This shows that for female and male
         each should thoroughly attend to the other.

11–20   Suppose that a house is shared by two women,
         of enchanting beauty and charm;
         and that Su Qin, the mediator,
         and Zhang Yi, the interceder,
         debate with sharp tongues,
         and with beautiful words propose
         that they arrive at an earnest accord,
         joining as husband and wife:
         their hair will fall, their teeth will rot,
         but not once shall they know one another.

21–24   With ingredients of unlike kinds,
         with names and types unmatched
         and mistaken doses and measures,
         your guiding thread is lost.

25–28   Then even if the Yellow Emperor tends to the furnace,
            the Great One looks after the fire,

the Eight Sirs pound and refine,
and Master Huainan adjusts the compound;

29–32   even if you set up space for a sumptuous altar,
            with steps made of jade
            and with dried meat of unicorn and phoenix fat,
            and you pay obeisance holding the records;

33–36   even if you pray invoking all spirits and gods,
            beg every demon with wails,
            and you bathe, fast, and keep to the precepts,
            hoping that what you long for would finally come —

37–42   all this would be like spreading glue to repair a pot,
            daubing a wound with sal ammoniac,
            using cold ice to cure a chill
            or hot water to heal a fever.
            Even seeing a flying turtle or a dancing snake
            would be easier than this!

BOOK 3

75   *The saints and the worthies of old*

1–4   The saints and the worthies of old
       cherished the Mystery and embraced the Truth.
       They refined the Nine Tripods,
       then altered their traces and sunk away in hiding.

5–8   Holding to their Essence, they nourished their Spirit
       and spread their virtue through the three luminaries;
       their corporeal fluids reached their skin,
       their sinews and bones were silken but firm.

9–12   Having removed every evil,
       they preserved pure Breath for a long time;
       gathering it longly,
       they transmuted their form and transcended the world.

76   *Wei Boyang and the* Cantong qi

1–4   Grieved and concerned for those in the future
       who will be fond of the Dao,
       they complied with the ways of the world
       and offered guidance on the writings of old.

5–10   They wrote charts and texts
       to aid posterity in seeing,
       but exposed only the branches
       and left the roots concealed;
       they disguised every name,
       enveiled every word.

11–16   As they came by these writings, those who studied this Art
        stored them in caskets for the whole of their life.
        The sons continued the ways of their fathers,
        and the grandsons trod their ancestors' paths.
        Delusion and doubt were passed down in the world,
        and in the end nothing was understood.

17–20   Thus officials did not attend to their duties,
        and farmers neglected to weed;
        merchants abandoned their goods,
        and the families of honorable men became poor.

21–24   Deeply saddened by this,
        I have written this book.
        Its words are concise and easy to ponder,
        the matter succinct and uncomplicated.

25–28   It unfurls the branches,
        that the fruit and kernel may be contemplated;
        its count of the mils and ounces
        can be trusted and relied upon.

29–32   Thus I have written an epilogue
        to open a gateway to my book.
        The wise should reflect,
        and, with attention, comprehend it.

77   *The order of Heaven*

1–2   "Among models and images, none is greater than Heaven
            and Earth,"
        and the Dark Ditch measures tens of thousands of miles;

3–4   if River's Drum faces Stellar Sequence,
        it will alarm and upset us all.

5–6 And if the sundial's shadow goes back and forth in a
haphazard way,
for nine years we will suffer misfortune and blame:

7–8 with the Ruler-on-High looking on,
the king should withdraw and reform.

9–10 Barriers and locks move up and down,
and the harmful breaths quickly depart,

11–12 as if the Yangzi and the Huai had been drained,
and their waters had poured to the sea.

13–14 The masculine and feminine in Heaven and Earth
move around between *zi* and *wu*;

15–16 *yin* and *shen*, the forefathers of Yin and Yang,
come and go, end and begin again:

17–18 complying with the Dipper and Rising Glimmer,
and holding to Scale, they set the prime sequence.

78   *Compounding the Elixir*

1–2 So that its heat may go up to Mount Zeng,
a blazing fire is made below;

3–4 the White Tiger leads the song ahead,
the green liquid joins after.

5–6 The Vermilion Sparrow soars into play,
flying upward in the hues of its five colors;

7–8 then it encounters the spread of a thin net —
caught, it can rise no more.

9–10 It screams deep in agony, "Wah! Wah!,"
      like an infant who yearns for its mother,

11–12 as it enters the boiling pot on its head,
       its feathers ripped off.

13–14 Before the water clock's notches have gone past the half,
       fish scales appear throughout;

15–16 the sheen of its five colors are dazzles and gleans,
       their transformations proceed without pause.

17–18 As the bubbling tripod stirs and seethes,
       ceaselessly gurgling and burbling,

19–20 coalescing continuously, one after the other,
       the dog's teeth form a lattice.

21–22 Their shape looks like ice in the winter's middle month,
       like stalactites issued forth from *langgan*:

23–24 they tower in tangles and jumbles,
       piling up upon one another.

79   *The Three Fives return to the One*

1–2   When Yin and Yang find one another in match
      they are faint and frail, but protect one another.

3–4   Green Dragon abides in Room, its number is 6;
      it is spring, the flowers, Zhen ☳, East, and *mao*.

5–6   White Tiger is at Pleiades, its number is 7;
      it is autumn, the awns, Dui ☱, West, and *you*.

7–8   Vermilion Sparrow is at Extension, its number is 2;
      it is pure Yang, Li ☲, South, and *wu*.

9–10 Together these three come to audience,
      like kin who belong to one family.

11–12 At first there are only two things,
       at the end they become the Three Fives;

13–14 the Three Fives together combine into One,
       they all gather and return to the two places.

15–16 Compound it according to the rules given above,
       and take from them the days and the measures.

17–18 First it is white, then it is yellow;
       red and black run through it, without to within.

19–20 Its name is First Tripod:
       ingest it in pills sized as a grain of millet.

80   *"It is made of its own"*

1–2   It is made of its own,
      and not through some artificial or evil way —

3–4   like the breaths of mountains and lakes that share steam,
      and the clouds that rise to make rain;

5–6   like the mud that has dried and comes to be dust,
      and the fire that, extinguished, turns into soil;

7–8   like the yellow dye from the cork tree,
      and the indigo plant that makes silk green;

9–10   like the leather that is boiled to form glue,
        and the yeast and the sprouts that change into liquor.

11–12   Like kinds yield results with ease;
        unlike types are a challenge to craft.

81   *The Way of Heaven renders no favors*

1–2   This alone is the wondrous Art,
        veritable, genuine, free of untruthful words.

3–4   Millions of generations have passed it down,
        yet still it gleams asking to be investigated,

5–6   brilliant as the stars of the Milky Way,
        luminous as a river that runs home to the sea.

7–8   Ponder it intensely,
        look at it all around, and above and below:

9–10   at one thousand changes, it is still vivid and splendid,
        at ten thousand transformations, you can still behold it.

11–12   On occasion the Numinous Light reveals itself to a man,
        and his Heart suddenly awakens:

13–14   investigate its beginnings, search its inception;
        without fail you will find its gate.

15–16   The Way of Heaven renders no favors:
        it is always transmitted to those who are worthy.

82   *Song of the Tripod*

1–4   3 and 5 around,
        an inch and one part,
        4 and 8 the mouth,
        the lips a pair of inches.

5–8   A foot and 2 tenths high,
        evenly thick and thin;
        its belly on the third day
        sits beneath the descending warmth.

9–12   Yin stays above,
        Yang rushes below;
        fierce are the head and the tail,
        gentle in between.

13–16   Seventy at the beginning,
        thirty days at the end;
        and for two hundred and sixty
        the balance well kept.

17–20   The whiteness of the Yin Fire,
        the lead of the Yellow Sprout:
        the Two Sevens assemble
        to support and assist man.

21–24   This suffices to order the brain
        and to make steady the ascent to the Mystery:
        the infant dwells within,
        gaining security and stability.

25–28   Roaming in its coming and going,
        it never exits the gates;
        gradually does it grow,
        until its qualities and nature are pure.

29–32   Then it returns to the One
         and reverts to the origin,
         as courteously and respectfully
         as a minister is to his lord.

33–36   At the end of each cycle,
         laboriously and assiduously
         protect it with utmost attention
         — let there be no lapse.

37–40   Long is the path
         to return to the Abyssal Mystery,
         but if you do arrive there,
         you will comprehend Qian and Kun.

41–44   Moisten one knife-point,
         and it will cleanse the *hun* and the *po*;
         you will obtain a long life
         and find a home in the town of the Immortals.

45–48   Lovers of the Dao
         should seek out its root:
         look into the five agents
         to settle the scruples and mils.

49–52   Think about this carefully;
         it need not be discussed.
         Hide it deep and guard it,
         do not transmit it in writing.

53–56   Riding a white crane,
         harnessing a scaly dragon,
         you will roam through Great Emptiness
         and pay homage to the Lord of the Immortals.

57–58   Your name will be inscribed in the Heavenly Charts,
         and you will be called a True Man.

83   *The Five Categories*

1–4   *The Seal of the Unity of the Three*
          sketches the contours:
          it can never be utterly complete;
          it speaks only of the surface.

5–8   As I have not brought forth the minute and the tenuous,
          and have omitted the dim and the indistinct,
          I now write again
          to fill the lacunae.

9–12   Giving luster to the deep and the obscure,
          my words bridge and complement one another:
          their intent is the same,
          their import equal.

13–15   Hence once again I put this in writing,
          and call it "The Five Categories";
          with this, the qualities and nature of the great *Book of
              Changes* are completed.

JIA	leftward floating	3	WOOD	rightward sinking	YI
BING	martial fire	2	FIRE	civil fire	DING
WU	Yang ingredient	5	SOIL	Yin ingredient	JI
GENG	worldly gold	4	METAL	worldly silver	XIN
REN	true mercury	1	WATER	true lead	GUI

"The five positions   "Each of them
match one another"   finds its equal"

84   *The three ways of the* Cantong qi

1–8   The qualities and nature of the great *Book of Changes*
              all follow their measures;
          with study, the Yellow Emperor's and the Old Master's teachings
              are simple to grasp;

the work with the fire of the furnace
    is based on the Truth.
These three Ways stem from one,
and together yield one path.

9–12   The branches and stalks, the flowers and leaves,
and also the fruits spread and unfold:
because the root and trunk are correct,
none of them loses its purity.

13–14   The words spoken by a sincere heart
are truthful and unerring.

85   *The timeless instant between end and beginning*

1–6   It is like the node of the winter's middle month,
when all bamboos and trees are wasted and injured.
As he attends to the Yang, and forbids travel and trade,
the ruler stays in deep seclusion:
complying with the ordinances in accord with the time,
he closes his mouth and does not use it for talking.

7–10   Vast and broad is the Way of Heaven,
and the Great Mystery has no form or appearance.
None can behold its emptiness and silence,
as it disappears within its own walls.

11–14   Commit an error, and you lose the thread of your pursuit;
your words turn against you and injure you.
One by one pursue these four images,
and awaken from blindness the students to come.

86   *Wei Boyang and the* Cantong qi

1–4   A lowly man born in Kuaiji,
I rust my life away in an obscure valley.
I cherish plainness and simplicity,
and find no joy in power or fame.

5–8   At leisure in a secluded place,
unconcerned with profit or name;
upholding calm and tranquility,
I seek quietness and serenity alone.

9–14   Unhurried, dwelling at ease,
I wrote this book
to sing and tell of the great *Book of Changes*
and of the words that the three sages handed down.
I have examined their import and meaning
and the principle that runs through them all.

87   *The three ways stem from one source*

1–4   Abide by these norms without fail,
let their essence and spirit shine far and wide:
when the divine transformations flow and pervade all
        things,
the Four Seas are in harmony and at peace.

5–8   Use them outwardly as a calendar,
with which ten thousand generations can comply.
Pursue them in carrying out governance,
and its practice will be uncomplicated.

9–12   Draw them within to nourish your nature:
this is the Dao of the Yellow Emperor and the Old Master,
        just as it is.

"Hold the fullness of virtue,"
and you will go back to the root and return to the origin.

13–16   It is there, near, in your Heart
and not separate from yourself:
embracing Unity without neglect,
"you will be able to maintain yourself for long."

17–22   Accord with it by preserving and ingesting,
so that male and female may be established.
Dispose of realgar,
discard the eight minerals!
Attentively use what you produce;
this is what is treasured by the world.

23–26   I have tendered three twigs,
but their branches and stalks are bound to one another:
"They come forth together but have different names,"
as they all stem from one gate.

27–32   These are not sentences merely strung together
in order to embroider my writing.
In them there is only the Truth,
as solid as stone to be seen.
Had I spoken falsely,
I would bear the fault.

33–36   The name of my book is *The Seal of the Unity of the
Three*;
examine its principles in detail.
"Its words are few," but its intent is great:
all future generations should abide by it.

88   *Wei Boyang's final words*

1–6   Forsaking the times, avoiding harm,
       I have entrusted myself to mountains and hills.
       I have wandered and roamed through the Unbounded,
       with demons as my neighbors.
       Transmuting my form, transcending the world,
       I have entered the depths of the Inaudible.

7–10   Once in a hundred generations I descend
       to roam in the human world;
       spreading my wings,
       I bend east, west, and south.

11–16 In times of adversity like those met by Tang,
       when flood is compounded by drought,
       when the stems and leaves shrivel and fade,
       losing their luster and glow,
       the good-natured man braves and endures the turn of
          events:
       steady and serene, and ready to live a long life.

Notes

BOOK 1

1. Qian and Kun, Kan and Li

Sections 1–17 of Book 1 are devoted to cosmology. The constant conjunction of Qian and Kun, the active and the passive principles, gives birth to all phenomena in the world of change. Therefore Qian and Kun are "the door and the gate" through which change arises, and "the father and the mother" of all emblems that represent change. As they join with one another, Qian ☰ entrusts his generative potential to Kun and, in doing this, becomes Li ☲; Kun ☷ receives the essence of Qian to bring it to fruition and, in doing this, becomes Kan ☵. Since Kan and Li embrace Qian and Kun, represented by the respective inner lines, they provide "inner and outer walls" to Qian and Kun: the Yin principle (☷) harbors True Yang (—), and the Yang principle (☰) harbors True Yin (- -).

If the two sets of walls are shaped as joined semicircles, they form a wheel (see fig. 3). The central hub is the emptiness from which existence comes forth; the axle passing through the hub is Qian and Kun, which hold the wheels in position; and the wheels with their spokes are the compass of space and the cycles of time governed by Kan and Li. The *Daode jing* (Book of the Way and its Virtue) uses the same images to illustrate the operation (or "function," *yong*) of emptiness at the center of the cosmos: "Thirty spokes share one hub: wherein there is nothing lies the function of a carriage. . . . Therefore in what is there lies the benefit; in what is not there lies the function" (*Daode jing*, 11).

Qian, Kun, Kan, and Li are also compared to a bellows and its nozzles. The bellows (Qian and Kun) is empty, but sends forth its breath through the nozzles (Kan and Li). This image too alludes to a passage in the *Daode jing*, which refers to the empty center that brings about existence by saying: "The space between Heaven and Earth — is it not like a bellows? As empty, it is never exhausted; as it moves, it continues to pour" (*Daode jing*, 5).

1. *"Qian and Kun are the door and the gate of change."* This sentence is an almost literal quotation from the "Appended Sayings" of the *Book of Changes*: "Qian and Kun are indeed the door and the gate of change!" (B.5; see Wilhelm, 343).

2. *The father and the mother of all hexagrams.* Compare *Book of Changes*, "Explanation of the Trigrams": "Qian is Heaven, therefore he is called the father. Kun is Earth, therefore she is called the mother" (sec. 9; see Wilhelm, 274). See also the "Commentary on the Judgement" on the hexagrams Qian (no. 1) and Kun (no. 2): "Great indeed is Qian, the Origin! The ten thousand things owe their beginning to him . . . Perfect indeed is Kun, the Origin! The ten thousand things owe their birth to her" (see Wilhelm, 370 and 386).

3. *Kan and Li are the inner and the outer walls.* In the trigrams Kan ☵ and Li ☲, the lower lines are the "inner wall," and the upper lines are the "outer wall." The central lines respectively belong to Qian ☰ and Kun ☷.

2. The artisan and the charioteer

The four artisan's tools are traditional images mentioned in several early Chinese texts (see the Introduction, § 6). They represent the devices that enable the ruler to measure the patterns of space and time, discern the cosmic laws, and conform his governance to those laws. Analogously, the charioteer who drives (*yu*) his carriage by following the tracks already found on the path is emblematic of the ruler who masters (*yu*) the properties and features of his domain, and governs (*yu*) his kingdom by complying with them.

Similar to an artisan and a charioteer, the sage ruler resides at the center of his domain and conforms his conduct to the patterns of space and time. The images and emblems used to explicate the functioning of the cosmos ("the system of pitch-pipes and the calendar") enable him to respond to change while maintaining himself in the state of non-action (*wuwei*).

1. *Enfolding and encompassing the Way of Yin and Yang.* Compare *Book of Changes*, "Appended Sayings": "Now, what is the *Changes*? The *Changes* begins things, completes affairs, and encompasses the Way of all under Heaven—this and nothing else" (A.10; see Wilhelm, 316).

7. *Abide in the Center to control the outside.* Compare *Huainan zi*: "Depend upon the small to embrace the great; stay in the Center to

control the outside; apply yieldingness and you will be firm; use weakness and you will be strong" (1.49; see Le Blanc and Mathieu, 28).

8. *The numbers are found in the system of the pitch-pipes and the calendar.* "Pitch-pipes and calendar" (*lüli*) refers not only in a literal sense to the musical and calendrical emblems, but also in an extended sense to the whole range of cosmological emblems.

3. The monthly cycle of the hexagrams

The first major cosmological cycle described in the *Cantong qi* concerns the thirty days of the lunar month. The alternation ("warp and weft") of Sun and Moon during the month occurs under the authority of the Sun: its light is reflected by the Moon along the course of the six "nodes" (or "sectors," *jie*) of five days in which the month is divided, and its rise and fall divides each day into its two main parts, daytime and nighttime. The movements of the Sun and Moon correspond to the stages of ascent and descent of Yin and Yang; they "set periods and measures" with respect to the terms of time (*qi*) and the spans of space (*du*), because each day on the scale of time corresponds to one degree in the compass of space.

Since the Yang and Yin principles respectively prevail at daytime and at nighttime, a Yang hexagram, called the "inner core," rules on the first part of the day, and a Yin hexagram, called the "outer function," rules on the second part (Yang is movement and Yin is quiescence, thus "movement precedes, quiescence follows"). Therefore altogether sixty hexagrams govern the thirty days of the lunar month, beginning with Zhun ䷂ and Meng ䷃ in the first day, and ending with Jiji ䷾ and Weiji ䷿ in the last day (see table 7). Moreover, the twelve lines of each pair of hexagrams are associated with the twelve earthly branches (*dizhi*; see fig. 4); the first six branches, going "from *zi* 子 to *chen* 辰 and *si* 巳," represent the rise of the Yang principle in the first part of the day, while the other six branches, going "from *wu* 午 to *xu* 戌 and *hai* 亥," represent the rise of the Yin principle in the second part of the day.

The cycle of the sixty hexagrams also establishes correspondences between each day, the four seasons, and the associated qualities in the human realm. In particular, daytime corresponds to spring, which is the time of "reward" (*shang*, when the Yang principles gives life), and to humanity (*ren*); nighttime corresponds to autumn, which is the time of "punishment" (*fa*, when the Yin principle takes life), and to righteousness (*yi*).

Just like space and time express the qualities of Qian and Kun in the cosmos, so do humanity and righteousness, "punishment" and "reward" express them in the human realm. Therefore the patterns of time and space provide models for the operation of the sage ruler. The emblems and the statements of the *Book of Changes* embody those patterns and suggest proper ways of responding to the different states of change: firmness, benevolence, and other qualities respectively related to Yin and Yang.

The four directions of space and the four seasons of time are related in turn to the five agents (*wuxing*; see tables 1 and 2). By conforming himself to the properties and the qualities of space and time, the ruler allows the five agents to function in accordance with their own principles.

1. *In one month there are six nodes of five days. Jie* ("node" or "sector") denotes a segment or subdivision of any temporal cycle. The five-day "nodes" are often called "periods" (*hou*). See, for instance, *Huangdi neijing, Suwen*, sec. 9: "Five days are called a period. Three periods are called a breath (i.e., the fortnightly "nodal breaths," *jieqi*). Six breaths are called a season. Four seasons are called a year."

4. *The firm is external, the yielding internal.* In this verse, "external and internal" denotes the first and the second hexagrams that rule on each day.

19. *The Statements on the Lines contain humanity and righteousness.* In the *Book of Changes*, the "Statements on the Lines" explain the meaning of the Yin and Yang lines in each hexagram. — Compare *Book of Changes*, "Explanation of the Trigrams": "In ancient times, the sages who made the *Changes* complied with the principles of nature (*xing*) and life (*ming*). Therefore they established the Way of Heaven, and spoke of Yin and Yang; they established the Way of Earth, and spoke of the yielding and the firm; and they established the Way of man, and spoke of humanity and righteousness" (sec. 2; see Wilhelm, 264).

4. Kan and Li, the functions of Qian and Kun

This section consists of a short commentary on the statement "Heaven and Earth establish their positions, and change occurs within them," found in the "Appended Sayings" of the *Book of Changes*. The Dao generates the world through Qian and Kun, and Qian and Kun operate in it through Kan and Li. These four modes are illustrated by different images. Heaven and Earth represent Qian and Kun; respectively placed above and below, they are immutably joined as one in the precosmic domain. The Moon and Sun are the main images of Kan and Li; they attest to cyclical alternation and change in the cosmic domain.

In the first place, Qian, Kun, Kan, and Li reside together in the center, undistinguished from one another (see 43:13–14). Their differentiation pertains to the perspective of the world of change. Here Qian and Kun are the substantive basis (*ti*) of Kan and Li, and Kan and Li are the function or operation (*yong*) of Qian and Kun.

The emblems of the *Book of Changes* illustrate these notions: the solid Yang line within Kan ☵ and the broken Yin line within Li ☲ represent the operation of Qian ☰ and Kun ☷, respectively, in the domain of space and time. The same Yin and Yang lines that belong in the first place to Qian and Kun also form the sixty-four hexagrams (see 1:1–2, where Qian and Kun are called "the father and the mother of all hexagrams"). Each hexagram consists of "six empty spaces" that are filled by lines of either sort to represent the nature and qualities of a particular state of change. Just as the solid and broken lines within the hexagrams are not fixed, but "flow in cycles" through the sixty-four emblems, so too are the states of the cosmos "not constant," and change occurs cyclically throughout space and time.

1–2. *"Heaven and Earth establish their positions, and change occurs within them."* This sentence is quoted from the "Appended Sayings" of the *Book of Changes* (A.5; see Wilhelm, 303).

8. *"Flowing in cycles they go through the six empty spaces."* Compare the "Appended Sayings": "Transformation and movement have no pause: they flow in cycles through the six empty spaces. Ascent and descent are not constant: the firm and the yielding change into each other" (B.7; see Wilhelm, 348).

9. *As their coming and going are not determinate.* The expression "coming and going" derives from the "Appended Sayings," where it refers to
the Yin and Yang principles: "Their coming and going without being
exhausted is called 'being pervasive'" (A.10; see Wilhelm, 318).

10. *So too "their ascent and descent are not constant."* See the passage of
the "Appended Sayings" quoted in the note to verse 8 above.

5. The emptiness within Kan and Li

The arising, transformation, and disappearance of all things occur
within the Dao, which does not generate them out of "nothing," but
out of itself. Thus the Dao embraces what it creates; the individual
objects and phenomena, in turn, are the instruments (*qi*) through
which the Dao operates in the cosmic domain.

This view is illustrated by a reference to a sentence in the *Daode
jing*: "One molds clay to make a vessel: wherein there is nothing lies
the function of a vessel" (sec. 11). The "vessel" is an object provided
with a form and, on that account, distinct from the formless Dao; yet
it holds formlessness in its concrete void, and that is its function.
Beyond the metaphor, the form of an object is the substantive basis
(*ti*, "body") that allows Emptiness to operate (*yong*, "function") in the
domain of change.

The distinction between emptiness and existence, or absolute and
relative, is meaningful only from the perspective of the relative domain. Here Kan and Li (Yin and Yang) follow cycles of ascent and
descent ("ebb and flow"), which can be deduced from the unfolding of
the three main emblematic time cycles: the day, the month, and the
year. However, Kan and Li are the operation (or "function," see 4:6)
of Qian and Kun: they harbor the emptiness and the timelessness of
the precosmic domain, and make it possible for them to operate in the
relative domain.

2. *"Therein occur the transformations."* This sentence is an almost literal
quotation from the "Appended Sayings" of the *Book of Changes*: "The
firm and the yielding follow one another, and therein occur the transformations" (B.1; see Wilhelm, 325). In the "Appended Sayings," the words
"therein occur the transformations" refer to the Yin and Yang lines that
alternate within the hexagrams; in the *Cantong qi*, they refer to the Dao
itself.

6. The Principle in words

The Numinous Light "is subtle and can hardly be beheld" (14:3), and "can hardly be envisaged" (37:16). Being "immeasurable" in itself (48:8), one can only "infer its rules and attest its tokens" (14:4). Certain images and emblems provide guidance to comprehend the principles by which the Formless manifests itself. They reveal the analogies that tie different domains—for example, the cosmos and the human being—to the absolute principle and to one another.

This is especially true of the trigrams and hexagrams of the *Book of Changes*. These emblems make it possible to discern the kinds or categories (*lei*) to which the different phenomena of the world pertain, and show how they relate to the primary modes—Qian and Kun— taken on by the Dao in its self-manifestation. Several words and images used in the *Cantong qi* perform the same function. The next section provides an example, concerned with the graph for the word "change" (*yi* 易).

7. Sun and Moon make change

The Moon is Kan ☵ and the Sun is Li ☲. However, although the Yin trigram Kan is associated with the Moon, it encloses a solid Yang line that belongs to Qian ☰. This line corresponds to the celestial stem *wu* 戊, an emblem of the active, creative aspect of the One. Analogously, the Yang trigram Li is associated with the Sun, but encloses a broken Yin line that belongs to Kun ☷. This line corresponds to the celestial stem *ji* 己, representing the passive, fulfilling aspect of the One. When Qian and Kun are contained within Kan and Li, they are called the "essence" (*jing*) of the Moon and the "radiance" (*guang*) of the Sun.

The alternation of the Sun and the Moon produces change. With regard to this, the *Cantong qi* observes that when the graphs that represent the Sun and the Moon are joined to one another, with the graph for "sun" (*ri* 日) placed above the graph for "moon" (*yue* 月), they form the graph for "change" (*yi* 易). This etymology of the word "change" does not pertain to philology, but is an example of the analogical function of images and forms.

In addition to being associated with True Yang (Qian) and True Yin (Kun), the celestial stems *wu* 戊 and *ji* 己 are also emblems of the central agent Soil, which, like the One, comprises Yin and Yang halves. Soil transmits the One Breath to the four directions and the four seasons—i.e., to space and time—which correspond to the agents Wood, Fire, Water, and Metal, referred to here by the colors green, red, black, and white. In reiterating the unity of Qian and Kun, Kan and Li, and *wu* and *ji*, Soil guarantees the conjunction of the world of multiplicity to the Absolute.

8. The greatest images of change

The opening sentences of this section are quoted from the "Appended Sayings" of the *Book of Changes*. "Images" (*xiang*) refers to the Sun and the Moon as the main emblems of Yin and Yang, whose alternation coincides with different states of change within the cosmos.

In another statement of the "Appended Sayings," Spirit is said to be that in which Yin and Yang are still joined as One and "cannot be fathomed." (*) Change, instead, is owed to Yin and Yang becoming separate from one another and cyclically alternating as Two. The One and the Two are indispensable to each other, but only the understanding of the One affords the understanding of the Two. Therefore comprehending Spirit (the unity of Yin and Yang) makes it possible to comprehend change (their alternation).

The unity of Yin and Yang underlies their transformations, which determine the appearance of time. Time moves in cycles, similar to a circle rotating around its axis or a wheel revolving around its hub. The axis and the hub represent Non-Being; the circle and the wheel are its operation in the domain of change.

(*) "That in which Yin and Yang cannot be fathomed is called Spirit" ("Appended Sayings," A.5; see Wilhelm, 301).

1. *"Change consists in images."* This sentence is quoted from the "Appended Sayings" of the *Book of Changes* (B.3; see Wilhelm, 336). In the *Book of Changes*, the word *yi* ("change") refers to the text itself, and the images are its lines, trigrams, and hexagrams; the full passage reads: "The *Changes* consists in images; these images are representations. The Judgements ("Tuan") provide the material. The lines [of the hexagrams] attest to the movements that occur under Heaven." The *Cantong qi*, instead, uses the word *yi* to refer to the notion of "change," which is owed to the

movements of the Sun and the Moon, the main images of Yin and Yang within the cosmos.

2–3. And *"among the suspended images that send forth their light, none is greater than the Sun and the Moon."* This sentence is quoted from the "Appended Sayings" (A.11; see Wilhelm, 319). "Suspended images" is a common expression that designates planets and asterisms, which appear to be hanging in the sky.

4. *"Probe the Spirit to understand the transformations."* This sentence is an almost literal quotation from the "Appended Sayings": "When one probes the Spirit and understands the transformations, this is the fullness of virtue" (B.3; see Wilhelm, 338).

5. *When Yang goes, Yin comes.* Compare the "Appended Sayings": "When the Sun goes, the Moon comes; when the Moon goes, the Sun comes. Sun and Moon follow one another, and light comes into existence. . . . Going means bending, and coming means stretching. Bending and stretching respond to one another, and benefit arises" (B.3; see Wilhelm, 338). With regard to the light generated by the alternation of the Sun and the Moon, note that *ming* 明 ("light") is the other graph formed when the graphs for "sun" (*ri* 日) and "moon" (*yue* 月) are placed not above and below one another, but next to one another.

9. Change and its emblems

The sixty-four hexagrams contain altogether 384 Yin or Yang lines. Based on the different positioning of the lines, the emblems of the *Book of Changes*—trigrams and hexagrams—symbolize different states of change within the cosmos. The next section, which refers to the trigram Zhen ☳, provides an example of this function.

10. The joining of the Sun and the Moon

The joining of Kan ☵ and Li ☲ (Sun and Moon) occurs in the night between a month's last day and next month's first day; it replicates within space and time the joining of Qian ☰ and Kun ☷ (Heaven and Earth) in the precelestial domain. When Kan and Li join one another, the active and the passive principles return to the original state of indistinction. Qian endows Kun with its essence (which is "mysterious," *xuan*, a word emblematic of Heaven), and the womb ("wrap") of Kun (which is "yellow," the color emblematic of Earth) is impregnated. Spirit produces that essence through its own coagulation (*ning*). Thus Kun receives the seed of Qian, and brings it to fruition. All forms of life are generated in this way.

In the cosmos, the joining of the Sun and the Moon gives birth to a new time cycle, the lunar month. The first half of that cycle is ruled by the Yang principle, which flourishes until it culminates at the middle of the month. The second half is ruled by the Yin principle, which similarly grows until it overcomes the Yang principle at the end of the month. Then the Sun and the Moon join once more, the Yang principle is reborn, and the cycle begins again.

The trigram Zhen ☳ (Thunder) symbolizes the first stage of the rebirth of luminous Yang after the obscurity of Yin. Its Yang line at the bottom (the position of the initial line) is an image of regeneration after stagnation, represented in the *Book of Changes* by the crack of thunder produced by the conjunction of Yin and Yang. At the beginning of the month, Heaven assigns Zhen the task of ruling over the first stage of the newly-born time cycle (the initial five days) and the corresponding sector of space (East). Having been reborn, the Yang principle begins a new cycle of ascent and descent. Section 13 describes this cycle.

4. *Heaven and Earth merge their essences*. Compare *Book of Changes*, "Appended Sayings": "Heaven and Earth mesh together, and the ten thousand things proliferate by transformation. Male and female join their essences, and the ten thousand things are born by transformation" (B.4; see Wilhelm, 342–43).

11. The signs of Heaven

"Boundless" approximates the sense of *hongmeng*, one of several terms that connote the inchoate state prior to the formation of the cosmos. At this stage—which is temporal only if the hierarchical states of Being are projected onto a metaphoric time scale—Yin and Yang are still joined to one another. Therefore the sages of antiquity, here represented by Confucius, emphasized the joining of Yin and Yang as that which lays the beginning of things.

The five verses that follow refer to the initial sections of five Confucian Classics (*Changes*, *Documents*, *Odes*, *Ceremonials*, and *Spring and Autumns*), in which the *Cantong qi* reads allusions to the conjunction of the male and female principles. The arrangement of these verses illustrates the generative process of the cosmos: taken together, they describe the unfolding of a process that sees Yin and Yang first joined in indistinction, then separated by the "opening of Heaven and Earth," then remaining apart, then joined again "in marriage," and finally producing their offspring (see the notes to sentences 2–6).

When the cosmos emerges from the initial state of indistinction, space and time are pervaded by the cycles of alternation of Yin and Yang. The Sun and the Moon, with their continuous and perfectly corresponding movements of ascent and descent, make those cycles apparent.

1. *Thereupon Confucius eulogized the boundless.* For the term *hongmeng* see, for instance, the *Huainan zi*: "In ancient times, when there were not yet Heaven and Earth, there were only images without forms. Deep and obscure! It was vast and measureless. Boundless and cavernous! No one knows where it came from" (7.503; see Le Blanc and Mathieu, 299; Larre, 53–54). This and analogous terms, for which no literal translation is possible, denote the initial state of formlessness, where "initial" has no temporal connotation except in a metaphoric sense.

2. *The virtue of Qian and Kun is cavernous and empty.* The first two hexagrams of the *Book of Changes*, namely Qian and Kun (Heaven and Earth), represent the True Yin and True Yang of the precosmic state, immutably joined to one another.

3. *"Inquiring into antiquity" we find the original sovereign.* The initial chapters of the *Book of Documents* (*Shujing*) begin with the phrase "Inquiring into antiquity" (for example, the "Canon of Yao" opens with these words: "Inquiring into the antiquity, [we find] Emperor Yao who was styled Fangxun"; see Legge, *The Sacred Books of China*, 3:32). According to some commentators, *yuanhuang* ("original sovereign") refers to the first two mythical sovereigns mentioned in the *Documents*, namely Yao and Shun, who established the foundations of Chinese civilization. According to others, it refers instead to the mythical ruler Pan Gu, who transformed his own body into the Sun, the Moon, wind, thunder, mountains, rivers, and so forth, thereby causing the "opening of

Heaven and Earth" (the creation of the world), which until then had been joined in his person.

4. *"Guan go the ospreys" to lay the beginnings.* Compare the *"Guan* Go the Ospreys" poem in the *Book of Odes (Shijing)*: *"Guan guan* go the ospreys / on the islet in the river" ("Guanya," no. 1; see Waley, *The Book of Songs*, 81–82). The entire first quatrain of this poem is quoted in section 74 below. This poem is often deemed to depict the correct relation between man and woman, and the ideals of morality and chastity. The *Cantong qi*, however, refers to it because ospreys are said to live on their own until the time of mating, and thus represent the state of separation of Yin and Yang while awaiting their rejoining.

5. *The auras of the capping and the marriage ceremonies are tied to one another.* The first ceremonies described in the *Book of Ceremonials (Yili)* are those for the coming of age and the marriage. These rites are deemed to be the most important ones in the life of a male and a female, respectively, who acquire social status through these rites. The capping ceremony, however, indicates not only that a male has reached adulthood, but also that he is ready for wedding. Both rites, therefore, denote the idea of "marriage." The *Cantong qi* takes them as images of the joining of Yin and Yang.

6. *And "in the first year" the sprouts are nurtured.* In the first entry in the *Springs and Autumns (Chunqiu)*, which describes the "first year" of rule by Duke Yin, the *Cantong qi* sees an allusion to the "sprouting forth" of offspring after the joining of Yin and Yang.

7–8. *The sage is not born in vain: he contemplates on high the manifest signs of Heaven.* Compare *Book of Changes*, "Commentary on the Judgement" on the hexagram Guan ䷓ (no. 20): "He contemplates the divine Way of Heaven, and the four seasons do not deviate from their rule. The sage uses the divine Way to establish his teaching, and the whole world submits to him" (see Wilhelm, 486).

12. The hexagram Fu and the trigram Zhen

At the end of a time cycle, the joining of the Sun the Moon does not only resume time; it also regenerates, after its apparent annihilation, the pure Light that belongs in the first place to the Center, the Heart of Heaven (*tianxin*). According to the traditional, symbolic etymology, the words "light" (*ming* 明) and "change" (*yi* 易) are both represented by the joined graphs of "sun" (*ri* 日) and "moon" (*yue* 月), placed next to one another in the former case, and one above the other in the latter case. This Light is carried throughout space and time by the different states of change that occur in the cosmos.

The hexagram and the trigram associated with the initial stages of the year and the month—the two time cycles respectively based on the Sun and the Moon—are images of the rebirth of Light. Fu ䷗, associated with the eleventh lunar month (the month of the winter solstice), is the first hexagram in the cycle of the year. Zhen ☳, which rules on the first five days of the month, is the first trigram born from the union of Qian ☰ and Kun ☷ (it is also the lower of the two trigrams that constitute Fu). Metaphorized as the "elder son," it inherits the Yang nature of Qian, its father, and after being brought to life by Kun, its mother, it establishes the foundation for a new cycle of change during the lunar month. Therefore the emblematic functions of Fu and and Zhen are the same: when cyclical change is represented by the year, Fu stands for the rebirth of Light and the first stage of a time cycle among the hexagrams (see section 51); when it is represented by the month, Zhen performs the same function among the trigrams (see sections 13 and 49).

"Ebb and flow respond to the bells and pitch-pipes" alludes to cycles based on the number 12 (the number of the bells and the pitch-pipes) and therefore refers to the annual solar cycle, initiated by Fu (for the bells and the pitch-pipes, see table 11). "Rise and fall accord with the axis of the Dipper" refers to the monthly lunar cycle, inaugurated by Zhen.

1–2. Therefore change encompasses the Heart of Heaven — The hexagram Fu lays the initial buds. Compare *Book of Changes*, "Commentary on the Judgement" on the hexagram Fu ䷗ (no. 24): "Fu indeed reveals the Heart of Heaven and Earth!" (see Wilhelm, 505).

3. The elder son inherits the body of his father. In their representations as trigrams, Qian and Kun generate three male trigrams, namely Zhen ☳, Kan ☵, and Gen ☶; and three female trigrams, namely Xun ☴, Li ☲, and Dui ☱. Zhen is the first male trigram and is, therefore, the "elder son." — "Body" (*ti*) refers to the frame of Qian ☰, from which Zhen ☳ draws the lower Yang line.

5. Ebb and flow respond to the bells and pitch-pipes. The twelve pitch-pipes—here called *zhonglü*, lit., "bells and pitch-pipes"—produce a musical scale based on the correct relations among the different sounds. The six pitch-pipes are Yang, and the six bells are Yin. In a purely emblematic function, they represent the items comprised in any duodecimal sequence, particularly the twelve "double hours" of the day and the twelve months of the year, and are therefore used to illustrate the increase and decrease of Yin and Yang along the stages of that sequence (see table 11).

13. The cycle of the Moon

In this section, the *Cantong qi* describes the second main cosmological pattern. The cosmological device known as *najia*, or Matching Stems, divides the lunar month into six parts of five days. Each of the six stages is associated with a trigram and with one of the ten celestial stems. The six trigrams illustrate the rise and the fall of Yin (the broken line) and Yang (the solid line) during the thirty days of the month:

☳	☱	☰	☴	☶	☷
震	兌	乾	巽	艮	坤
Zhen	Dui	Qian	Xun	Gen	Kun

In the present section, verses 1–6 describe the rise of the Yang principle during the former half of the month, and verses 13–18 the rise of the Yin principle during the latter half of the month. (The *Cantong qi* describes the lunar cycle again in section 49.)

At dusk on the third day of the lunar month, the crescent Moon appears in the West, associated with the stem *geng* 庚; its clear light is an image of the beginning of the rise of Yang and is represented by Zhen ☳. On the eighth day, the Moon at dusk appears in the South, associated with the stem *ding* 丁; being in its first quarter, its light is "level as a string" and is represented by Dui ☱. At dusk on the fifteenth day, the full Moon appears in the East, associated with the stem *jia* 甲; it is an emblem of Pure Yang and is represented by Qian ☰. Now "the Breaths of Sun and Moon shine together," because Yang is at the peak of its growth and Yin is at its lowest: the Moon is entirely exposed to the light of the Sun, and thus appears as full. While the toad, which represents the Essence (*jing*) of the Moon, ensures that the cycle progresses without error, the hare, which represents its Breath (*qi*), exhales the Moon's radiance.

After Yang has reached its highest point, it begins to wane, and Yin begins to rise. At dawn on the sixteenth day, the Moon appears in the West, associated with the stem *xin* 辛; its decreasing light illustrates the emergent Yin and is represented by the trigram Xun ☴. At dawn on the twenty-third day, the Moon appears in the South, associated with the stem *bing* 丙; now in its last quarter, it is represented by Gen ☶. Finally, at dawn on the thirtieth day, the Moon is lightless in the East, associated with the stem *yi* 乙; it is now an emblem of Pure Yin and is represented by Kun ☷.

The trigrams Li ☲ and Kan ☵ are not part of the lunar cycle, because they represent the Center; but precisely for this reason, they constitute a major feature of the Matching Stems device. In the night of novilune, between the end of one month and the beginning of the next one, the Sun (日) and the Moon (月) move to the center of space. They join their essences to regenerate the light (明) of the Yang principle, and give birth to the next cycle of change (易). At that time, the trigram Zhen ☳ "inherits" the body of Qian ☰, its father, as its the lower Yang line, and "regenerates the dragon." (Zhen corresponds to the East and thus has the "green dragon," *qinglong*, as its emblem. The ascent of this dragon through the six stages of the lunar month is one of the subjects of section 49.)

Since Kan and Li represent the operation of Qian and Kun within the cosmos, the unfolding of all time cycles is ultimately governed by Qian and Kun. The final verses refer to this by means of the celestial stems (see table 9). Qian corresponds to the stems *jia* 甲 and *ren* 壬, and Kun to the stems *yi* 乙 and *gui* 癸; therefore "*ren* and *gui* match *jia* and *yi*." Moreover, since *jia* 甲 and *ren* 壬 are the last two stems and *yi* 乙 and *gui* 癸 are the first two stems, Qian and Kun "enclose beginning and end."

Even though they do not take part in the lunar cycle, Qian, Kun, Kan, and Li determine its development. The *Cantong qi* sees a confirmation of this in the numerical values associated with the celestial stems. Qian is associated with number 9 (the number of "great Yang," *taiyang*) and Kun with number 6 ("great Yin," *taiyin*); Li is associated with number 7 ("minor Yang," *shaoyang*) and Kan with number 8 ("minor Yin," *shaoyin*). The sum of these numbers is 30, corresponding to the number of days in the lunar month.

7. *The toad is with the hare and its lightless soul.* The hare is referred to in this passage as *tupo.* *Po* here denotes the lightless side of the Moon, i.e., its Yin "soul."

9–10. *The toad beholds the trigram nodes, the hare exhales the radiance of life.* The "trigram nodes" are the time segments associated with the individual trigrams, each of which rules over six days during the lunar month. For example, the first "node" is associated with Zhen ☳ (see table 10).

18. *"Forego your friends in the northeast."* This sentence is quoted from the *Book of Changes,* "Judgement" on the hexagram Kun ䷁ (no. 2; see Wilhelm, 11). According to several commentaries to the *Cantong qi,* however, *peng* 朋, "friends," is used in this verse to mean *ming* 明, "light," with reference to the obscuration of the Yang principle at the end of the lunar cycle.

14. Heaven, Earth, Man

When the eight trigrams are projected onto the celestial vault, they are distributed among the directions of space, arranged around a central axis represented by the Northern Dipper. The trigrams represent the segments of space to which the Dipper points during its apparent rotation around itself, as well as the corresponding terms of time. Although only one trigram is active at a given time, none of them ever strays from its place.

These and other emblems illustrate how Original Essence (*yuanjing*), the seed from which the Dao gives birth to its self-manifestation, operates within the cosmos. Its patterns determine, and are revealed by, the regular movements of the Sun and the Moon. Trigrams and hexagrams make it possible to represent these patterns and the corresponding states of change. Therefore they provide guidance to the ruler.

The *Hetu* (Chart of the Yellow River, based on the five agents) and the *Luoshu* (Writ of the Luo River, based on the the eight trigrams) are among the other images and emblems that are used for the same purpose (see figs. 1 and 2). Relying on these emblems, and on the writings that illustrate their functioning, the ruler assists Heaven and Earth in maintaining and nourishing all creatures, and ensures that everything within his domain accords with the operation of Qian and Kun.

4. *Infer its rules and attest its tokens.* "Inferring the rules" (*tuidu*, an expression that also means "inferring the measures" or "the degrees") refers to observing and reckoning the patterns underlying the different phenomena; in particular, the cyclical alternation of the Sun and the Moon.

5. *"When you dwell, contemplate its images."* This sentence is quoted from the "Appended Sayings" of the *Book of Changes*: "When the noble man dwells, he contemplates the Images and reflects on the Statements" (A.2; see Wilhelm, 290).

6. *"Adjust and conform to its forms and appearances."* This sentence is an almost literal quotation from the "Appended Sayings": "The sages were able to survey the multiplicity under Heaven, and observed its forms and appearances" (A.6; see Wilhelm, 304; and A.12, see Wilhelm, 324). In the quotation, the *Cantong qi* replaces *ni* ("observe") with *zhunni* ("abide by, conform to"), changing somewhat the meaning.

7. *Let the gnomon function as your norm.* The gnomon (*libiao*), which measures the progression of the time cycles, is also mentioned in 51:4.

8. *Divine and forecast "to determine good and ill fortune."* The second half of this verse is quoted from the "Appended Sayings": "The eight trigrams determine good and ill fortune" (A.11; see Wilhelm, 310).

11–12. *Above, examine the signs of the Chart of the River, below, pursue the flow of the forms of the earth.* For these verses, compare the "Appended Sayings": "When in early antiquity Bao Xi (i.e., Fu Xi) ruled the world, he looked upward and contemplated the images in Heaven, he looked downward and contemplated the models on the Earth" (B.2; see Wilhelm, 328).

14. *Combine them to investigate the Three Powers.* Compare the "Appended Sayings": "As a book, the *Changes* is vast and great. The Way of Heaven is in it, the Way of the Earth is in it, and the Way of Man is in it. It combines the Three Powers and doubles them. Therefore [an hexagram has] six lines. The six lines are nothing but the Ways of the Three Powers" (B.8; see Wilhelm, 351–52).

16. *In quiescence, rely upon the Judgements and the Statements.* In the Book of Changes, the "Judgements" explain the meaning of the whole

hexagram, and the "Statements" explain the meaning of its individual
lines.

15. The essential course

As a symbol of the Heart of Heaven (the center of the cosmos), the
Northern Dipper presides over the directions of space and the cycles
of time. Designated by terms Head (*kui*) and Handle (*bing*), which
respectively refer to its first four and last three stars, the Dipper aligns
the patterns of space and time with the apparent rotation around its
own axis. (*)

The trigrams and hexagrams of the *Book of Changes* illustrate
those patterns. By adhering to them, the ruler is enabled to manage
the events that occur in his kingdom, and even to know the favorable
or unfavorable outcome of his actions. Although the task of government is demanding, if he follows the directions or the *Book of
Changes*, the king brings harmony to the kingdom, just as the five
planets ("five wefts") intersect in their orbits in complex ways, and yet
move harmoniously along their paths. If he goes against them, instead,
the king induces adversities, comparable to the calamities that would
occur if the twenty-eight lunar lodges parted from one another.

The celestial administration governed by the Northern Dipper is a
model for the earthly administration governed by the king. Just as the
Dipper rules in the cosmos with the support of its subordinate constellations and stars, so should the ruler govern the kingdom with the
assistance of his ministers and officials.

(*) A passage of the "Book of Celestial Offices" in the *Records of the
Historian* illustrates this function: "The Dipper is the chariot of the
Emperor [of Heaven]. It revolves at the Center and presides over the four
hamlets (i.e., the four quarters of space). It divides Yin and Yang, establishes the four seasons, regulates the five agents, shifts the nodes [of time]
and the degrees [of space], and establishes the various sequences (*ji*). All
this is related to the Dipper" (*Shiji*, 27.1291; see Chavannes, *Les Mémoires historiques*, 3:342).

3. *Be watchful in exercising control.* Compare the "Appended Sayings" of
the *Book of Changes*: "If the ruler is not watchful, he loses his ministers;
if the ministers are not watchful, they lose their life. If one is not watchful
toward things that are germinating, harm develops. Therefore the noble

man is cautious and watchful, and does not let anything go out" (A.7; see Wilhelm, 307).

5. *The essential course lies in Head and Handle.* The term "essential course" (*yaodao*) derives from the opening passage of the *Book of Filial Piety*: "For the kings of old there was a perfect virtue and an essential course, through which they were in accord with all under Heaven. By the practice of it, the people were brought to live in peace and harmony, and there was no ill-will between superiors and inferiors" (*Xiaojing*, 2/1/1; see Legge, *The Sacred Books of China*, 3:465). — Head (*kui*) refers to the first four stars of the Dipper, and Handle (*bing*) to its last three stars. Other sources use the term *biao* ("ladle") to refer to the last three stars of the Dipper.

6. *They are the strings to manage all transformations.* Gangniu (literally translated as "strings") is analogous in meaning to *gangji* ("guiding thread"), a term found in 32:4, 38:17, 73:14, and 74:24. In an extended sense, both terms mean "guiding principle, standard, key."

7–8. *"As lines and images move on the inside, good and ill fortune rise on the outside."* These sentences are an almost literal quotation from the "Appended Sayings": "As the lines and the images move on the inside, good and ill fortune reveal themselves on the outside" (B.1; see Wilhelm, 327).

9. *The five wefts intersect in their routes.* The "five wefts" are the five planets, namely, Mercury, Venus, Earth, Mars, and Jupiter. They are so called in contrast to the Sun and the Moon, which are the "warp." According a different interpretation, the five planets are the "weft" because they rotate in Heaven from the right to the left, while the twenty-eight lunar lodges are the "warp" because they rotate from the left to the right. The latter explanation may also relevant here, since the lodges are mentioned immediately below in verses 11–12.

11. *If the twenty-eight lodges opposed one another.* The twenty-eight lunar lodges in this verse are referred to as *siqi*, "four [times] seven" (i.e., "if the four-seven run opposed one another . . ."). The lodges are subdivided into four sets of seven, corresponding to the four quarters of space (see table 16).

13. *Literary Glory manages the registers.* Literary Glory (*wenchang*) is a constellation formed by six stars above the Northern Dipper. The six stars represent the six ministers that assist the ruler in the earthly administration. The phrase "manages the registers" refers in particular to the

fourth star, the Controller of Destinies, or *siming*, which manages life and death.

14. *Terrace and Assistant inquire and adjure.* Terrace (*tai*) is another constellation below the Northern Dipper, made of six stars grouped into three sets of two and therefore often referred to as the Three Terraces (*santai*). Assistant (*fu*) may be a star located near the sixth star of the Northern Dipper, but the reference here is more likely to be to another group of four stars around the north pole, called the Four Assistants (*sifu*).

16. Space and time correspond to one another

According to several commentators, this section alludes to the six periods of five days (*ri* 日 means both "sun" and "day") contained in the lunar month (*yue* 月 means both "moon" and "month"; compare 3:1: "In one month there are six nodes of five days"). The five days correspond to the five agents, and the six periods of the month correspond to the six Yin items within the series of the twelve pitch-pipes (see the note to 12:5).

By virtue of the rule of the Northern Dipper, the spans of space and the terms of time correspond to one another without error. The numeric symbolism used in this passage provides an example of this correspondence: the thirty days of the Moon cycle agree with the thirty degrees of space crossed by the Sun in one month along its course.

17. The ruler and the Pole Star

The *Book of Changes* enables the ruler to trace the origin of things and know their end. Inauspicious events and errors, however, may occur as he performs his tasks. When this happens, he should rely on his subordinates to have knowledge of those incidents, and respond appropriately.

The king conducts government from the Hall of Light (*mingtang*), a building that performed the symbolic and ritual function of aligning the center of the kingdom with the center of the cosmos. Taking as his model the Pole Star that rules at the center of Heaven (see 2:7: "abide in the Center to control the outside"), the sage ruler may respond to the events that occur in the kingdom while maintaining himself in the state of non-doing.

1. *"Going back to the beginning and pursuing the end."* This sentence is quoted from the "Appended Sayings" of the *Book of Changes*: "The *Changes* is a book that goes back to the beginning and pursues the end" (B.7; see Wilhelm, 349).

2. *Is the thread to understand existence and extinction.* Compare the "Appended Sayings": "Yes, even that which is most important in regard to existence and extinction, in regard to good or ill fortune, can be known staying fixed in place" (B.7; see Wilhelm, 350).

8. *Adverse events and "ill fortune" and "blame" occur.* "Ill fortune" and "blame" are two standard terms in the divinatory portions of the *Book of Changes*.

9. *The Upholder of the Law denounces and reproaches.* The *zhifa*, or Upholder of the Law, is usually known as Censor (*yushi*), one of the main officers in the imperial administration. In the context of the present portion of the *Cantong qi*, which compares the administration of the kingdom with the administration of Heaven, it is significant that *zhifa* is also the name of a constellation.

11. *Just as the Pole Star holds its correct position.* Compare *Lunyu* 2.1: "Carrying out governance by virtue is like the Pole Star staying fixed in place, while all the other stars go along with it" (see Legge, *Confucian Analects*, 145).

12. *And effortlessly drifts relying on what is below.* Compare *Huainan zi*: "The art of rulership consists in dwelling in the pursuit of non-doing and in practicing the teaching without words. Clear and quiescent, [the king] does not move; he uses a single measure and does not hesitate; he complies with the course of things and relies on those who are below; he instructs others to fulfill their tasks and does not toil himself" (9.605; see Le Blanc and Mathieu, 367).

18. Nourishing inner nature

This is the first of ten sections (18–27) that illustrate the main features of "superior virtue" (*shangde*) and "inferior virtue" (*xiade*). The import of these chapters is made clear in sections 20–21: superior virtue is the way of non-doing (*wuwei*), and consists in the cultivation of inner nature (*xing*); inferior virtue is the way of doing (*youwei*), and focuses on the cultivation of one's existence (or "vital force," *ming*) by means of practices such as the alchemical ones.

The subject of sections 18–19 is the principles of superior virtue. Emptiness is the fundament from which all things arise and to which they return; quiescence is the state required to contemplate Emptiness. The first stanza expresses these principles with allusions to an exemplary passage of the *Daode jing*: "Attain the ultimate of emptiness, guard the utmost of quiescence. The ten thousand things are brought about together: accordingly, I observe their return. . . . Returning to the root means quiescence; being quiescent means reverting to one's destiny; reverting to one's destiny means being constant; knowing the constant means being luminous" (*Daode jing*, 6). The subjects of the present section of the *Cantong qi* are the same as those of this passage: Emptiness, the return to the root, and the luminous quality of those who achieve quiescence.

Attaining the state of Emptiness requires closing the "openings" through which we deal with the world of multiplicity. This principle, and its formulation, also originate in the *Daode jing*: "Shut the openings, close the gates, and to the end of your life you will not toil. Unlock the openings, meddle with affairs, and to the end of your life you will not attain salvation" (*Daode jing*, 52).

For the *Cantong qi*, the openings are the "three luminaries": the eyes, the ears, and the mouth, or the functions of sight, hearing, and speech. When the "three luminaries" do not turn their light toward the external world, they "sink into the ground." This expression, which derives from the *Zhuangzi*, denotes the attitude of the saintly man who conceals his sainthood (see the note to verse 7). Established in quiescence, he does not turn himself toward the external objects, allowing the radiance of the luminaries to illuminate and nourish his true Nature (the "numinous trunk"). Maintaining himself in the state of non-doing, he contemplates the arising of all entities and phenomena from Emptiness and their return to it, and nurtures the Pearl spontaneously generated in him by the One Breath prior to Heaven.

This attitude and nothing else constitutes the way of superior virtue and the realized state according to the *Cantong qi*. As we are reminded with another sentence drawn from the *Daode jing* (see the note to verse 9), no pursuit is necessary: the Dao is invisible, inaudible, and imperceptible, but is "nearby and easy to seek."

4. *And innerly illuminate your body.* In later times, *neizhao* ("to illuminate within") became the name of an inner alchemical practice, as seen, for instance, in the expression *huiguang neizhao,* "circulating the light to illuminate within." From the perspective of the *Cantong qi,* however, this term does not refer to a practice, or at least not to a practice in the ordinary sense: *neizhao* describes the state of the realized person, whose inner being is constantly illuminated.

5. *"Shut the openings."* Compare 58:1–2, which refers to the "three luminaries" as the "three treasures" (*sanbao*), saying: "Ears, eyes, and mouth are the three treasures: shut them, and let nothing pass through."

7. *As the three luminaries sink into the ground.* The term *luchen* ("sinking into the ground") derives from this passage of the *Zhuangzi*: "[The saint] has buried himself among the people, hidden himself among the fields. . . . Perhaps he finds himself at odds with the age and in his heart disdains to go along with it. This is called 'sinking into the ground'" (25.895; see Watson, 285–86).

9. *"Watching, you do not see it."* This verse is quoted from *Daode jing*, 14, where it refers to the Dao: "Watching, you do not see it: it is called invisible. Listening, you do not hear it: it is called inaudible. Grasping, you do not get it: it is called imperceptible."

19. The Yellow Center

The One Breath of the Dao is invisible and unknown to all, but embraces all things. This Breath is distributed from the Yellow Center (*huangzhong*), the spaceless point that ensures the conjunction of the cosmos and the human being with the absolute principle. In the cosmos, that point is the Heart of Heaven (*tianxin*); in the human being, it is the Heart (*xin*).

1. *"From the Yellow Center" it gradually "spreads through the veining."* This verse is an almost literal quotation from the "Commentary on the Words of the Text" on the hexagram Kun ䷁ (no. 2) in the *Book of Changes. Tongli* can mean both "to comprehend the principle(s)" and "to spread through (*or*: pervade) the veining." In the original context of the *Book of Changes,* the sentence refers to the operation of the sage in the world, and the first meaning of *tongli* applies: "The noble man from the Yellow Center comprehends the principles [of things]." Several other translations of this sentence are possible, but the main point is that the

central position occupied by the "noble man" enables him to comprehend the principles of constancy and change. The *Cantong qi* uses part of this sentence to refer to the One Breath; in this context, the second meaning of *tongli* applies. — In several Taoist traditions, Yellow Center (*huangzhong*) is a name of the central Cinnabar Field (*dantian*), which is located in the region of the heart. It is, moreover, a name of the spleen, the organ that represents the Center when the framework of reference is not the three Cinnabar Fields, but the five viscera.

20. Superior Virtue and Inferior Virtue

Sections 20–21 define the difference between superior virtue and inferior virtue. The *Cantong qi* upholds two ways of realization. Quoting the *Daode jing*, the present section defines the two ways as "superior virtue" (*shangde*) and "inferior virtue" (*xiade*). In superior virtue, nothing needs to be searched or investigated; the unity of the state "prior to Heaven" (*xiantian*, the Absolute, Emptiness, constancy) and the state "posterior to Heaven" (*houtian*, the relative, the world of change) is immediately realized. Inferior virtue, instead, seeks the One Breath prior to Heaven (*xiantian yiqi*) within the state posterior to Heaven. Superior virtue is the way of "non-doing" (*wuwei*), inferior virtue is the way of "doing" (*youwei*, or *wei zhi*). As a practice, alchemy—in any of its forms, "external" or "internal"—pertains to the way of inferior virtue. (On this subject, see also the Introduction, § 7.)

1–2. *"Superior virtue has no doing": it does not use examining and seeking.* The first sentence is quoted from *Daode jing*, 38: "Superior virtue has no doing: there is nothing whereby it does."

3–4. *"Inferior virtue does": its operation does not rest.* The first sentence is quoted from *Daode jing*, 38: "Inferior virtue does: there is something whereby it does."

21. Non-Being and Being, the "two cavities"

Qian ☰ and Kun ☷ signify the precelestial state. Qian (Heaven) is above and represents the principle of Non-Being; Kun (Earth) is below and represents the principle of Being. As they join, Qian enters Kun and becomes Li ☲; Kun receives Qian and becomes Kan ☵. The joining of Qian and Kun gives rise to the postcelestial state. Here Li (Fire) dwells above and Kan (Water) dwells below. Li encloses the principle of Being, represented by its inner line that originally belongs to Kun. Kan encloses the principle of Non-Being, represented by its inner line that originally belongs to Qian.

The apparent symmetry of this process hides a significant distinction between what is "above" and what is "below." Above, Non-Being embraces Being. Discerning this is the way of "superior virtue": nothing needs to be sought, and one resides in the state of "non-doing." Below, Non-Being is enclosed within Being. The hidden principle demands to be sought, and one enters the state of "doing" in order to enable the inner line of Kan to rise again "above," where Spirit dwells, and reconstitute Qian. Allowing this to occur is the way of "inferior virtue," and is the function of alchemy.

The way of superior virtue centers on the "cavity" of Li ☲, the Breath of Water (*shuiqi*) that originally belongs to Kun. The way of inferior virtue centers on the "cavity" of Kan ☵, the Essence of Metal (*jinjing*) that originally belongs to Qian. (*) As the *Cantong qi* upholds both ways, it is concerned with the "two cavities."

(*) Li ☲ is Fire, but its inner line—its "breath"—represents Water; therefore Breath of Water should be intended to mean "the Breath that is Water." Analogously, Kan ☵ is Water, but its inner line—its "essence"—represents Metal, or True Lead; therefore Essence of Metal means "the Essence that is Metal."

5. *These are the methods of the two cavities.* The "methods" are those of doing and non-doing, which correspond to the ways of inferior and superior virtue, respectively.

22. The principles of alchemy

Sections 22–25 concern the way of inferior virtue. This portion of the *Cantong qi* begins with a description of the principles of alchemy.

Alchemy seeks the principle that gives birth to, and is hidden within, the manifest cosmos. Among the emblems of the *Book of Changes*, this principle is represented by the solid Yang line contained within Kan ☵ (Water), which originally belongs to Qian ☰. Alchemically, it is represented by the True Lead found within "black lead," or native lead.

The opening sentence, borrowed from the *Daode jing*, states that one should "keep to the black" in order to "know the white." Black (Yin) represents the agent Water, the outer Yin lines of Kan ☵, and native lead; it is the world in which we live. White (Yang) represents the agent Metal, the inner Yang line of Kan, and True Lead; it is the One Breath sought by the alchemist. "Keeping to the black" and "knowing the white" generates the Numinous Light (*shenming*), which in the alchemical metaphor is the Elixir.

Therefore the precelestial Breath is to be sought within Water. As a cosmological principle, Water is the first of the five agents (here called the "five metals"); it is "the beginning of Yin and Yang," and is represented by number 1 and by the northern direction. Because of its primal position within the cosmos, Water is the "axis of the Dao," and all changes and transformations derive in the first place from it. For the same reason, Water is also the element that supports the River Chariot (*heche*), the vehicle that transports the One Breath (Metal, True Lead, True Yang) back and forth in its cycles of ascent and descent within the cosmos.

Water is the "mystery" (*xuan*): it stands for obscurity, the north, and black lead, but it holds light and, being the "axis of the Dao," is intimately connected to the center. In alchemical language, this hidden principle is referred to as the Yellow Sprout (*huangya*), a term that connotes both the essence of Metal (True Yang) found within Water (Yin), and the first intimation of the birth of the Elixir (denoted as "yellow" for its association with Soil, the agent that represents the center). Analogously, lead is black outside, but harbors the white and luminous Golden Flower (*jinhua*) within. Quoting another passage from the *Daode jing*, the *Cantong qi* likens the authentic principle hidden in the darkness of the world to the treasure concealed by the saintly man, who disguises himself as a common mortal.

1. *"Know the white, keep to the black."* This sentence is quoted from *Daode jing*, 28: "Know the white, keep to the black, and be a mold for the world. If you are a mold for the world, the constant virtue does not depart from you, and you return to the Ultimateless."

2. *And the Numinous Light will come of its own.* Compare *Daode jing*, 73: "The Dao of Heaven does not contend but is good at overcoming, does not speak but is good at responding, is not summoned but comes of its own, seems to be slack but excels in planning."

3–4. *White is the essence of Metal, Black the foundation of Water.* For several commentators, "white" stands for True Lead; for others, it means either mercury, or silver, or gold. These varying views reflect different configurations of the alchemical emblems, in whose contexts the same principle can be represented by different terms and symbols. "White," in all cases, alludes to the authentic principle contained within the "black." Being the True Yang within Yin, this authentic principle is the opposite of black lead, and therefore is called True Lead. For the same reason, it may be called "mercury," which in Chinese alchemy stands in a polar relation to lead. Because of its white color, it can also be called "silver," in contrast to black native lead. Finally, since True Yang is the precelestial One Breath, it may be called "gold," the metal that more than any other represents the Elixir.

6. *Its number is 1.* Compare the "Monograph on the Pitch-pipes and the Calendar" in the *History of the Former Han Dynasty*: "By means of number 1, Heaven generates Water. By means of number 2, Earth generates Fire. By means of number 3, Heaven generates Wood. By means of number 4, Earth generates Metal. By means of number 5, Heaven generates Soil" (*Hanshu*, 21A.985; the same passage is also found in several other texts). These are the so-called "generation numbers" (*shengshu*) of the five agents. The "accomplishment numbers" (*chengshu*) are obtained by adding 5 to each "generation number." See table 4.

9. *It is the ruler of the five metals.* The five metals are gold, silver, copper, iron, and lead. Here they are meant as mere emblems of the five agents: Water is the first of the five agents, and lead, which is related to Water, is "the ruler of the five metals."

10. *The River Chariot of the northern direction.* In Neidan, River Chariot refers to path of the circulation of Breath (*qi*) through the *renmai* and *dumai* vessels, respectively running along the back and the front of the body. This circulation is analogous to the circulation of the One Breath in the cosmos along the cycles of time and the compass of space.

13. *Like the man who "wears rough-hewn clothes but cherishes a piece of jade in his bosom."* This sentence is quoted from *Daode jing*, 70: "It is only because they have no understanding that they do not understand me; but since those who understand me are few, I am honored. Thus the saint wears rough-hewn clothes, but cherishes a piece of jade in his bosom."

23. Metal and Water, mother and child

This short section describes two movements. The first is the movement of "ascent" from the postcelestial (*houtian*, the relative) to the
precelestial (*xiantian*, the absolute); the second is the movement of
"descent" from the precelestial to the postcelestial. The precelestial
domain is symbolized by Metal; the postcelestial domain, by Water. In
a strict sense, alchemy deals only with the first movement, which is the
way of "inferior virtue," but its path is fulfilled when the second
movement, the way of "superior virtue," is also performed.

The return from the postcelestial to the precelestial is described as
the inversion of the generative sequence of the five agents. In this
sequence, Metal (the "mother") generates Water (the "son"), but in
the alchemical process it is Water ("black lead") that generates Metal
(True Lead). Thus the son generates the mother, and "the mother is
hidden in the embryo of her son." The extension of the precelestial
into the postcelestial, which occurs after the first movement has been
completed, is represented as the common course of the generative
sequence of the five agents. In this movement, Metal (the "mother")
once again generates Water (the "son"). Thus "the child is stored in
the womb of its mother."

After the first, "ascensional" part of the alchemical work is
completed, the movement of "descent" does not lead to a new shift
from the precelestial to the postcelestial. It realizes, instead, the unity
the precelestial and the postcelestial.

24. Born before Heaven and Earth

This section is characterized by frequent switches of topics, which
additionally are not always explicitly stated. The True Man alludes to
Metal, i.e., True Lead, and the "great abyss" alludes to Water. Metal
ordinarily is the "mother" of Water, which is its "son." The alchemical process inverts these roles. In the cosmological metaphor, Metal,
whose color is white, emerges from Water, whose color is black; in the
alchemical metaphor, True Lead emerges from native lead, or "black
lead." Placed within the vessel, the white True Lead is compounded
with True Mercury and generates the Elixir, whose color is vermilion.

The Elixir is equivalent to the One Breath prior to Heaven. It contains the True Yin and True Yang principles joined together as one, and accordingly it is said to be both "square and round," two traditional attributes of Heaven and Earth. Its size of "one inch" alludes to the Two joined as One.

11. *"Square and round, one inch is its diameter."* Compare the "Inner" version of the *Scripture of the Yellow Court* (*Huangting neijing jing*, sec. 7): "Each of the Nine True Men in the Muddy Pellet has his room. / Square and round, one inch is its size, and they abide within it." In the *Scripture of the Yellow Court*, these words refer to the upper Cinnabar Field, one of whose names is Muddy Pellet (*niwan*), which is represented as made of nine palaces or nine rooms each of which is inhabited by a divine being. For this reason, several commentators have suggested that the present verse of the *Cantong qi* also refers to the upper Cinnabar Field.

13. *"Born before Heaven and Earth."* This sentence is found in both the *Daode jing* and the *Zhuangzi*. The *Daode jing*, 25, says: "There is something inchoate and yet accomplished, born before Heaven and Earth. Silent! Still! It stands alone and never alters, it goes all around and never ends. One can say that it is the mother of Heaven and Earth. I do not know its name, but call it Dao." The *Zhuangzi* has: "[The Dao] is its own fundament, its own root. Before Heaven and Earth existed it was there, firm from ancient times. . . . It is born before Heaven and Earth, and yet you cannot say it has been there for long; it is earlier than the earliest time, and yet you cannot call it old" (6.246–47; see Watson, 81).

25. The Elixir in the tripod

The alchemical vessel is compared to one of the mythical mountain-islands that lie in the midst of the ocean, and to a palace with surrounding walls and intricate passageways. Thus the vessel guards and shields the Elixir, making its compounding possible.

The most essential stage of the compounding is the final one, as it consists in entering the state of non-doing (*wuwei*). If this state is attained, the Elixir is accomplished; otherwise, it vanishes. But once the Elixir is obtained, it is never lost.

2. *And in shape it resembles Penghu.* Penghu is another name of Penglai, one of five mythical mountain-islands located in the Eastern Ocean.

4. *It is interwoven at every turn.* "At every turn" approximates the sense of *sitong*, an expression that connotes the four directions, i.e., "everywhere."

8. *In order "to prevent the unforeseen."* Compare the "Outward Demeanor" poem in the *Book of Odes*: "Address what concerns the people, / be careful of your duties as a prince, / to prevent the unforeseen" (*Shijing*, "Yi," no. 256; see Waley, *The Book of Songs*, 301). See also the "Image" on the hexagram Cui ䷬ (no. 45) in the *Book of Changes*: "The noble man renews his weapons to prevent the unforeseen" (see Wilhelm, 175). After these early instances, the same sentence is found in the *Huainan zi* (20.1391; see Le Blanc and Mathieu, 962) and in several other works.

11–12. *When Spirit and Breath fill the house, no one can detain them.* Compare *Daode jing*, 9: "Gold and jade fill your halls, but no one can guard them." While this sentence has a negative import in the *Daode jing* (it is pointless to keep ephemeral possessions under guard), the *Cantong qi* uses it to denote something precious.

26. Incorrect practices

Sections 26–27 conclude the portion of Book 1 concerned with the general principles of superior virtue and inferior virtue. The present section consists in an admonition against fruitless practices.

The *Cantong qi* repeatedly warns against the performance of practices deemed to be incorrect or unproductive for true realization. This section rejects meditation methods, breathing practices, sexual techniques, and the worship of minor deities and spirits. "Passing through the viscera" (*lizang*) is an early term that refers to visualizing in succession the gods residing within the five viscera. "Inner contemplation" (or "inner observation," *neishi*, the reading found in other redactions of the *Cantong qi*) also refers to meditation on the inner deities. "Treading the Dipper and pacing the asterisms" denotes the meditation methods of "pacing the celestial net" (*bugang*). "Six *jia*" alludes to protective calendrical deities, and in particular to those associated with the talismans of the "six decades," each of which begins on a day marked by the celestial stem *jia* 甲. "Way of Yin" indicates the sexual techniques, and the expression "nine-and-one" hints to the phrase *jiuqian yishen* ("nine shallow and one deep" penetrations in intercourse). "Ingesting breath" designates the breathing practices.

Not only does the *Cantong qi* reject these methods; it also refers to them with irony. "Exhaling the old and inhaling the new [breath]" (*tugu naxin*), a common designation of the breathing practices, becomes "exhaling the pure and inhaling the evil without" (from the perspective of the *Cantong qi*, the "pure" is to be found in the first place within). Breath is ingested "till it chirps in your stomach." The adept who devotes himself to these practices is "vague and indistinct," an image that in the *Daode jing* denotes the Dao itself, but here quite literally refers to the practitioner who "looks like a fool." Apart from this, the rejected practices, says the *Cantong qi*, are ineffective because they focus on the body and on the hope of extending one's lifetime. For this reason, they go against the true Taoist teaching, which the *Cantong qi* associates with the Yellow Emperor and with Laozi, the Old Master.

4. *Using the six* jia *as markers of time.* The six *jia* (*liu jia*) are the six days of the sexagesimal cycle marked by the celestial stem *jia* 甲 (see table 15). Being especially important in hemerology, these days are associated with deities and with talismans that grant communication with those deities. — The word *chen* in *richen* (here rendered as "markers of time") refers to the twelve earthly branches, which are used to mark the individual stages of duodecimal time cycles—in particular, the twelve "double hours" of the day and the twelve months of the year.

24. *For you were defiant and let slip the hinge.* The term *shuji* denotes the pivot, mainspring, or "vital point" of something, and derives from the "Appended Sayings" of the *Book of Changes*: "Words and deeds are the hinge of the noble man. As the hinge moves, it determines honor or disgrace" (A.6; see Wilhelm, 305).

25. *The arts are so many.* Shu, here translated as "art," refers to various cosmological sciences and techniques—for instance, divination, physiological techniques, and alchemy—including both their doctrinal foundations and their specific methods.

28. *Their winding courses oppose the Nine Capitals.* Quzhe ("winding courses," "crouchings and bendings") connotes pointless and unproductive pursuits. See this passage of the *Zhuangzi*: "The crouchings and bendings of rites and music, the smiles and beaming looks of humanity and righteousness, which are intended to comfort the hearts of the world,

in fact destroy their constant naturalness" (8.320; see Watson, 100). — The precise connotation of the term *jiudu* ("nine capitals") is unclear in this context; it may refer to the Nine Palaces (*jiufu*) of the administration of Fengdu, the subterranean realm of the dead. The implication, nevertheless, is clear: the death of the adept of incorrect practices is a punishment delivered by Heaven.

27. The Great One sends forth his summons

Having rejected several methods that it deems to be erroneous, the *Cantong qi* portrays the attainment of those who devote themselves to alchemy, the only practice that it regards as correct if performed according to its own principles.

For the adept who performs both stages of the alchemical path— those that lead him first to ascend to the Dao and then to realize the non-duality between the Dao and the world—existence and non-existence are one. He maintains himself in the world as long as the conditions to do so persist, hiding his state and giving benefit to his surroundings by his mere presence, until God, the Great One, summons him to Heaven.

1. *"Assiduously practice it."* This sentence is quoted from *Daode jing*, 41: "A superior gentleman hears of the Dao, and assiduously practices it."

3. *For three years preserve and ingest.* On the expression "preserve and ingest" (also found in 35:5, 35:1, 61:13, and 87:17), see the textual note on the present verse.

5–6. *"Stepping across the fire you will not be scorched, entering the water you will not get wet."* Sentences similar to this one are found in many Taoist texts. The earliest instance is in the *Zhuangzi*, which describes the True Man saying: "He enters the water and does not get wet; he enters the fire and is not burned" (6.226; see Watson, 77).

7. *You will be able to retain your life or depart from this world.* Compare the description of the True Man in the *Huainan zi*: "He dwells in what has no shape, he abides in what has no place. He moves in what has no form, he settles in what has no body. *He retains his life but looks as if he had departed this world*, he is alive but looks as if he were dead" (7.526; see Le Blanc and Mathieu, 308).

8. *Forever content and undistraught.* For the term *wuyou* ("undistraught, without grief") compare *Daode jing*, 19: "Appear unadorned and embrace the uncarved block, diminish personal interest and lessens desires, cut off learning and be undistraught."

12. *And you move your abode to the Central Land.* The Central Land (or Continent, or Island, *zhongzhou*) is found in the Eastern Sea, surrounded by three mythical archipelagos each of which consists of three islands. It is the earthly residence of the supreme God, the Great One (Taiyi), correlated with his celestial abode in the Pole Star.

13. *Your work concluded, you ascend on high.* This verse can also be translated as "your merit completed, you ascend on high."

14. *To obtain the Register and receive the Chart.* On this phrase, which denotes the adept's achieving the highest degree of transcendence, see the Introduction, § 3.

28. White Tiger and Green Dragon

The remaining portion of Book 1 (sections 28–42) is concerned with alchemy. The Sun and the Moon, the main emblems of the *Book of Changes*, perform multiple roles in the alchemical process. For example, the "fire times" (*huohou*) used for compounding the Elixir are modeled on the yearly cycle of the Sun (see the Introduction, § 6); and the alchemical tripod, shaped as two semicircles—vessel and lid— reproduces the forms of the waxing and waning quarters of the Moon.

The essences of the Sun and Moon, moreover, correspond to the ingredients of the Elixir, True Mercury and True Lead. In this role, Sun and Moon can be referred to by multiple but equivalent sets of emblems, some of which are mentioned in this and the next sections of the *Cantong qi*:

(1) The Moon (Yin) is associated with the agent Water, the direction North, the color black (darkness), the trigram Kan ☵, and "black lead" (native lead). The essence of the Moon (True Yang within Yin) is represented by the White Tiger, which is the emblem of the agent Metal, the direction West, and the trigram Dui ☱.

(2) The Sun (Yang) is associated with the agent Fire, the direction South, the color red (light), the trigram Li ☲, and cinnabar. The radiance of

the Sun (True Yin within Yang) is represented by the Green Dragon, which is the emblem of the agent Wood, the direction East, and the trigram Gen ☶.

Therefore the White Tiger signifies the True Lead found within native lead (True Yang within Yin), and the Green Dragon signifies the True Mercury found within cinnabar (True Yin within Yang). The joining of Dragon (East) and Tiger (West) forms the Elixir. The two ingredients are also referred to as the *hun* and the *po* souls, which here are abstract emblems just like those mentioned above: True Lead is the *po*, and True Mercury is the *hun*. With regard to the human being, *hun* stands for one's true nature (*xing*), and *po* for one's true qualities (*qing*).

1. *The Records of Fire are not written in vain.* The expression "records of fire" (*huoji*) designates the alchemical texts.

2. *Look into the* Changes *to comprehend them.* Apart from its explicit meaning—i.e., *Book of Changes*—the word *yi* 易 in this verse also refers to the Sun and the Moon according to the traditional etymology adopted by the *Cantong qi* (see section 7). This allusion is reinforced by the use, in the same verse, of the word *ming* 明 ("light," or, as a verb, "to comprehend"), written with the other graph that is formed by the graphs for "sun" (日) and "moon" (月).

3. *The supine Moon is the model of tripod and furnace.* "Supine Moon" (*yanyue*) is a name of the crescent Moon, also attested outside alchemical sources.

4. *The White Tiger is the hinge of the heating.* The White Tiger is called "the hinge of the heating" with regard not only to its association with the tripod and the furnace, but also to its being the emblem of True Lead, which represents the One Breath of the precelestial world sought by the alchemist in the postcelestial world.

5. *The mercurial Sun is the Flowing Pearl.* "Mercurial Sun" (*hongri*) refers to the Sun as the emblem of Yang containing True Yin, i.e., True Mercury. "Flowing Pearl" (*liuzhu*) is a common alchemical synonym of mercury obtained from the refining of cinnabar. The name alludes to the physical aspect of mercury and to its ability to escape in both a factual and a figurate way, including its tendency to volatilize when it is heated.

29. The "two eights"

In addition to the inner line of Kan ☵, True Lead (True Yang within Yin) is also represented by Dui ☱, the trigram associated with the West and the White Tiger. Analogously, True Mercury (True Yin within Yang) is represented not only by the inner line of Li ☲, but also by Gen ☶, the trigram associated with the East and the Green Dragon.

Dui and Gen, in turn, respectively connote the first and the last quarter of the Moon (see table 10). In this role, they are both assigned the symbolic number 8, derived from the sequence of the lunar cycle. Dui is the waxing quarter, which occurs at the middle of the first half of the month, eight days after the black Moon (see 13:3–4: "On the eighth day, when Dui ☱ matches *ding* 丁, the waxing quarter is level as a string"). Gen is the waning quarter, which occurs at the middle of the second half of the month, eight days after the full Moon (i.e., on the twenty-third day; see 13:15–16: "When Gen ☶ aligns with *bing* 丙 in the south, it is the twenty-third, the waning quarter").

Therefore Dui and and Gen, in addition to being emblems of True Yang and True Yin, also signify the first and the second halves of the lunar month, respectively distinguished by the growth of the Yang and the Yin principles. As emblems of True Yang and True Yin, Dui and Gen are equivalent to the inner lines of Kan ☵ and Li ☲. Saying that "the two quarters join their essences," thus, is equivalent to saying that Kan and Li join to one another and exchange their inner lines, reestablishing Qian ☰ and Kun ☷.

The sum of the numeric values of Dui and Gen is 16. In the traditional Chinese weight system, 16 ounces (*liang*) correspond to one pound (*jin*). The symbolic pound of Elixir, therefore, incorporates and unifies the whole set of cosmological and alchemical correspondences represented by its two ingredients, True Lead and True Mercury. (*)

(*) An additional correspondence between the Elixir and the emblems of the *Book of Changes* is mentioned in two verses not found in Chen Zhixu's redaction of the *Cantong qi*. See the textual note to verse 29:6.

5. *Two times 8 corresponds to one pound.* In the later alchemical tradition, the expression "two eights" (*erba*, lit., "two times 8") designates by

antonomasia the Elixir, which is formed by True Lead and True Mercury joined to one another in equal parts.

30. Constancy and change

Incorruptible and unchanging, gold withstands the action of fire. Similarly, the Sun and the Moon have been following their courses in heaven since the beginning of time, without ever becoming depleted or exhausted. Gold is a metaphor for the One Breath prior to Heaven, and the Sun and the Moon are images of Yin and Yang.

31. The true nature of Metal

The previous section has mentioned gold (*jin*), which is capable of enduring the heat of fire, and the Sun and the Moon, which do not degenerate despite their continuous movements in the heavens. This section concerns the operation of Metal (also denoted by the word *jin*, and standing for the One Breath of the Dao), whose nature persists unchanged through the innumerable cycles of change brought about by the Sun and the Moon.

Metal is the inner line of Kan ☵, the trigram that represents the Moon. This Yang line is, in the first place, the One Breath sought by the alchemist, the essence bestowed by Qian ☰ (Heaven) upon Kun ☷ (Earth) and now hidden within the world. The conjunction of Qian and Kun is reiterated by the joining of Kan ☵ (Moon) and Li ☲ (Sun) at the end of each time cycle (see sections 10 and 48). In the postcelestial world, therefore, Metal is "born from the Moon," and is sought within Kan (Water).

The inner line of Kan has the same nature as the lower line of Zhen ☳, the trigram that represents the rebirth of the Yang principle after its extinction at the end of each lunar month. Brought to life by Kun ☷, the Yang principle begins a new cycle of ascent and descent, until it is obscured again in the night of novilune (see sections 13 and 49). On that night, the Moon is lightless. Since Kun rules on the final segment of the month, Metal, i.e., the Yang principle, is said to have "returned to its mother."

The Moon receives its light from the Sun; when the Yin principle prevails in the last night of the month, this is because the light of the

Moon is entirely contained in the Sun. In the instant between the end of a time cycle and the beginning of the next one, therefore, Metal is liberated from Kan and returns to Qian ☰, "its ancient nature."

The formation of the Elixir within the tripod reproduces this process. In the alchemical metaphor, the instant in which Metal (True Yang, light) is liberated from "black lead" (Yin, obscurity) and returns to its nature signifies the formation of Gold.

2. *When the Sun receives the token at dawn on the month's first day.* For the expression *shoufu* ("receive the token") compare 10:1–2: "Between the month's last day and dawn on next month's first day, Zhen ☳ comes to receive the token." The two verses are equivalent: Zhen represents the newly reborn light, which belongs to the Sun.

5–6. *Hidden within its inner and outer walls, sinking into the depths of cavernous emptiness.* In these verses, *kuangguo* ("inner and outer walls") alludes to Kan ☵, which holds Metal between its upper and lower lines; and *dongxu* ("cavernous emptiness") alludes to Qian ☰, the "ancient nature" of Metal. See verse 1:3, where *kuangguo* denotes the upper and lower lines of Kan and Li (i.e., the Moon and the Sun) that respectively enclose True Yang and True Yin; and verse 11:2, where *dong* and *xu* are adjectives ("cavernous and empty") that describe the qualities of Qian and Kun. The two verses, therefore, refer to the return of the inner line of Kan to Qian.

32. Water and Fire return to Soil

Water, Fire, and Soil are the three main components of the Elixir. Water and Fire (Yin and Yang) are referred to by the respective earthly branches and "generation numbers" (see tables 4 and 13): Water is the branch *zi* 子 and its number is 1; Fire is the branch *wu* 午 and its number is 2. The third agent, Soil, whose "generation number" is 5, is referred to by the celestial stems *wu* 戊 and *ji* 己, which respectively stand for its Yang and Yin aspects.

Water and Fire have an inherent bond with Soil, the agent that represents the original unity of Yin and Yang: Water is Kan ☵, Fire is Li ☲, and the Yang and Yin inner lines of these trigrams respectively correspond to *wu* 戊 and *ji* 己 (see section 7). Having come forth from a state of unity, Water and Fire wish to join again one another; Soil is the intermediary element that makes their conjunction possible.

Therefore "3 (Water and Fire) and 5 (Soil) harmonize with one another." The agreement among Oneness, Yin, and Yang underlies all emblems that represent the vertical and horizontal dimensions of the cosmos (typically represented in the Chinese tradition by the numbers 3 and 5, respectively), as well as its spatial and temporal extensions (the eight directions, *baji*, and the eight "nodal days," *bajie*). (See also the note to verses 3–4.)

The second and third stanzas consider Water, Fire, and Soil from the point of view of the sequences of "generation" and "conquest" that occur among the five agents (see table 3). In the generation sequence, Soil gives birth to Metal (True Lead), and Water gives birth to Wood (True Mercury, referred to here with its alchemical name of Flowing Pearl). In this emblematic context, the Elixir is formed when Metal and Wood join to one another. In the conquest sequence, instead, Water conquests Fire, and Soil conquests Water. Since Fire— whose emblem is the Vermilion Sparrow—in turn generates Soil, it is said to be responsible for the equitable conquest and vanquishment that occur among the five agents.

In the alchemical process, Water conquers Fire, and Soil conquers Water; when Water and Fire return to Soil, the three merge their natures. This happens by virtue of Soil, which represents the original unity of Water and Fire.

3–4. *As 3 and 5 harmonize, the eight minerals set the guiding thread in line.* There are several lists of the eight minerals; one of them includes cinnabar, realgar, malachite, sulphur, mica, salt, saltpetre, and orpiment. The eight minerals, however, are not part of the discourse of the *Cantong qi* either as a group or—with the single exception of cinnabar—individually. In fact, the other mention of the eight minerals, found in 87:19–20, is definitely negative: "Dispose of realgar, discard the eight minerals!" This suggests that in the present passage, the expression "eight minerals" is used in a purely metaphoric way: "eight" is the sum of the numerical values of Water (1), Fire (2), and Soil (5), and "minerals" refers to the subject of the present section, which is obviously alchemical. (Compare 22:9, where, for an analogous reason, the five agents are called "five metals.") — According to another interpretation, instead, the "eight minerals" are the alchemical equivalent of the eight trigrams.

7. *The Yellow Soil is the father of Metal.* Yellow is the color associated with Soil in the system of the five agents.

8. *The Flowing Pearl is the child of Water.* Flowing Pearl (*liuzhu*) is a common alchemical synonym of mercury. On this verse, see also the Textual Notes.

9. *Water treats Soil as its demon.* In the context of the divination techniques, "demon" (*gui*, or *guangui*) denotes an item within a series of emblems that "conquers" another item in the same series. In the present case, which refers to the series of the five agents, Soil conquers Water.

33. Soil and the Elixir

Being positioned at the center of the horizontal plane, Soil upholds the vertical axis that conjoins the precosmic and cosmic domains. It distributes the One Breath to the other agents, setting the principles by which they alternately rule. This enables the cosmos to function without error.

Analogously, the Elixir is made of Yin and Yang joined as One. It allows an adept to return to the Center, from where he raises to the higher states of being; and it benefits the entire person, affording health and prolonging life.

7–8. *Soil roams the four seasons, guarding the boundaries and setting the rules.* Compare 7:5: "Soil rules over the four seasons." — *Guiju*, translated here as "rules," literally means "compass and square." This expression connotes rules and regulations, in this case those governing the relations among the five agents. In addition, compass and square respectively allude to Heaven and Earth, and thus to the Yin and Yang halves of Soil.

9. *When the Golden Sand enters the five inner organs. Jinsha*, translated here as "Golden Sand," might also be translated as "Metal and Sand." In fact, according the several commentators, this expression refers to the Elixir made of True Lead, whose emblematic agent is Metal, and True Mercury, which in Waidan is obtained from cinnabar (*dansha*, "cinnabar sand," or *zhusha*, "vermilion sand"). — The five inner organs are the five viscera (*wuzang*), namely liver, heart, spleen, lungs, and kidneys.

34. The true nature of all things

This and the next two sections are devoted to the notion of *tonglei*, "belonging to the same kind" or "category," one of the main alchemi-

cal principles of the *Cantong qi*. The true nature of all things underlies their particular forms or states. If ceruse (white lead) is placed in a
stove, it reverts to black lead; if ice or snow are heated, they return to
being water. The same is true of cinnabar ("the Sand"): its original
essence and authentic nature is mercury ("quicksilver"), and it yields
mercury when it is heated. Since lead (the "Metal") forms the Elixir
by joining with mercury, lead is said to honor cinnabar.

All transient objects and forms harbor the principle that generates
them. This principle is their true nature, and they revert to it at the
end of their existence ("end and beginning, of their own accord,
depend one on the other"). As long as it complies with the requirement presented in the next section, the alchemical work reveals that
principle.

1–2. *When you throw ceruse into the fire, its color spoils and it reverts to
lead.* There have been several explanations of the chemical import of
these verses and their possible relation to the alchemical content of the
Cantong qi. As this section makes clear, however, the transformation of
ceruse (white lead, *hufen*) into lead is mentioned only as an instance of a
form reverting to its original state, not different in nature from the return
of ice or snow to the state of water.

4. *It dissolves to form the Great Mystery.* Great Mystery (*taixuan*) is an
alchemical synonym of water. See also the use of the word
"mystery" (*xuan*) to mean the agent Water in 22:11: "Mystery holds the
Yellow Sprout."

5–6. *As its ruler Metal takes the Sand, which by nature is joined with
quicksilver.* "Sand" (*sha*) is an abbreviation of the common names of
cinnabar, *dansha* ("cinnabar sand") and *zhusha* ("vermilion sand"). —
According to a different interpretation, instead, the "sand" is the Vermilion Sand (*zhusha*), which here is not the common name of cinnabar but
denotes the True Mercury within cinnabar (True Yin within Yang).
Shuiyin (lit., "water silver") is not the common name of quicksilver, but
denotes the Silver within Water, i.e., True Lead within native lead (True
Yang within Yin; on the use of the word "silver" to denote Lead see the
note to 22:3–4). This reading is based on these verses of *Awakening to
Reality* (*Wuzhen pian*): "If in the Golden Tripod you want to detain the
Mercury within the Vermilion, first from the Jade Pond send down the
Silver within the Water" ("Lüshi," no. 4). In these verses, the Golden
Tripod is Li ☲, and the "Mercury within the Vermilion" is its inner Yin

line; the Jade Pond is Kan ☵, and the "Silver within the Water" is its inner Yang line.

35. "Things of the same kind follow each other"

To compound the Elixir, the ingredients must fulfill the principle of *tonglei*, an expression that literally means "to be of the same kind" or "of the same category." This section illustrates this principle only by means of images; their sense becomes clear by reading this section in conjunction with the previous one and the next one.

The principle of *tonglei* requires that the ingredients agree with Qian and Kun. Only then can they join one another and generate the Elixir: if the ingredients do not agree with Qian and Kun, "could they ever will to be joined in one body?" (36:16). In the alchemical path illustrated in the *Cantong qi*, therefore, the ingredients—whether they are material or immaterial—should not only match one another, but also enable the conjunction of Qian and Kun.

Within the cosmos, Qian ☰ operates through Kan ☵, and Kun ☷ operates through Li ☲. Qian and Kun are the true natures of Kan and Li. Black lead and cinnabar represent this configuration. In the alchemical process, they reveal their true nature: the true nature of black lead (☵) is True Lead (☰), and the true nature of cinnabar (☲) is True Mercury (☷).

9. *"Things of the same kind follow each other."* This sentence is an almost literal quotation from the *Zhuangzi*: "Creatures [*or*: things] of the same kind follow each other, and a voice will answer to the voice that is like itself. This has been the principle of Heaven since time began" (31.1027; see Watson, 346).

13–14. *Water streams and does not blaze by rising up, fire stirs and does not wet by flowing down.* These verses allude to a passage in the "Great Plan" ("Hongfan") chapter of the *Book of Documents* (*Shujing*): "Water is the name given to what wets by flowing down; fire is the name given to what blazes by rising up" (12.76b; see Legge, *The Sacred Books of China*, 3:141).

36. Erroneous alchemical methods

Any alchemical practice that does not involve the conjunction of True Lead and True Mercury is deemed by the *Cantong qi* to be ineffective, because its ingredients do not represent Qian and Kun, or True Yin and True Yang. The present section illustrates this view with examples drawn from Waidan. Adepts of the alchemical arts often hope to make elixirs by refining such minerals as chalcanthite, mica, alum, and magnetite; or by compounding sulphur and mercury with one another (the classical Waidan method in traditions not based on the *Cantong qi*; see the note to verses 11–12); or by making compounds of minerals and metals. These methods do not comply with the principle of *tonglei*, described in the previous section: their ingredients do not represent the state in which Heaven and Earth, or Qian and Kun, are joined to one another as "one body," and cannot make it possible to revert to that state.

This is not criticism of Waidan per se: even though the *Cantong qi* deems all alchemy to be the way of "inferior virtue" (see section 20), it uses explicit Waidan terminology and imagery to describe the only kind of alchemical practice that it supports (see sections 39–40 and 62). The criticism, instead, is addressed to methods that do not allow the conjunction of Qian and Kun, alchemically represented by the union of True Lead and True Mercury.

3. *Unless they suddenly have the "unexpected encounter."* The term *xiehou* ("unexpected encounter") is first found in "On the Moor is the Creeping Grass," one of the love poems of the *Book of Odes*. The first half of this poem says: "On the moor is the creeping grass, / And how heavily is it loaded with dew! / There was a beautiful man, / Lovely, with clear eyes and fine forehead! / We met together unexpectedly, / And so my desire was satisfied" (*Shijing*, "Ye you mancao," no. 94; see Waley, *The Book of Songs*, 21). Later, *xiehou* was used to denote the "unexpected meeting" with a master.

11–12. *They roast sulphur above camphor wood, and refine it with mercury made into a mud.* These verses allude to the fundamental method in the Waidan traditions not based on the *Cantong qi*. Cinnabar (Yang) is refined to obtain mercury (Yin), which is then compounded with sulphur (Yang) to recompose cinnabar. At the end of several cycles of refining—typically nine, sometimes seven—one obtains an elixir whose properties are entirely Yang. Authors belonging to Waidan traditions based on the *Cantong qi* would later criticize this method for being based only on the refining of Yang, without a corresponding method for the refining of Yin (see the Introduction, § 9).

13. *Blowing on the fire to melt the five minerals and copper*. This verse probably refers to Waidan techniques similar to the one described in the *Baopu zi neipian*: "Let [the crucible] cool, remove the contents, and blow to melt the copper" (16.288; see Ware, 272). — There are several lists of the five minerals. One of them includes cinnabar, realgar, arsenolite, malachite, and magnetite.

16. *Could they ever will to be joined in one body?* Compare *Zhuangzi*: "Heaven and Earth are the father and mother of the ten thousand things. When they join they become one body; when they part they become a beginning" (19.632; see Watson, 198). According to the *Cantong qi*, only True Yin and True Yang (Heaven and Earth, and what represents them by "being of their kind") can "join in one body."

37. The *Book of Changes* and the *Cantong qi*

Sections 37–38 concern the relation between the *Book of Changes* and the *Cantong qi*. They introduce the method for making the Elixir described in sections 39–40.

According to the traditional account, the composition of the *Book of Changes* began with the mythical emperor Fu Xi, who drew the eight trigrams. King Wen of the Zhou later created the sixty-four hexagrams by combining the trigrams in pairs, and added the short "Statements on the Lines" on each hexagram and its individual lines. Finally Confucius wrote the Ten Wings (or Ten Appendixes, "Shiyi").

Heaven chose Fu Xi, King Wen, and Confucius to instruct humanity by means of the *Book of Changes*. Wei Boyang took those three sages as his masters, and thus become awakened. Following his masters' example, he wrote his *Cantong qi* to enable us to use forms and signs in order to comprehend what is devoid of forms and signs.

3. *"He was the first to draw the eight trigrams."* This sentence is an almost literal quotation from the "Appended Sayings" of the *Book of Changes*: "When in early antiquity Bao Xi (i.e., Fu Xi) ruled the world, he looked upward and contemplated the images in Heaven, he looked downward and contemplated the models on the Earth. . . . Thus he was the first to make the eight trigrams. Through them he communicated with

the virtue of Numinous Light (*shenming*) and classified the qualities (*qing*) of the ten thousand things" (B.2; see Wilhelm, 328–29).

6. *Joined them together and added the Statements on the Lines.* For "joined them together," the text literally has "joined their bodies together." This refers to the figures of the eight trigrams being combined in pairs to form the sixty-four hexagrams.

8. *Appended the Ten Wings.* The Ten Wings, or Ten Appendixes, consist of seven texts, the first, second, and fourth of which are in two parts, making ten parts altogether: Commentary on the Judgements ("Tuanzhuan"); Commentary on the Images ("Xiangzhuan"); Commentary on the Words of the Text ("Wenyan zhuan," concerning only the hexagrams Qian ☰ and Kun ☷); Appended Sayings ("Xici"); Explanation of the Trigrams ("Shuogua"); Hexagrams in Sequence ("Xugua"); and Hexagrams in Irregular Order ("Zagua").

13–14. *In what they produced they trod one path, inferring the measures and inspecting the minutest details.* On the expression *tuidu* see the note to 14:4. The compound word *fenzhu* connotes something exceedingly small (*fen* and *zhu* are the smallest units of length and weight, respectively).

18. *On behalf of the world I have composed this book.* On this verse, see the Textual Notes.

38. Wei Boyang's hesitancy

As does the *Book of Changes*, all alchemical texts deal with one and the same subject: the unity underlying the Dao and the world. In alchemy, this unity is represented by the Elixir made of Lead and Mercury. At first, Wei Boyang thought that he would communicate the method for compounding the Elixir only by means of oral instructions to those who were worthy of receiving it. Later, he decided to transmit it also in written form. Fearing to disclose the "token of Heaven" (*tianfu*), however, he provided only a brief summary of the method, veiled by the use of images and metaphors. The next two sections contains that summary.

1. *The Records of Fire count six hundred chapters.* The expression "records of fire" (*huoji*) is used to define the alchemical texts in 28:1–2: "The Records of Fire are not written in vain; look into the *Changes* to

comprehend them." *Pian* generally denotes either a piece of writing or a unit within a larger composition.

5–6. *Should they quest for the origin, they would see that, at first, darkness and light dwell together.* Compare the "Appended Sayings" of the *Book of Changes*: "Looking upward, we use [the *Book of Changes*] to contemplate the signs in heaven; looking downward, we use it to examine the lines of the earth. Thus we understand the reasons for darkness and light" (A.3; see Wilhelm, 294, whose comments on this passage deserve attention). As we have seen, the unity of darkness and light is represented by the graphs for "sun" (*ri* 日, i.e., Yang, light) and "moon" (*yue* 月, i.e., Yin, darkness), which combined together form the graphs for the words "light" (*ming* 明) and "change" (*yi* 易).

14. *I have looked upward and downward, and have written these trifles.* In writing his *Cantong qi*, Wei Boyang does what Fu Xi did when he created the eight trigrams: "He looked upward and contemplated the images in Heaven, he looked downward and contemplated the models on the Earth" (see note to 37:3).

39. Compounding the Elixir (First part)

Sections 39–40 contain the main description of the method for compounding the Elixir found in the *Cantong qi*. The description is divided into two parts: the first ends with the compounding of the Yellow Carriage, and the second one, with the compounding of the Reverted Elixir proper. Although most later commentators have explained these verses from the perspective of the tradition to which they belonged, namely Neidan, terminology and images in both sections are explicitly Waidan. Nevertheless, the emblematic functions of the ingredients and the process described here can apply to both Waidan and Neidan.

The Elixir is made of two ingredients, here called Metal and Water. Metal is True Lead, and Water is True Mercury. The two ingredients are placed in the vessel, so that mercury circulates but does not volatilize when it is heated. Each ingredient is assigned a symbolic weight of fifteen ounces. Together, their weights correspond to the number of days in the lunar month.

In addition, the weights have another and more important symbolic connotation: 5 and 10 respectively are the "generation number" and the "accomplishment number" of the central agent Soil (see table 4).

This correspondence ties both Lead and Mercury to Soil, an association that is already implicit in the emblematic functions of the two ingredients: the Yang line within Kan ☵ (True Lead) is equivalent to the celestial stem *wu* 戊, which is the active, Yang aspect of Soil, while the Yin line within Li ☲ (True Mercury) is equivalent to the celestial stem *ji* 己, which is its passive, Yin aspect (see section 7). Being comprised within both ingredients, Soil can play a mediating function between them, enabling the Yin and Yang principles to conjoin.

Five parts of Water (Mercury) are suitable—"more than enough"—for compounding the Elixir, together with the same amount of Metal (Lead); at the end, Metal will weigh as it did at the beginning. The agent Fire, whose "generation number" is 2, is used for heating the compound. Through the action of fire, which is placed underneath the open vessel, the "three things"—Metal, Water, and Soil—undergo transmutation, taking at first a liquid form and then a solid form, similar to ashes or dust. The compound obtained at the end of the first part of the method is called Yellow Carriage (*huangyu*). It serves as the basis for making the Elixir in the second part of the method, which is described in the next section.

9–10. *The other three are thus not used, but Fire, which is 2, is fastened to them.* Other redactions of the *Cantong qi* contain significant variant readings for these verses; see the Textual Notes.

12. *In their transformations their shapes are divine.* This verse might also be translated as "in their transformations their shapes are like [those of] a spirit." Compare *Huainan zi*: "In its movements, [the Dao] is formless; in its transformations, it is like a spirit" (1.60; see Le Blanc and Mathieu, 33–34).

16. *It is given the name Yellow Carriage.* Yellow is the color associated with the central Soil in the system of the five agents. *Yu* primarily means "carriage," but this word also includes "earth" among its meanings. The term "Yellow Carriage," therefore, alludes to the Center as the unity of Yin and Yang, respectively represented in alchemy by Mercury and Lead.

17–18. *When its time is about to come to an end, it wrecks its own nature and disrupts its life span.* Suiyue, here translated as "time," literally means "years and months."

19. *Its form looks like ashes or soil.* Note again the mention of Soil, the agent that represents the conjunction of Lead and Mercury.

40. Compounding the Elixir (Second part)

The description of the refining of True Lead and True Mercury that had began in the previous section continues here. The compound obtained in the first part of the method is placed in a tripod and is heated in a furnace. The vessel, this time, should be hermetically closed, as even the slightest leakage of Breath (*qi*) would prevent the Elixir from being compounded. The intensity of heat is regulated according to the system of the "fire times" (*huohou*), which subdivides each heating cycle into twelve stages ("twelve nodes") modeled on the growth and decline of the Sun during the year (see section 51). Fire is mild at the beginning, then grows stronger until it reaches the highest intensity, then decreases until it is finally extinguished. After several cycles of heating, Lead and Mercury go through a symbolic death. When Yin and Yang cease to exist as separate entities, the *hun* soul returns to Heaven, the *po* soul returns to the Earth, and the luminous Reverted Elixir (*huandan*) is achieved.

18. *Even one knife-point is supremely divine.* The term *daogui*, translated above as "knife-point," more precisely means "tip of a spatula." According to an interpretation, the word *dao* 刀 ("blade, spatula, knife") alludes to Metal (i.e., Gold, the Elixir); *gui* 圭, instead, stands for the "two Soils 土" (one on top of the other, representing *wu* 戊 and *ji* 己, or Yin and Yang) incorporated into the Elixir. The symbolic "knife-point" of Elixir evokes, therefore, the ingredients that have made its compounding possible.

41. Yin and Yang feed on each other

The ingredients of the Elixir are named here Water and Fire. Water (Kan ☵, containing Metal, or True Lead) conquers Fire (Li ☲, containing Wood, or True Mercury); when Soil in turn conquers Water, the Elixir is attained (see above, section 32). The relation that ties the agents to one another is the same as the one that occurs among the corresponding natural phenomena: when water is poured over fire, fire is extinguished, and "when soil invades, water cannot rise" (32:10).

The same relations of mutual "conquest" are also observed in the heavens. In night of novilune, the Yin principle is at the height of its development and obscures the Yang principle: the Sun cannot send its light upon the Moon, and the Moon therefore is black. On that day, however, the Yang principle begins a new cycle of ascent. Then, in the night of plenilune, the Yang principle culminates and overcomes the Yin principle: the Moon is entirely exposed to the rays of the Sun, and appears as full. On that day, the Yin principle in turn begins its ascending cycle that will result in a new obscuration of the Yang principle. Despite the apparent contest between them, the Sun and the Moon ceaselessly giving way to one another provide an example of the harmony that exists between Yin and Yang.

The same event that occurs at the beginning of the month also happens in the alchemical process. Kan ☵ (Water) conquers Li ☲ (Fire), which is obscured; therefore Li, which is the Sun, "turns from daylight to dusk." The consequences of this event are all but negative. When Water conquers Fire, Metal (the inner line of Kan ☵) is liberated from its temporary dwelling and returns to Qian ☰, its "initial nature" (see section 31). The name "metal" expresses the outer qualities (*qing*) of Metal as one of the two ingredients of the Elixir. But Qian is also Pure Yang, the One Breath of the Dao, the principle sought by the alchemist: it is the Elixir itself. When Metal regains its true, precelestial nature (*xing*), it acquires a different name (a "cognomen") and is called Reverted Elixir.

5–6. *The Sun and the Moon always encroach upon one another on the month's first day and the day of full moon.* Compare 70:9–10: "Between the month's last day and next month's first, [Yin] encroaches, overcasting and upsetting." In these verses, the reciprocal encroaching of the Sun and the Moon in the novilune and the plenilune is compared to an eclipse, which in Chinese divination is deemed to be an ill omen.

13–14. *When Metal goes back to its initial nature, then you can call it Reverted Elixir.* In addition to the one reported above, there have been several other interpretations of these verses. According to one of these interpretations, Metal (Yang) refers to the "qualities" (*qing*) and Wood (Yin) refers to the "nature" (*xing*); when they join, Metal reverts to its nature and is called Reverted Elixir. According to another interpretation, "qualities" refers to the Yang dyad made of Metal and Water, and "nature" to the Yin dyad made of Wood and Fire.

42. The tradition of the *Cantong qi*

This section ends Book 1 of the *Cantong qi*, and serves as a concluding statement on the author's purpose and accomplishment in writing this part of his work. The teachings of the *Cantong qi* are based on a timeless doctrine that has no creators, but only exemplary figures. Wei Boyang wrote his work by taking them as his models. Since a tradition like the one reflected in the *Cantong qi* is devoid of history in the common sense of the word, there is no difference between the teachings of the past and those of the present. Therefore, even though Wei Boyang's work uses concise statements and obscure expressions, those who are qualified to receive its teachings find here an integral exposition of the doctrine.

3. *The ancient records told of the Dragon and the Tiger*. According to several commentators, this verse refers to the *Longhu jing* (Scripture of the Dragon and Tiger), the text on which the *Cantong qi* is supposedly based (see the Introduction, § 3).

4. *The Yellow Emperor praised the Golden Flower*. The Yellow Emperor (Huangdi) was the patron deity of the early Chinese alchemists. He received alchemical teachings and, according to some versions of his legend, ascended to Heaven after compounding an elixir. See Kaltenmark, *Le Lie-sien tchouan*, 50–53. — On the Golden Flower see the notes to section 22.

5. *Master Huainan refined the Autumn Stone*. Liu An (179?–122, also known as Huainan zi, or Master of Huainan) is credited with alchemical knowledge and is believed to have become an immortal after ingesting an elixir. — The term Autumn Stone (*qiushi*) has several meanings in Waidan, but only one of them applies to the present context: the association of autumn with Metal in the system of the five agents (see tables 1 and 2) makes this term a synonym of Metal, or Gold.

6. *And Wang Yang commended the Yellow Sprout*. Wang Yang has been identified as Wang Jie, a well-known Han-dynasty scholar who was said to be able to "make gold." (On this name, see the Textual Notes.) On the Yellow Sprout (*huangya*) see the notes to section 22. As its name also indicates, the alchemical meaning of this term is essentially equivalent to Golden Flower.

BOOK 2

43. Qian and Kun, Kan and Li

As does Book 1, Book 2 of the *Cantong qi* opens with several sections
(43–52) that concern cosmology. The images of Qian and Kun are
Heaven and Earth; those of Kan and Li are the Moon and the Sun.
Just like Heaven and Earth are unchanging and in constant conjunction, so do Qian and Kun "join and embrace one another." As they
join, the active and the passive principles respectively give and receive.
Thus the Essence of Qian and the Breath of Kun are distributed, and
creatures and phenomena are generated.

Qian ☰ in the act of bestowing its essence upon Kun is Li ☲; Kun
☷ in the act of receiving the essence of Qian is Kan ☵. Kan and Li are
the counterparts of Qian and Kun within the cosmos. They follow
one another like the Sun and the Moon, and nourish all beings with
their light, which actually is the light of Qian and Kun. This function
of Kan and Li is mysterious and unfathomable, but the sages have
provided a way to comprehend it by means of images and emblems.

Although Qian, Kun, Kan, and Li, from our perspective, appear to
differ from one another, they all reside within the Center, indistinct
and not separated from each other. The other emblems of the *Book of
Changes* represent the operation of this motionless Prime Mover
within time and space. They arrange themselves like a carriage
around the Center. The saintly ruler is its driver, and uses those
emblems to manage and respond to change.

Earth brings the generative faculty of Heaven to accomplishment;
without the Earth, Heaven would not fulfill its power, and without
Heaven, the Earth would be fruitless. The "bright noble man" embodies and makes manifest the creative action of Heaven within the
human world: what the Earth is for Heaven is the world for the saint,
and is the kingdom for the ruler. When the ruler conducts government
according to the principles set forth by the saintly men, he brings
harmony to his kingdom.

1. *Qian the firm and Kun the yielding.* Compare *Book of Changes*,
"Appended Sayings": "Qian is something Yang, Kun is something Yin.
When Yin and Yang join their virtues, the firm and the yielding take
form" (B.5; see Wilhelm, 343–44).

5. *Attending, they create and transform.* Compare the "Appended Sayings": "The firm and the yielding follow one another and generate change and transformation" (A.2; see Wilhelm, 288); and "The firm and the yielding follow one another, and therein occur the transformations" (B.1; see Wilhelm, 325).

6. *Unfolding their Essence and Breath.* Compare the "Appended Sayings": "Essence and Breath become the creatures" (A.4; see Wilhelm, 294). Essence refers to Qian, and Breath to Kun.

17. *Harnessing a dragon and a mare.* Dragon and mare are associated with Qian and Kun, respectively; see *Book of Changes*, hexagrams no. 1 and no. 2.

19. *In harmony there are following and compliance.* This verse refers to the "noble man" who drives his carriage by following the right path (compare section 2; the word *sui*, "to follow," is used in both passages). It also refers to the ruler who leads the kingdom in accordance with the principles of humanity and righteousness, and thus obtains the compliance of his people. Compare *Book of Changes*, "Commentary on the Judgement" on the hexagram Xian ☲ (no. 31): "The sage stimulates the hearts of men, and the world attains harmony and peace" (see Wilhelm, 541).

20. *The path is level and begets no evil. Ping*, "level," also connotes "equality" and "peace," and thus applies not only to driving a carriage, but also to governing a kingdom. The simile of the "path" (or "road") is also found in section 2, where the "noble man" is urged to "follow the tracks and the ruts."

44. Awaiting the time

This section consists of a short commentary on a passage of the "Appended Sayings" of the *Book of Changes*. The sage ruler resides in the Center (see 2:7) and is mindful of the visible and the unseen patterns that tie his own person, his palace, his kingdom, and the whole world to one another. As he fulfills his tasks by conforming to those patterns, the influence of his words and actions extends throughout his kingdom and beyond.

Like the saintly man, who conceals his skills and discloses them only when the circumstances allow or require him to do so, the sage ruler should know when the circumstances demand him to respond by quiescence or action. For this purpose, he relies on the emblems of the *Book of Changes*, arranged into meaningful patterns. The first of these patterns is the cycle of the hexagrams during the thirty days of the lunar month, which is described in the next section.

1–3. *"The noble man dwells in his house; if he speaks his words well, even those from more than a thousand miles away respond to them."* This sentence is quoted from the "Appended Sayings" of the *Book of Changes* (A.6; see Wilhelm, 305).

4. *This means that the ruler of a kingdom of ten thousand chariots.* The phrase "ruler of [a kingdom of] ten thousand chariots" is found in several early texts to denote the ruler of a large kingdom.

5. *Resides in a house surrounded by nine layers of walls. Jiuzhong,* lit. "nine layers," connotes, by extension, not only the ruler's palace itself, but also its central location: a nine-layered wall is also said to be found on Mount Kunlun, at the center of the world. The nine horizontal layers of walls, in turn, mirror the nine vertical layers of Heaven.

7. *He complies with the nodes of Yin and Yang.* In other words, the ruler complies with the properties of each stage of the time cycles determined by the ascent and descent of Yin and Yang. — For the translation of *jie* as "nodes," see the note to 3:1. In a more specific sense, *jie* here could also refer to the twenty-four "nodes" or periods of the year (*jieqi*), each of which lasts approximately fifteen days. These time spans are mentioned in section 46 below.

8. *"Hiding his skills and awaiting the time."* This sentence combines two sentences of the "Appended Sayings": "The noble man hides his skills within himself. He awaits the time and then acts" (B.4; see Wilhelm, 340).

45. The monthly cycle of the hexagrams

The *Cantong qi* has described the cycle of the hexagrams during the thirty days of the month in section 3. The present section reiterates its basic features. Qian ☰, Kun ☷, Kan ☵, and Li ☲ reside at the Center and are not part of the time cycles. The remaining sixty hexagrams are associated in pairs with the thirty days of the month, beginning with Zhun ䷂ and Meng ䷃ that rule on the daytime and the nighttime of the first day (see table 7).

The earthly branches related to each pair of hexagrams reflect a different system of associations compared to the one used in section 3 (see table 8). Despite this difference, the cycle of the sixty hexagrams again provides a model for the conduct of the ruler, who uses the qualities pertaining to each stage of time to determine his tasks. In particular, he uses them to determine whether he should operate according to the principles of humanity or righteousness, respectively associated with the Yang and the Yin phases of the time cycles. Before making decisions, he carefully examines the principles set forth by the saintly men, and accordingly responds by activity or quiescence.

3–4. *Of the remaining sixty hexagrams, each has its own day.* "The remaining sixty hexagrams" means the sixty-four hexagrams except for Qian, Kun, Kan, and Li, which are not part of the cycle.

5–6. *Let me present just these two emblems, for here I cannot be exhaustive.* The entire cycle consists of sixty hexagrams, of which Zhun ䷂ and Meng ䷃ are the first two (see table 7).

9–10. *"Those who transgress this have ill fortune; those who comply with it have good fortune."* The terms "good fortune" and "ill fortune," as well as "regret" and "remorse" (found in verse 16 below) belong to the vocabulary of the *Book of Changes*. See, for example, these passages of the "Appended Sayings": "Good fortune and ill fortune are the images of gain and loss; regret and remorse are the images of sorrow and distress" (A.2; see Wilhelm, 288); and "'Good fortune' and 'ill fortune' refer to gain and loss, 'regret' and 'remorse' to minor imperfections" (A.3; see Wilhelm, 291; for other similar passages see Wilhelm, 325 and 337).

13. *Cautiously watch the markers of time.* On the term *richen* see the note to 26:4.

14. *Attentively inspect the ebb and the flow.* "Ebb and flow" refers to the ascent and the descent of Yin and Yang during the time cycles.

15–16. *Even with the smallest of errors, regret and remorse would possess you.* See the note to verses 9–10 above.

46. The regular phenomena of Heaven and Earth

The time cycles and the related phenomena in Heaven and on Earth are regular and function without error; therefore they serve as exemplary patterns for the operation of the ruler. If the rise and fall of Yin and Yang deviated from their regular course, the whole cosmos would be thrown into confusion. Likewise, if the ruler does not conform to those patterns, his kingdom is endangered.

3–4. *In deep winter we would have the Great Heat, and in full summer, frost and snow.* "Great Heat" (*dashu*) is one of the twenty-four periods of the year (*jieqi*). The words "frost" and "snow" appear in the names of three of the twenty-four periods: Descent of Frost (*shuangjiang*), Lesser Snow (*xiaoxue*), and Great Snow (*daxue*).

6. *And did not agree with the water clock's notches.* Water clocks bore "notches" (*ke*) that divided the day into one hundred equal parts, each of which corresponds to about fifteen minutes by modern reckoning.

47. Complying with the cycles of Yin and Yang

The patterns of Yin and Yang pervade and unify the domains of Heaven, Earth, and Man. Since the ruler's task is to guarantee and maintain the agreement of Man with Heaven and Earth, this requires that he operates in accordance with those patterns. If he does so, the influence of his words extends throughout and even beyond his own kingdom, bringing about different effects according to the circumstances.

The sage ruler complies with the alternation of Yin and Yang and with the qualities associated with the four seasons. He is active in the times corresponding to spring and summer (Yang), and quiescent in the times corresponding to autumn and winter (Yin). Therefore he ensures that Yin and Yang, the five agents, and all other forces operating within his kingdom keep to their respective places and perform their respective functions.

2. *Bringing the August Ultimate to move in response.* Compare *Book of Changes*, "Appended Sayings": "Words and deeds are the hinge of the noble man. As the hinge moves, it determines honor or disgrace. Through words and deeds the noble man causes Heaven and Earth to move. Must one not, then, be cautious?" (A.6; see Wilhelm, 305). "August Ultimate" (*huangji*) refers to the principle that originates and sustains the cosmos. This principle, which coincides with the Center, is represented in Heaven by the Celestial Emperor (*tiandi*). On Earth, it is represented by the sage king, who rules in accordance with the principles of humanity and righteousness and thereby induces his subjects to follow him.

3–4. *What comes forth from his mouth anear flows to little-known regions afar.* Compare again the "Appended Sayings": "Words go forth from his own person and exert their influence on the people. Deeds are born close at hand and become visible afar" (A.6; see Wilhelm, 305).

5–8. *Sometimes it provokes calamities . . . at others it engenders battles and wars.* Compare the passage of the *Book of Changes* quoted in the note to verse 2 above, according to which the words and deeds of the noble man "determine honor or disgrace."

11. *"Movement and quiescence have constancy."* This sentence is quoted from the "Appended Sayings": "Movement and quiescence have constancy; in accordance with this, the firm and the yielding are distinguished" (A.1; see Wilhelm, 280).

12. *Therefore he abides by the marking-cord and the plumb-line.* On these tools symbolic of rulership see the notes to section 2 above.

15. *"The firm and the yielding are distinguished."* This sentence is quoted from the passage of the *Book of Changes* translated in the note to verse 11 above.

19–20. *The course of change flows in cycles—it bends and it stretches, and goes back and forth.* For the term *zhouliu* ("flowing in a cycle") compare 3:7–8: "The two functions have no fixed positions in the lines: 'flowing in cycles they go through the six empty spaces.'" — For *qushen* ("bend and stretch") compare the "Appended Sayings": "When the Sun goes, the Moon comes; when the Moon goes, the Sun comes. Sun and Moon follow one another, and light comes into existence. . . . Going means bending, and coming means stretching. Bending and stretching respond to one another, and benefit arises" (B.3; see Wilhelm, 338). — For *fanfu* ("go back and forth," "go to and fro") see *Book of Changes*, hexagram Qian ䷀ (no. 1), third line, "Commentary on the Images": "All day long [the noble man] is creatively active. He goes back and forth on the path" (see Wilhelm, 374).

48. The joining of the Sun and the Moon

This section mirrors the description of the joining of the Sun and the Moon found in section 10. In the last night of each lunar month, Sun and Moon meet at the Center of the cosmos and exchange their essences. Thus they fulfill the function of generating and sustaining life on behalf of Qian and Kun: "emanation" (*shi*, "giving forth") is the function of Qian, "transformation" (*hua*, also meaning "bringing to life") is the function of Kun.

The conjunction of the Sun and the Moon does not only produce change; it also renovates, within the cosmos, the Numinous Light in which Heaven and Earth are joined to each other. This light leads the saintly man, whose operation in the world attains the perfection of non-doing.

7. *The Numinous Light of Heaven and Earth.* Compare the "Appended Sayings" of the *Book of Changes*: "Qian is something Yang, Kun is something Yin. When Yin and Yang join their virtues, the firm and the yielding take form. Thus they give form to the phenomena of Heaven and Earth, and spread the virtue of Numinous Light" (B.5; see Wilhelm, 343–44).

9. *"Use it for benefit and to bring serenity to yourself."* This sentence is quoted from the "Appended Sayings": "Let pure thoughts enter your Spirit, and you will achieve the utmost of operation. Use it for benefit and to bring serenity to yourself, and you will exalt your virtue" (B.3; see Wilhelm, 338).

10. *Hide yourself and remain secluded.* For 'hide yourself," the text literally has "hide your form" (*yinxing*), the principle of individuality of all creatures and objects.

49. The cycle of the Moon

This section describes again the lunar cycle according the *najia*, or Matching Stems, cosmological device (another description of the same cycle is found in section 13). This time the focus is not on the rise of Yang and Yin in the first and the second halves of the lunation, but on the ascent and the descent of the Yang principle alone. Moreover, each of the six stages of the cycle is associated not only with one trigram, but also with one line of Qian ☰, the hexagram that represents Pure Yang, and is illustrated with a sentence drawn from the Statements on the Lines on that hexagram in the *Book of Changes*. Their subject is the dragon, the animal that represents Qian. (*)

The Moon begins its cycle in the northeast. On the third day (represented by Zhen ☳), the Yang principle begins to rise. On the eighth day (Dui ☱), Yin and Yang are equal to each other when the Moon is in the first quarter: half of it is illuminated by the Sun and the other half is dark. On the fifteenth day (Qian ☰), the Moon's illuminated side faces the Earth. Now the Yang principle, having reached its culmination, is about to begin its descent: Yin and Yang invert their courses of "flourishing and decay."

On the sixteenth day (Xun ☴), Yin begins to advance, and Yang begins to recede. On the twenty-third day (Gen ☶), Yin and Yang are again in balance; now the dragon is "sitting in the throne of heaven," because this stage corresponds to the fifth line of Qian, and the fifth line is the ruling line of an hexagram. On the thirtieth day (Kun ☷), finally, Yang has been overcome. The "arrogant dragon" here denotes the Yin principle, which has defeated the Yang principle and attempts to prevent its rebirth.

The end of the lunar cycle is represented by the words "all nines" (*yong jiu*), which in the language of the *Book of Changes* signify that all the Yang lines of Qian change into Yin lines. This final change generates Kun ☷, the hexagram that embodies Pure Yin. In addition, number 9 is the last of the Yang numbers (which are 1, 3, 5, 7, and 9), and after it, the numeric sequence starts again.

Although Kun represents the supremacy of the Yin principle at the end of the lunar cycle, she gives birth again to the Yang Breath when the Sun and the Moon join with one another in the night of the thirtieth day. Therefore Kun "binds and encloses end and beginning," and "is like a mother to all things in the world." When Kun regenerates the Yang principle, a new time cycle begins.

(*) The association among the six time stages, the lines of Qian, and the dragon is not a creation of the authors of the *Cantong qi*. It agrees with a description of the "noble man" found in the *Book of Changes*: "Because he is clear as to the end and the beginning, as to the way in which each of the six stages (i.e., the six positions of the lines of an hexagram) completes itself in its own time, in due time he mounts on the six dragons and rides through heaven" ("Commentary on the Judgements" on the hexagram Qian; see Wilhelm, 371–72). Richard Wilhelm's comments on this passage deserve to be quoted: "The holy man, who understands the mysteries of creation inherent in end and beginning, in death and life, in dissolution and growth, and who understands how these polar opposites condition one another, becomes superior to the limitations of the transitory. For him, the meaning of time is that in it the stages of growth can unfold in a clear sequence. He is mindful at every moment and uses the six stages of growth as if they were six dragons on which he mounts toward heaven."

11. *It rises in the northeast.* The first stage of the lunar cycle represents the rebirth of the Yang principle. Compare the *Huainan zi*: "The Yang Breath rises in the northeast and expires in the southwest; the Yin Breath rises in the southwest and expires in the northeast" (14.1037; see Le Blanc and Mathieu, 691).

12. *The hamlet of Winnowing Basket and Dipper.* These two lunar lodges represent the northeast (see table 16).

13. *Revolving and turning to the right.* That is, from East to West, according to the orientation of traditional Chinese cartography, where the West is on the "right."

17. *Above Pleiades and Net.* Pleiades (*mao*) and Net (*bi*) are the fourth and the fifth lunar lodges assigned to the western quarter of heaven. On the third day of the lunar month, the crescent Moon appears in the West (see 13:1–2).

20. *"Initial nine, withdrawn dragon."* Compare *Book of Changes*, hexagram Qian ䷀ (no. 1), first line: "Initial nine: Withdrawn dragon. Do not act" (see Wilhelm, 7); and the "Commentary on the Images": "The Yang is still below" (see Wilhelm, 373). See also the "Commentary on the Words of the Text": "This means a person who has the virtue of a dragon but remains concealed" (see Wilhelm, 379).

25. *"Nine in the second place, appearing dragon."* Compare *Book of Changes*, hexagram Qian, second line: "Nine in the second place: Dragon appearing in the field" (see Wilhelm, 8); and the "Commentary on the Images": "Already the influence of virtue reaches far" (see Wilhelm, 373). See also the "Commentary on the Words of the Text": "This means a man who has the virtue of a dragon but is moderate and correct" (see Wilhelm, 380).

26. *In harmony and equality there is light.* Compare the "Commentary on the Words of the Text" on the hexagram Qian, second line: "Dragon appearing in the field. Through him (i.e., through the "great man," *daren*) the whole world attains refinement and light" (see Wilhelm, 380).

29. *"Nine in the third place, at nightfall he is watchful."* Compare *Book of Changes*, hexagram Qian, third line: "Nine in the third place: All day long the noble man is creatively active. At nightfall he is watchful as if in danger" (see Wilhelm, 8). See also the "Commentary on the Words of the Text": "He is creatively active and, as circumstances demand, careful, so that even in a dangerous situation he does not make a mistake" (see Wilhelm, 381).

35. *"Nine in the fourth place, wavering flight."* Compare *Book of Changes*, hexagram Qian, fourth line: "Nine in the fourth place: Wavering flight over the depths" (see Wilhelm, 9); and the "Commentary on the Images": "Advance is not a mistake" (see Wilhelm, 374). See also the "Commentary on the Words of the Text": "In advance or retreat there is no permanence, except that one should not depart from one's fellows. . . . Here the way of the Creative (Qian) is about to transform itself" (see Wilhelm, 381 and 382).

37–38. Gen *rules over arrest and advance, so that nothing contravenes the timing.* Compare *Book of Changes*, "Commentary on the Judgement" on the hexagram Gen ☶ (no. 52): "Gen (Keeping Still) means stopping. When it is time to stop, then stop. When it is time to advance, then advance. Thus movement and quiescence do not miss the right time, and their course becomes bright and clear" (see Wilhelm, 653).

41. *"Nine in the fifth place, flying dragon."* Compare *Book of Changes*, hexagram Qian, fifth line: "Nine in the fifth place: Flying dragon in the heavens" (see Wilhelm, 9). See also the "Commentary on the Words of the Text": "This is the place appropriate to heavenly virtue" (see Wilhelm, 382).

47. *"Nine at the top, arrogant dragon."* Compare *Book of Changes*, hexagram Qian, sixth line: "Nine at the top: Arrogant dragon will have cause to repent" (see Wilhelm, 9); and the "Commentary on the Images": "What is at the full cannot last" (see Wilhelm, 375). See also the "Commentary on the Words of the Text": "In time he exhausts himself" (see Wilhelm, 383).

48. *Fighting for power in the wild.* Compare *Book of Changes*, hexagram Kun ☷ (no. 2), sixth line: "Dragons fighting in the plains. Their blood is black and yellow" (see Wilhelm, 15). These two colors are emblematic of Heaven and Earth, or Yang and Yin, respectively.

49–50. *"All nines," flutter flutter, are the compass and square of the Dao.* The expression "compass and square" (*guiju*) connotes the idea of a rule, standard, or law. Compare the "Commentary on the Words of the Text" on the hexagram Qian ☰ (no. 1), "All nines": "When Qian, the Origin, undergoes change in all the nines, one perceives the law of Heaven" (see Wilhelm, 383).

50. The "ancestor of change"

This section concludes the description of the monthly lunar cycle found in the previous section, and introduces the description of the annual solar cycle found in the next section. Its subject is the Yang line that rises and declines along the six lines of the hexagram Qian ☰, which illustrates the course of Yang during the six periods of the month (described in the previous section); and along the six lines of the twelve "sovereign hexagrams," which illustrate the course of Yang during the twelve months of the year (described in the next section).

The rise and decline of the Yang principle accord with the apparent rotation of the Northern Dipper, referred to here with the names of two of its stars, Jade-cog and Armil. Rotating around its own axis, the Dipper distributes the One Breath to the sectors of space and the nodes of time. This Breath sustains the world, and operates through and by means of the cycles of change produced by the alternation of Yin and Yang.

1. *Moving in a ring in accordance with Jade-cog and Armil. Xuan* (Jade-cog) and *ji* (Armil) are the second and the third stars in the constellation of the Northern Dipper. By extension, they also denote the first four stars of the Dipper (i.e., the so-called Head, *kui*), as well as the entire constellation.

2–3. *Rising and falling, ascending and descending, it flows in cycles through the six lines.* Compare 4:7–10: "The two functions have no fixed positions in the lines: 'flowing in cycles they go through the six empty spaces.' As their coming and going are not determinate, so too 'their ascent and descent are not constant.'" See also the passage of the "Appended Sayings" of the *Book of Changes* quoted in the note to 4:8.

51. The cycle of the Sun

After the descriptions of the ascent and descent of Yin and Yang during the day (sections 3 and 45) and the month (sections 13 and 49), the present section is concerned with the third major cosmological pattern described in the *Cantong qi*: the cycle of the Sun during the twelve months of the year.

Each stage of the cycle—which begins with the eleventh lunar month—is associated with one of twelve hexagrams of the *Book of*

Changes, one of the twelve pitch-pipes, and one of the twelve earthly branches (see also the Introduction, § 6). The hexagrams chosen to represent the months are the so-called "sovereign hexagrams" (*bigua*). Analogously to the six trigrams that represent the lunar phases (see sections 13 and 49), they illustrate the ascent and descent of Yin and Yang during the twelve months:

䷗	䷒	䷊	䷡	䷪	䷀	䷫	䷠	䷋	䷓	䷖	䷁
復	臨	泰	大壯	夬	乾	姤	遯	否	觀	剝	坤
fu	lin	tai	dazhuang	guai	qian	gou	dun	pi	guan	bo	kun

In the eleventh month, with Fu ䷗ (Return), the Yang principle is reborn and begins its new cycle of ascent and descent during the year. Lin ䷒ (Approach) rules on the twelfth and last month, which connects the current year ("what is above") to the upcoming year ("what is below"). In the first month of the new year, the Yang principle continues to grow ("looks upward") and reaches a correct state of balance with the Yin principle, represented by Tai ䷊ (Peace). In the second month, with Dazhuang ䷡ (Great Strength), Yang prevails over Yin: the days begin to grow longer and the nights to grow shorter. The Yin principle has retired but is still powerful; the elm seeds that "fall to the ground" represent the strength of Yin within Yang, and prepare its rebirth in the second half of the year. In the third month, corresponding to Guai ䷪ (Parting), the Yin principle has almost entirely vanished, and thus "the time has come for Yin to move into retreat." The fourth month is the sixth stage of the solar cycle; Yang reaches its culmination and is represented by Qian ䷀ (The Creative), the hexagram that depicts pure Yang.

Then the second half of the cycle starts. In the fifth month, with Gou ䷫ (Encounter), the Yang principle begins its descent, and the Yin principle begins its ascent; since Yin will overcome Yang, Yin is the "host" and Yang is the "guest." In the sixth month, ruled by Dun ䷠ (Withdrawal), the Yang principle, aware of its eventual obliteration, "leaves its worldly place." With Pi ䷋ (Obstruction), in the seventh month, the Yin principle continues to increase; for the Yang principle, this month marks the actual time of defeat, symbolized by the hexagram that represents the inversion of the correct relation between Yin and Yang. Guan ䷓ (Contemplation) rules on the eighth month, when Yin prevails over Yang. The Yang principle has retired, but paves the way for its rebirth and puts forth new sprouts, representing the strength of Yang within Yin. In the ninth month, corresponding to Bo ☷ (Splitting Apart), Yang is vanquished. In the tenth and last month, at the end of the solar cycle, Yin reigns alone and is represented by Kun ☷ (The Receptive), the hexagram that symbolizes pure Yin. Kun, however, fulfills her motherly function: "she receives Heaven in herself," and once again gives birth to the Yang principle.

3. *"Going out and coming in without error."* This sentence is quoted from the *Book of Changes*, "Judgement" on the hexagram Fu ☷ (no. 24): "Return: Success. Going out and coming in without error" (see Wilhelm, 97).

17. *As Yin and Yang conjoin.* Compare the "Image" on the hexagram Tai ☷ (no. 11) in the *Book of Changes*: "Heaven and Earth are conjoined: Peace" (see Wilhelm, 49).

18. *"The small departs, the great approaches."* This sentence is quoted from the *Book of Changes*, "Judgement" on the hexagram Tai: "Peace. The small departs, the great approaches. Good fortune and success" (see Wilhelm, 48). The "small" is the Yin principle, which is decreasing, and the "great" is the Yang principle, which is increasing.

25–26. *Punishment and virtue are opposed one to the other.* "Punishment" corresponds to Yin, the time of "taking life"; "virtue" corresponds to Yang, the time of "giving life." Since at this time Yin and Yang are still contending for supremacy, they are "opposed one to the other."

31. *Qian (The Creative) is strong, flourishing, and bright.* Compare the "Commentary on the Words of the Text" on the hexagram Qian ☰ (no. 1) in the *Book of Changes*: "Great indeed is Qian, the Origin! He is firm, strong, central, and upright; he is pure, incorrupt, and uncontaminated" (see Wilhelm, 378).

32. *And lays itself over the four neighborhoods.* "Four neighborhoods" (*silin*) connotes the four quarters of the world.

33. *Yang terminates at* si. In the cycle of the twelve "sovereign hexagrams," Qian represent the end of the ascent of the Yang principle, which occurs in the month marked by the earthly branch *si* 巳.

36. *For the first time "there is hoarfrost underfoot."* Compare *Book of Changes*, hexagram Kun ☷ (no. 2), first line: "When there is hoarfrost underfoot, solid ice is not far off" (see Wilhelm, 13).

37. *"In the well there is a clear, cold spring."* Compare *Book of Changes*, hexagram Jing ䷯ (The Well, no. 48), fifth line: "In the well there is a clear, cold spring from which one can drink" (see Wilhelm, 188). The well underneath the earth is the lowest Yin line of the hexagram Jing, whose nature is represented by the image of a cold spring.

45. *At Pi (Obstruction) there are stagnation and blockade.* Compare the "Commentary on the Judgement" on the hexagram Pi ䷋ (no. 12): "The great departs and the small approaches; therefore Heaven and Earth do not conjoin, and the ten thousand things are blocked off from each other" (see Wilhelm, 447).

57. *The vital Breath is drained.* Literally, the "transmuting Breath" or "Breath of transformation" (*huaqi*), the energy that gives birth to all forms of life and nourishes them.

59. *The course comes to its end and turns around.* Compare *Book of Changes*, "Appended Sayings": "When change comes to an end, it alters; as it alters, it has continuity; having continuity, it has duration" (B.2; see Wilhelm, 331–332). Compare also *Daode jing*, 40: "Return is the movement of the Dao."

62. *She receives Heaven in herself, allowing it to unfold.* Compare the "Commentary on the Judgement" on the hexagram Kun ䷁ (no. 2): "Perfect indeed is Kun, the Origin! The ten thousand things owe their birth to her, because she receives Heaven with devotion" (see Wilhelm, 386). See also the "Commentary on the Words of the Text" on the same hexagram: "The Way of Kun is following: she receives Heaven with devotion and moves in accordance with the time" (see Wilhelm, 392).

69–70. *"Going ahead of it brings on delusion" and you lose your track, "go behind it," and you are a ruler and a lord.* Compare the "Judgement" on the hexagram Kun: "If the noble man goes somewhere, going ahead brings delusion; going behind he finds guidance and benefit" (see Wilhelm, 11). The "Commentary on the Judgement" adds: "If the noble man goes somewhere, going ahead brings on delusion and he goes astray; going behind and following he finds constancy" (see Wilhelm, 388). See also *Daode jing*, 7: "Thus the saint places himself before by placing himself behind."

52. End and beginning

Change follows a cyclical course. After the path of the Sun reaches the stage represented by Kun (the tenth lunar month), it begins again from the stage represented by Fu (the eleventh lunar month). Like the other two main time cycles described in the *Cantong qi*—the day and the month—the cycle of the year provides an exemplary pattern for the ruler. By modeling his governance on the qualities of each stage, he grants harmony and permanence to his kingdom.

1. *"There is no plain that is not followed by a slope."* This sentence is quoted from the *Book of Changes*, hexagram Tai ䷊ (no. 11), third line, which continues by saying: "There is no going that is not followed by a return" (see Wilhelm, 50).

53. Non-Being and existence

Sections 53–61 concern the way of "superior virtue." This portion of the text begins with four sections (53–56) on the principles that govern birth and life.

To cultivate one's nature (*xing*) and life (*ming*), one should comprehend the circumstances that initiate existence. Existence originates in Non-Being; our birth is owed to the joining of the Original Essence (*yuanjing*) issued by Qian, the active principle, with the Original Breath (*yuanqi*) yielded by Kun, the passive principle. (See the "Appended Sayings" of the *Book of Changes*, A.4: "Essence and Breath become the creatures"; and *Cantong qi*, section 43: "Yang endows, Yin receives . . . unfolding their Essence and Breath.")

After we are generated, Yin and Yang govern our life. The Original Essence of Qian exists in us as the Yang Spirit, and the Original Breath of Kun, as the Yin Spirit. The Yang Spirit and the Yin Spirit manifest themselves as the *hun* and the *po* souls, respectively. In the first place, *hun* and *po* are one, just like Qian and Kun; after they emerge as separate entities, they operate through one another.

1–2. *In order to nourish your nature, prolong your life and hold off the time of death.* In addition to the translation given above, these verses have been understood in two other ways. At the basis of these different interpretations is the question of whether the cultivation of *xing* ("inner nature") should precede or follow the cultivation of *ming* ("life, existence," or in certain contexts, "vital force"). This was one of the points under discussion within the Neidan traditions, to which most commentators of the *Cantong qi* belonged. According to the first view, the two verses are understood as: "In order to nourish your nature (*xing*), [and then] prolong your life (*ming*) holding off the time of death . . ." According to the second view, they are understood as: "In order to nourish your nature (*xing*), [first] prolong your life (*ming*) and hold off the time of death . . ." The translation given above attempts to express the possible dual meaning of the two verses.

3–4. *Attentively reflect upon the end and duly ponder what comes before.* According to one of the interpretations of this passage, the words *hou* ("after," in the compound *houmo* "end") and *xian* ("before") respectively refer to the postcelestial and the precelestial states of being (*houtian* and *xiantian*).

7. *As the Original Essence spreads like the clouds.* Compare *Book of Changes*, "Commentary on the Judgement" on the hexagram Qian ☰ (no. 1): "Great indeed is Qian, the Origin! . . . Like clouds passing and rain being distributed, all the individual things flow into form" (see Wilhelm, 370).

9. *Yin and Yang set the measures.* Compare 3:11: "The Sun and the Moon set periods and measures."

54. Nature and qualities

One's true nature (*xing*) should be guarded and fostered. The individual "qualities," or *qing*, provide protection for it, and allow it to manifest itself, to different degrees of actuality, in the external world. These qualities pertain to the sphere of individual existence (*ming*); they embrace a wide range of features, including the outward personality or temperament, feelings, emotions, desires, and passions. In the postcelestial world in which we live, it is these properties of *qing*— which include love, in all of its aspects—that induce the conjunction of precelestial Qian and Kun: the coupling of the male and the female leads to the birth of a new life. (*)

(*) Liu Yiming writes in his commentary to this section: "Man and woman join one another because of their *qing*, like Qian above and Kun below."

6. *Can people be secure*. The expression *renwu*, rendered here as "people," can also mean "people and things."

55. Water, the beginning

As does the passage of the *Book of Changes* from which verses 1 and 3 derive, the first stanza of this section describes the process that create life. Qian is movement, Kun is quiescence. Complying with their natures and qualities, Qian gives forth the Essence that generates life, and entrusts it to Kun; Kun receives the Essence of Qian, and brings creation to achievement.

The joining of essence and substance, or male and female, is in the first place a return to the state of Unity of Qian and Kun. This process can be portrayed in several ways, two of which are alluded to in the present section. The second stanza uses images related to the numeric values of the five agents. Unity here is not represented by Soil, which stands for the joining of Qian and Kun per se, but by Water, the first agent in the cosmogonic sequence (see section 22): the conjunction of Qian and Kun is now the precondition for the creation of a new life, the first stage of a process that awaits its unfolding, a reiteration of the process that leads to the birth of the whole cosmos.

The symbolism of verses 7–8 is complex, but deserves attention as this passage of the *Cantong qi* is quoted in several later texts. The return of the four external agents—Water, Fire, Wood, and Metal—to the state of Unity is described as "the 9 reverts, the 7 returns, the 8 goes back, the 6 remains." These sentences refer to the "generation" and "accomplishment" numbers (*shengshu* and *chengshu*) of the agents, which respectively are 1 and 6 for Water, 2 and 7 for Fire, 3 and 8 for Wood, and 4 and 9 for Metal (see table 4). The state of Unity, to which the four external agents must return in order to generate life, is represented by number 1, which belongs to Water. Therefore Metal (9) "reverts," Fire (7) "returns," and Wood (8) "goes back" to the 1 of Water. Instead, Water (6) owns number 1 as its "generation" number; since it does not need to perform any movement, it "remains."

In the third stanza, the male and female principles are represented by the respective essences, semen and blood. Their colors, white and red, are associated with the agents Metal and Fire. These images lead to another description of the same process, based on the sequence of conquest among the agents (see table 3). Metal and Fire contend with one another, until Fire conquers Metal; then Water conquers Fire. Here Water is again the symbol of the return of Qian and Kun to the state of Unity, the very instant in which a new life is generated. Then this Unity "alters itself and distributes by parting": duality and multiplicity emerge, and life begins its course.

1. *"Qian is movement and is straight."* This sentence derives from the "Appended Sayings" of the *Book of Changes*: "Qian is collected in a state of quiescence, and straight in a state of movement" (A.5; see Wilhelm, 301).

3. *"Kun is quiescence and is gathered."* This sentence derives from the "Appended Sayings": "Kun is gathered in a state of quiescence, and open in a state of movement" (A.5; see Wilhelm, 301).

13. *"Superior goodness is like water."* This sentence is quoted from the *Daode jing*: "Superior goodness is like water. Water is good at giving benefit to the ten thousand things without contending, and dwells in places that all people dislike; therefore it is close to the Dao" (sec. 8).

16. *But True Unity can hardly be charted.* Compare 14:3–4: "Original Essence is subtle and can hardly be beheld; infer its rules and attest its tokens"; 37:15–16: "What has form is easy to gauge, but the signless can hardly be envisaged"; and 43:9: "Mysterious and obscure, this can hardly be fathomed."

56. The birth of the embryo

This section concludes the description of the origins of life that had begun in section 53. Its purport is clear: the embryo, produced by the joining of Yin (the "black") and Yang (the "white"), grows until it comes to life. Later commentators and authors belonging to the Neidan traditions have seen in this section a description of the generation of the Internal Elixir, with its three stages: conception, gestation, and birth. In this, as in many other instances, the *Cantong qi* has provided a model that the later tradition has applied to the alchemical process.

9. *"Its bones are weak" and are pliant.* This verse is partly quoted from the *Daode jing*: "Holding the fullness of virtue is being similar to an

infant. . . . Its bones are weak, its sinews are yielding, but its grasp is tight" (sec. 55).

57. The Breaths of Yin and Yang

All things and phenomena within the cosmos and the human being occur through the operation of Yin and Yang. The *yangsui* and the *fangzhu* bronze mirrors illustrate the principle that things of the same kind or "category" (*lei*) respond to one another (see section 35). The *yangsui* is round like Heaven, and receives the essence of the Yang principle (fire), which is sent forth by the Sun; the *fangzhu* is square like Earth, and gathers the essence of the Yin principle (water or dew), which is sent forth by the Moon.

The fire and the water obtained by means of these mirrors demonstrate that the Breaths of Yin and Yang extend their influence throughout the cosmos. If the Sun and the Moon, which are so remote from us, produce those transformations, how much more can be achieved by the Breaths of Yin and Yang that innately reside within the human being?

9. *"Yin and Yang match the Sun and the Moon."* Compare the "Appended Sayings" of the *Book of Changes*: "The meaning of Yin and Yang matches the Sun and the Moon" (A.5; see Wilhelm, 302).

58. The three treasures

Sections 58–60, which are closely related to sections 18–19, describe other features of the path of superior virtue. The "three treasures" spoken of here are the "three luminaries" of section 18: the ears, the eyes, and the mouth, respectively corresponding to the functions of hearing, seeing, and speaking. These treasures should be guarded and cherished, and their light should be turned within.

The mention of Breath (*qi*) in conjunction with Li ☲, the trigram that represents the eyes, shows that this passage refers to certain fundamental correspondences that pertain to the Taoist view of the human being:

(1) The ears are represented by Kan ☵ (Water, Yin), which is placed below (in correspondence with the lower Cinnabar Field) and holds the Original Essence (*yuanjing*).

(2) The eyes are represented by Li ☲ (Fire, Yang), which is placed above (in correspondence with the upper Cinnabar Field) and holds the Original Breath (*yuanqi*).

(3) The mouth is represented by Dui ☱ (Metal), which is placed in the center (in correspondence with the middle Cinnabar Field) and holds the Original Spirit (*yuanshen*).

When the "three treasures" are secured, Essence does not flow downward, as water does, but instead ascends; Breath does not rise upward, as fire does, but instead descends; and one's individual traits (*qing*, i.e., attitudes, temperament, personality, and other features related to one's individual existence) do not spring forth as emotions or passions, but emerge as qualities that enable Spirit, or one's own true nature (*xing*), to operate.

The true nature is referred to in this passage as the True Man. Withdrawn "in the depths of the abyss" (compare the expression "sinking into the ground" in section 18), the True Man leads his carriage (see sections 2 and 43) and meets no obstructions. Quiescence and activity are equivalent for him, and he enters and exits the world without distinction. Seeing, hearing, and speaking are turned inward: he watches and listens to the boundless, and communicates with it in words that no one can hear.

2. *Shut them, and let nothing pass through.* Compare 18:5: "Shut the openings," and the passage of *Daode jing*, 52, quoted in the notes to section 18.

3–4. *The True Man withdraws in the depths of the abyss; drifting and roaming, he keeps to the compass.* Compare 24:1–4: "The True Man is supremely wondrous: sometimes he is, sometimes he is not. Barely perceptible within the great abyss, now he sinks, now he wafts." For "keeping to the compass," see the note to the next verse.

5. *Watch and listen while wheeling around.* The images of the carriage and its driver occur again in this section. For the expressions "wheeling around" (*xuanqu*) in this verse and "keeping to the compass" (*shou guizhong*) in the previous verse, compare this passage of the *Liezi* that describes the art of charioteering as a metaphor of the state of the True Man: "What you sense within in your innermost heart will accord outside with the horse's temper. In this way you will be able to drive back and forth as straight as a stretched cord, and *wheel around as exactly as a compass*" (5.185; see Graham, 114).

6. *And opening and closing will always accord.* According to the explications given by Liu Yiming, this verse means that the two phases of activity and inactivity are fulfilled in a non-dual state. In his commentary, Liu Yiming defines this state as follows: "'One's mind (*xin*) is dead and one's Spirit lives; one severs evil and preserves sincerity; one neither forgets nor assists." In his commentary to the *Awakening to Reality* (*Wuzhen pian*), Liu Yiming also makes clear that the two movements of "opening and closing" are parallel to, or even synonymous of, movement and quiescence: "Opening and closing are timely; movement and quiescence are spontaneous" (commentary to "Qiyan jueju," poem no. 33) Here Liu Yiming certainly alludes to the present section of the *Cantong qi*, which mentions "opening and closing" in verse 6, and "movement and quiescence" in verse 8.

59. Achieving constancy

Those who attain the realized state guard the "three treasures" and turn their light within. Being focused on the Heart, the center of the human being, they do not let their sight, hearing, and voice drive them astray; whether they are in the states of wake or sleep, they do not lose their union with Spirit and their awareness of the unity of existence and extinction. Even their physical features benefit from this: the negative qualities that, in the relative domain, are associated with the Yin principle are removed, and are replaced by the corresponding qualities associated with the Pure Yang, the state prior to the emergence of duality.

5. *Going back and forth brings obstruction.* Lit., "if you experience difficulties, they are due to movement," i.e., to the operation of thinking.

10. *And your bones will grow solid and strong.* Lit., "and your bones and joints will grow solid and strong."

12. *You can establish pure Yang.* "Pure" is only one of several meanings of the words *zheng*. Other senses include "correct, upright, right, proper, aligned," etc. In this verse, *zhengyang* is equivalent to *chunyang*, the term that ordinarily denotes the state of Pure Yang, before the One divides itself into the two.

60. The breathing of the True Man

This section describes the way of breathing of the True Man. His breath is joined with the One Breath, and circulates within his entire person. This is not a description of a practice: it happens spontaneously to the realized beings who take the operation of the Dao as a model for their operation in the world.

5. *It will stream from the head to the toes.* Compare the *Zhuangzi*: "The True Man breathes through the heels" (6.228; trans. Watson, 78).

9–10. *Return is the attestation of the Dao, weakness is "the handle of virtue."* For these verses, compare *Daode jing*, 40: "Return is the movement of the Dao, weakness is the operation of the Dao"; and the *Book of Changes*, "Appended Sayings": "The hexagram Modesty (Qian ䷎, no. 15) is the handle of virtue; the hexagram Return (Fu ䷗, no. 24) is the fundament of virtue" (B.6; see Wilhelm, 345).

61. Incorrect practices

As it does in Book 1 (see section 26), the description of the way of superior virtue in Book 2 ends with a warning against the performance of incorrect practices. The "minor arts" (*xiaoshu*) are methods such as those mentioned in section 26. From the perspective of the *Cantong qi*, those practices seem to be easier than alchemy, but do not afford real benefits. On the contrary, using True Yin and Yang may at first appear to be more difficult, but is in fact easier because the Elixir is based on the same principles that generate and nourish life.

6. *Or the deaf bent on listening to the* shang *and the* gong. *Gong* and *shang* are the first and the second notes in the Chinese musical scale.

62. Compounding the Elixir

The remainder of Book 2 (sections 62–74) is concerned with alchemy. The present section reiterates the main features of the alchemical process already illustrated in sections 39–40. It describes the conjunction of True Yin and True Yang, the Flowing Pearl and the Golden Flower, volatile mercury and firm lead. The volatilization of Mercury when it is heated illustrates the principle that True Yin, by its own nature, tends to leave and become dispersed.

The Flowing Pearl is True Yin and True Mercury; it is the central Yin line within Li ☲, the trigram associated with cinnabar and the agent Fire, which in turn are emblems of Great Yang (*taiyang*); hence the name Flowing Pearl of Great Yang. The Golden Flower is True Yang and True Lead; it is the central Yang line within Kan ☵, the trigram associated with black lead and the agent Water, which are emblems of Great Yin (*taiyin*). When the Golden Flower is heated, it liquefies and takes on a white color (white is the color of Metal, the agent corresponding to True Lead). Then it joins with the Flowing Pearl, which as a consequence will not escape and vanish. The two ingredients coagulate into a dry amalgam, merging their natures and their qualities. The amalgam is pounded and is placed in the tripod. Controlled and nurtured by fire, which at first should be as mild as a "loving mother" and then as vigorous as a "stern father," the Pearl and the Flower transmute themselves into the Golden Elixir.

5–6. *They transform into a white liquid, coagulate and are perfectly solid.* The two stages of alchemical transmutation (liquid and solid: *solve et coagula*) are also mentioned in 39:15–16: "First it liquefies, then coagulates; it is given the name Yellow Carriage."

7. *The Golden Flower is the first to sing.* The compound *xianchang*, literally translated as "is the first to sing," means "to take the lead."

10. *Horse-tooth and* langgan. *Langgan* is a mythical gemstone, said to be found on Mount Kunlun at the center of the world. In his commentary, Liu Yiming explains that this verse describes the appearance of Metal: "Horse-tooth is a metaphor of its strength and whiteness; *langgan* is a metaphor of its warmth and softness." Note, in addition, that *chi* (tooth) is a synonym of *ya*, and thus alludes to *huangya* ("yellow sprout"), a name of True Metal; see the notes to section 22.

11. *The Yang is next to join it.* "Yang" here refers to the Flowing Pearl of Great Yang.

14. *Seize it and store it within the Forbidden Gates.* "Forbidden gates" (*jinmen*) is a common name for the king's or the emperor's palace. In a Waidan reading, this term refers to the tripod; in a Neidan reading, to the lower Cinnabar Field.

63. The Three Fives

In addition to the alchemical emblems, the compounding of the Elixir can also be described by means of the five agents. The most common arrangement of the agents is the generation sequence (*xiangsheng*), in which Water generates Wood, Wood generates Fire, Fire generates Soil, Soil generates Metal, and Metal generates Water. Instead of this sequence, the alchemical process utilizes two others. The first is the conquest sequence (*xiangke*), in which Water is conquered by Soil, Soil is conquered by Wood, Wood is conquered by Metal, Metal is conquered by Fire, and Fire is conquered by Water. The second consists of the reversal of the generation sequence, in which, in particular, Fire generates Wood, and Water generates Metal. The two quatrains of this section are respectively devoted to these two sequences.

The first quatrain mentions Metal, Wood, and Fire (the agents that correspond to the subjects of section 62): the Golden Flower is Metal, the Flowing Pearl is Wood, and fire makes their conjunction possible. The conquest sequence is at work here; yet in the alchemical process, the "conquest" does not merely cause the extinction of the individual ingredients, but also their transmutation into the Elixir. When the Golden Flower (Metal) is heated in the tripod, it undergoes liquefaction ("Fire by its nature melts Metal"); only because it has been subjugated by fire can it join the Flowing Pearl. Similarly, when the Flowing Pearl (Wood) is controlled by the Golden Flower, it flourishes instead of vanishing ("when Metal cuts it, Wood blooms"); only then can the Golden Flower and the Flowing Pearl merge in the Elixir.

The other sequence active in the alchemical process is based on the inversion of the generation sequence. Water, instead of being generated by Metal, generates Metal; and Fire, instead of being generated by Wood, generates Wood. In other words, Yin generates True Yang, and Yang generates True Yin. This configuration is expressed in the sentence "The Three Fives combine into One," which alludes to the numeric values of the agents. The pair made of Wood (3) and Fire (2) forms the first 5; the pair made of Water (1) and Metal (4) forms the second 5; and the central Soil, of its own, is the third 5, representing the Oneness of the five agents and the Unity underlying multiplicity. The alchemical process first restores Yin and Yang to their authentic state, represented by Wood and Metal, then joins the Two into the One. As the last quatrain points out, this is the secret of the alchemical work.

64. Inverting the course

This section uses other cosmological emblems to illustrate the alchemical process and the principles of "conquest" and "inversion." The twelve earthly branches, arranged in a circle, represent the whole compass of space and a complete time cycle. Among the branches, *zi* 子 corresponds to Water, and *wu* 午 corresponds to Fire; *mao* 卯 corresponds to Wood, and *you* 酉 corresponds to Metal.

When the circular pattern of the twelve branches is used to represent the alchemical process, the sequence is reversed compared to the customary cycle (see table 14; another description of this cycle is found in section 73). Starting at *zi* 子 (the branch emblematic of the North, which traditional Chinese cartography places at the bottom), it moves westward (i.e., to the right) to reach *you* 酉 (West) and then *wu* 午 (South, at the top), where it ends the ascending phase. Then from *wu* it continues its rotation, proceeding eastward to *mao* 卯 (East), and terminating at *zi* to complete the descending phase. The first half of the cycle is governed by the Yang principle: Water (*zi*) generates Metal (True Yang) at due West, the position corresponding to *you* 酉. Analogously, the second half is governed by the Yin principle: Fire (*wu*) generates Wood (True Yin) at due East, the position corresponding to *mao* 卯. In the first half of the cycle, *you* is prominent and thus is the "host," *mao* is subordinate and thus is the "guest"; in the second half, vice versa, *mao* is the "host" and *you* is the "guest." Therefore "the host and the guest are two."

In addition, *mao* 卯 and *you* 酉 perform another function: they are the boundaries between Yin and Yang, the intermediate positions of balance between them. When the alchemical process is represented in this way, *mao* and *you* are the locations in which Yin and Yang conjoin. Their union is represented as the union of Dragon (Wood, True Mercury) and Tiger (Metal, True Lead). The principle of inversion is again at work, for a Yang emblem (the Dragon) denotes True Yin, and a Yin emblem (the Tiger) denotes True Yang.

Among the planets, Mars (the Sparkling Wonderer, *yinghuo*) corresponds to Fire, and Venus (the Great White, *taibai*) corresponds to Metal. The description given in this section alludes to the exchange of their positions, and again applies the conquest sequence of the five agents. Since Fire subdues Metal, Mars takes the place that belongs to Metal in the West; since Metal subdues Wood, Venus "across the sky" takes the place that belongs to Wood in the East. When the "life-taking Breath" of True Lead (Venus) subdues True Mercury (Mars), the Elixir is achieved.

The different phenomena of conquest and defeat among agents and ingredients in the alchemical process are comparable to those that occur in nature, where each individual component plays its active or passive role without conceit or objection.

4. *The host and the guest are two.* Lit., "the host and the guest have two names," with reference to the fact that both *mao* and *you* are "hosts" and "guests" in the first and the second halves of the cycle.

11. *Sparkling Wonderer keeps to the West.* "Sparkling Wonderer" (*yinghuo*) is the name of Mars. This planet is associated with the South (Yang), but is mentioned here as an image of Yang (Fire) generating True Yin (True Mercury).

65. Erroneous alchemical methods

Once more, the *Cantong qi* admonishes against the performance of practices based on erroneous theories. With regard to alchemy, the only correct practice is the one that applies the principles described in the previous sections. There is no need of searching for minerals and metals that are hard to find in order to compound the Elixir: its ingredients are only True Yin and True Yang.

6. *Millions are those who have devoted themselves to this Art.* In premodern Chinese, *yi* can mean both "one million" and "one hundred thousand."

66. The course of all things

One's focused intention and the teachings of a master are required to comprehend the fundament of all things. Creatures, objects, and phenomena arise by receiving the essence from Qian, the father, and by taking form through Kun, the mother. Having been generated, they are bound to the laws of the cosmos, exemplified by the generation and the conquest cycles of the five agents.

1. *If you look into this and have the blessed encounter. Shen* is translated here as a verb meaning "to examine, look into." According to another interpretation, it is an adverb and the verse means: "If you truly have the blessed encounter." — The expression *zaofeng*, translated as "blessed encounter," is found in several Han and later texts to mean the encounter with a master, usually seen as a result of predestination. Compare the similar expression "unexpected encounter" (*xiehou*) found in 36:3.

9. *Essence coagulates and they flow into form.* "Flow into form" (*liuxing*) is a set phrase that refers to the coming to life of all things. It is found, for example, in the *Book of Changes*, "Commentary on the Judgement" on the hexagram Qian ☰ (no. 1): "Great indeed is Qian, the Origin! The ten thousand things owe their beginning to him, and thus he permeates Heaven. Like clouds passing and rain being distributed, all the individual things flow into form" (see Wilhelm, 370).

10. *Metals and minerals do not decay.* Several commentators suggest that this verse should be understood as a metaphor: "like metals and minerals they (i.e., the five agents) do not decay."

67. The perfect image of Heaven and Earth

The subject of this section is the principle of "non-doing" (*wuwei*), the self-less, coincident, and indispensable response to any circumstance that arises. "Non-doing" is the perfection of "doing." Shadow and echo exemplify this principle, which governs the operation of Heaven and Earth: "The Dao constantly does not do, yet there is nothing that is not done" (*Daode jing*, 37).

To comply with this principle, the alchemical work must conform to the rule of "belonging to the same kind" (*tonglei*, see section 35 above). Only the Elixir made of True Lead and True Mercury accords with that rule. Using ingredients, either material or immaterial, that do not accord with it would bear harmful consequences. Ultimately, the same principle of "response" would be at work in that case as well; but instead of granting eternal life, it would lead to inevitable death. When that happens, even kings, masters, physicians, or sorcerers could not be of any help.

5–6. And yet, if you take an inch of yege *or an ounce of* badou. *Yege* and *badou* are identified as the elegant jessamine and the croton seeds, respectively. Both are poisonous.

10–13. King Wen of the Zhou can sort out the stalks . . . and shaman Xian can beat on his drum. King Wen and Confucius are both attributed with the authorship of parts of the *Book of Changes* (see the comments to section 37). "Stalks" refers to the milfoil stalks used in divination, and "images" to the trigrams and hexagrams. Bian Que is a legendary doctor said to have lived around 500 BCE. Wu Xian is a "shaman" who owns multiple identities and reappears at different historical or pseudo-historical times.

68. The Lovely Maid and the Yellow Sprout

The Lovely Maid of the River (*heshang chanü*) is True Mercury; she is the Yin line within Li ☲, referred to as the "second daughter" in the terminology of the *Book of Changes*. Aroused by fire, she escapes and flies away. Only the Yellow Sprout (*huangya*), which is True Lead, can hold her. When they meet, they join and generate the Elixir.

The argument poetically expressed in these verses resounds at different levels and can be understood in different ways. From the perspective of the *Cantong qi*, all of them are instances of one and the same principle. In a material sense, the Lovely Maid of the River can be mercury, which escapes (volatilizes) when it is heated by fire. In a spiritual sense, referred to the human being, the Lovely Maid can refer to sentiments and passions. When one's own Fire is used to stimulate those sentiments and passions, they escape and run uncontrolled. When they are presided over by one's own True Nature (Lead, the Yellow Sprout), they turn into qualities—instincts, intuitions, propensities—that express one's Nature.

69. "Heaven and Earth as they are of themselves"

When the male and female principles conjoin, each finds in the other not only its match, but in the first place its own truth. This joining is the foundation of life, and no teaching or technique is necessary to make it happen. It occurs naturally as long as both parts fulfill the requirement of belonging to the "same kind" (*tonglei*, see section 35).

This section provides several examples of this principle: natural phenomena like fire and water; the conjunction of man and woman; and the processes that lead to birth and death. The three similar sentences found at the end of the last three stanzas —"No teacher instructs them to behave in that way . . . No skill and no craft is required to be accomplished in this . . . It is not our father and mother who teach us to do so"—clearly express the gist of this section.

7. *The 3 and the 5 did not merge with each other.* The expression "3 and 5" (*sanwu*) denotes Yin and Yang and their joining. The respective numeric values of Water and Fire are 1 and 2, which together make 3. The numeric value of Soil, representing the merging of Yin and Yang, is 5.

9–10. *The Essences emanated and transformed are Heaven and Earth as they are of themselves.* Qian ☰ "emanates" or "gives forth" (*shi*), Kun ☷ "transmutes" or "transforms" (i.e., "gives life," *hua*). Compare 10:6–7 ("the masculine Yang spreads his mysterious emanation, the feminine Yin transforms her yellow wrap"), 48:6 ("their emanations and transformations flow and spread all through"), and 55:5–6 ("the firm gives forth and then recedes, the yielding transmutes and thereby nurtures").

11–12. *Fire stirs and blazes by rising up, water streams and wets by flowing down.* For the passage of the *Book of Documents* (*Shujing*) at the origin of these verses, see the notes to 35:13–14 above.

15. *"They owe their beginning to this," and are permeated and made good by it.* Compare *Book of Changes*, "Commentary on the Judgement" on the hexagram Qian ☰ (no. 1): "Great indeed is Qian, the Origin! The ten thousand things owe their beginning to him, and thus he permeates Heaven" (see Wilhelm, 370).

19. *The firm and the yielding are bound to one another.* Compare the similar sentences found in the "Appended Sayings" of the *Book of Changes*: "The firm and the yielding stroke one another" (A.1; not translated by Wilhelm); "The firm and the yielding follow one another" (A.2 and B.1; see Wilhelm, 288 and 325); and "The firm and the yielding change into one another" (B.7; see Wilhelm, 348).

20. *"And cannot be untied."* This sentence is quoted from the *Daode jing*: "Those who are good at binding need no cords and knots, yet what they bind cannot be untied" (sec. 27).

24–25. *Males face downward after birth, females lie reclined on their back.* This statement is said to reflect the notion that the Yang *qi* in men gathers in the front of the body, while the Yin *qi* in women gathers in the back of the body.

70. "When Yang loses its token"

When the relations among the eight trigrams are represented by means of those within a family, Qian ☰ (Heaven) is the father and Kun ☷ (Earth) is the mother; Kan ☵ (the Moon) is the middle son and Li ☲ (the Sun) is the middle daughter (see table 5). The male and female natures of Kan and Li depend on the nature of their inner lines.

The inner lines of Kan and Li also represent the exchange of essences between Qian and Kun. The Sun emanates its light upon the Moon (the essence given forth by Qian is the inner line of Li), and the Moon receives the light of the Sun (the essence acquired by Kun is the inner line of Kan). If the bond between Yin and Yang complies with the proper rules—one "gives forth" and the other "receives" along their regular cycles of ascent and descent—Yin and Yang suffer no damage: the Sun and the Moon "are not harmed, not depleted."

The event that occurs at the end of each lunar cycle illustrates the potential negative consequences of the Yin principle overcoming the Yang principle. During the second half of the month, the power of Yin progressively increases and the power of Yang decreases. At the end of the month, Yang entirely "loses its token," and the complete supremacy of Yin brings about darkness and stagnation. It is only because the Sun and the Moon newly join to one another in the night between the end of the month and the beginning of the next month that the balance between Yin and Yang is restored, and life can continue. At that time, the Yin principle receives again the essence of the Yang principle, and a new time cycle is generated (see sections 10 and 48).

This example shows that the male and the female should constantly be joined to each other, and exchange their breaths "in accordance with their kind." This is possible only if they comply with the natures and the qualities of Qian and Kun, to which they owe their existence.

1–2. *Kan is man and is the Moon, Li is woman and is the Sun.* Compare 7:1–2: "*Wu* in Kan ☵ is the essence of the Moon, *ji* in Li ☲ is the radiance of the Sun."

7. *When Yang loses its token.* It might seem possible to introduce the translation of this verse with "if" instead of "when." The event described here, however, is deemed to regularly occur between the end of each lunar cycle and the beginning of the next one. At that time, the Yang principle loses its power, and is momentarily overcome by the Yin principle until the two newly join to create the next time cycle (see sections 10 and 48).

14. *Inhaling and exhaling onto one another, each nourishing the other.* The compound word *hantu* is translated literally as "inhaling and exhaling," but also means "to nurture" and "to harmonize."

71. "If man goes past the measure"

The notions treated in the previous section are illustrated again with an example drawn from the five agents and their cycles of generation and conquest. In the generation sequence, Metal gives birth to Water. By its nature, water—an image of the Yin principle—tends to "flow everywhere." In the figurative language of the five agents, its rampant spread should be controlled by the firmness of the central Soil, which is generated by Fire and therefore, in this emblematic configuration, represents the essence of the Yang principle. In the conquest cycle of the five agents, Soil conquers Water, which thus "can proceed no further."

Analogously, but from the opposite point of view, the Yin principle should exercise proper control on the Yang principle, which by its nature tends to exceed in giving forth its essence. If this happens, Yin (here represented by the *po* "earthly" soul) should "latch" Yang (the *hun* "celestial" soul) to prevent Yang from squandering its power.

Only when Yin and Yang are properly balanced, following their natural cycles of predominance and subordination, can each of them join with the other.

3–4. *When Fire transforms into Soil, water can proceed no further.* Compare 32:9–10: "Water treats Soil as its demon: when soil invades, water cannot rise."

72. "The three things are one family"

The Elixir is made of two ingredients, which in terms of the five agents respectively correspond to Metal and Wood, and in alchemical terms respectively correspond to True Lead and True Mercury. In the generative sequence of the agents, Metal generates Water, and Wood generates Fire. Through the inversion of this sequence that occurs in the alchemical process, Water (Yin) generates Metal (True Yang), and Fire (Yang) generates Wood (True Yin). In the language of alchemy, "black lead" (Water, Yin) generates True Lead (Metal, True Yang), and cinnabar (Fire, Yang) generates True Mercury (Wood, True Yin).

This inversion causes the postcelestial (*houtian*) aspects of Yin and Yang to be reintegrated within their precelestial (*xiantian*) aspects, which are of the opposite signs: the postcelestial Yin (Water) returns to precelestial True Yang (Metal), and the postcelestial Yang (Fire) returns to True Yin (Wood). The precosmic and cosmic aspects of Yin and Yang are now joined again to one another: "Metal and Water dwell in conjunction, Wood and Fire are companions."

Since the four initial elements are merged "in indistinction," they are reduced to two, symbolized by the Yang Dragon (whose numerical emblem is 3) and the Yin Tiger (whose numerical emblem is 4). With the addition of the central Soil, which enables True Yin and True Yang to conjoin, there are three sets, each of which has a numerical value of 5. The first set is made of Water and Metal (1+4); the second, of Fire and Wood (2+3); and the third, only of Soil (5). The main symbolic associations of each element are shown below:

(1)	WATER	1	north	dark warrior	black lead	kidneys	son
	METAL	4	west	white tiger	true lead	lungs	mother
(2)	FIRE	2	south	vermilion sparrow	cinnabar	heart	daughter
	WOOD	3	east	green dragon	true mercury	liver	father
(3)	SOIL	5	center	yellow dragon		spleen	forefather

The next verses mention the standard associations of the five viscera (liver, heart, spleen, lungs, and kidneys) with the five agents, here represented by their colors (green, red, yellow, white, and black) and by the family relations that occur among them (father, daughter, "forefather," mother, and son). (*) The verse translated as "the son is at the origin of the five agents" can be understood in two ways, and the double meaning is certainly intended. In the first sense, zi 子 means "son"; the son is Water, which is generated by the One and is the first element in the "cosmogonic sequence" of the five agents (see above the notes to section 22). In the second sense, zi 子 is the name of the first earthly branch (see table 13), and the verse should be translated as "*zi* is the origin of the five agents." In any of the two interpretations, the sense is the same: *zi* is the branch emblematic of the North, and the North corresponds to the agent Water.

The final two verses reiterate the reversion process: from 5 to 3 (Metal and Water; Wood and Fire; Soil), and from 3 to 1, when True Yin and True Yang are joined to one another in the Elixir. The One is indicated by *wu* 戊 and *ji* 己, the two celestial stems that represent Soil with its Yin and Yang halves.

(*) The associations of the five viscera with the five agents will play an important role in Neidan, where the Elixir is often said to be formed by joining the "fire of the heart," which holds True Yin, with the "water of the kidneys," which holds True Yang.

5. *These four, in indistinction.* This expression is also found in 43:13 with reference to Qian ☰, Kun ☷, Kan ☵, and Li ☲.

9–13. *The liver is green and is the father . . . The spleen is yellow and is the forefather.* For the variants found in these verses among different redactions of the *Cantong qi*, see the Textual Notes.

73. Inverting the course

This section is based on the same principles described in section 64. In the postcelestial domain, any time cycle—the day, the month, or the year—can be represented by a circle marked by the twelve earthly branches (see tables 13–14). The branches *zi* 子, *mao* 卯, *wu* 午, and *you* 酉 are placed at the four directions (North, East, South, and West) and correspond to four of the five agents (Water, Wood, Fire, and Metal). The first and the second halves of each cycle are ruled by the Yang and the Yin principle, respectively. Yang rises from *zi* in the North (placed "below" in traditional Chinese cartography), goes through *mao* in the East (placed on the left), and reaches completion at *wu* in the South (placed "above"); then it begins to decline. At that time, the Yin principle begins to rise; from *wu* in the South, it goes through *you* in the West (on the right), and culminates at *zi* in the North.

This "leftward" rotation is the customary route of the Yin and Yang Breaths in the postcelestial world. The cycle goes through the agents according to the sequence of generation—in particular, Wood is followed by Fire, and Metal is followed by Water—and replicates the ordinary course of the corresponding natural elements: Water flows downward (from North to South), and Fire rises upward (from South to North).

In alchemy, the sequence is inverted. The Breaths of Yin and Yang follow a "rightward" rotation: the Yang principle grows from *zi* to *you* and culminates at *wu*, the Yin principle grows from *wu* to *mao* and culminates at *zi*. The courses of Water and Fire are also reversed: Water moves upward, and Fire moves downward. Therefore *zi* (the branch associated with Water) now looks as though it is in the South, and *wu* (Fire) looks as though it is in the North.

When the inverted course reaches *you* and *mao*, Water generates Metal, and Fire generates Wood. This corresponds to the inversion of the sequence of generation: Yin generates True Yang, and Yang generates True Yin; alchemically, black lead generates True Lead, and cinnabar generates True Mercury. In the cycle of the year, these two times respectively correspond to the second lunar month, when the Northern Dipper points to *mao*, and to the eighth lunar month, when it points to *you*. During these months, the Yin "life-taking breath" (*shaqi*, "punishment") is born on the spring equinox, and the "life-giving breath" (*shengqi*, "virtue") is born on the autumn equinox. True Yin and *mao* correspond to the Dragon, and True Yang and *you* correspond to the Tiger. The positions of Dragon and Tiger are also inverted: the Dragon is in the West instead of the East, and the Tiger is in the East instead of the West. Now the Dragon (Yang) has become an emblem of True Yin (Mercury), and the Tiger (True Yin) has become an emblem of True Lead (True Yang).

The numbers 1 and 9 represent the beginning and the completion of a cycle, but here they also stand for the North and the South, respectively, according to the pattern of the *Luoshu* (Writ of the Luo River; see fig. 2). When the Breaths of Yin and Yang pass through Emptiness and Rooftop (the two lunar lodges related to the North, and also representing the joining of the Sun and the Moon), they generate the Original Breath (Yin) pertaining to Kun; when they pass through *zi* (now in the South), they generate the Original Essence (Yang) pertaining to Qian.

1. *The firm and the yielding rise in turn.* Compare the "Appended Sayings" of the *Book of Changes*: "The firm and the yielding follow one another and generate change and transformation" (A.2; see Wilhelm, 288).

4. *Across the way are* mao *and* you. This verse refers to *mao* (East) and *you* (West) being found halfway between *zi* (North) and *wu* (South). The meanings of *wei* include "horizontal," "east to west."

9. *In the second month, the elm seeds fall.* Compare 51:23–24: "The elm seeds fall to the ground, returning to their roots." This related verse clarifies that the subject here is the elm seeds, even though the Chinese text mentions only the elms.

10. *When Head faces* mao. Head (*kui*) denotes the first four stars of the Northern Dipper.

11. *In the eighth month, wheat grows.* Compare 51:53–54: "Shepherd's purse and wheat sprout and shoot anew, through their bravery they are able to survive."

12. *When Celestial Net accords with* you. Celestial Net (*tiangang*) is another name of the first four stars of the Dipper, i.e., its Head.

74. Using ingredients of unlike kind

Beyond its prevalent interpretation in terms of morals, the poem quoted from the *Book of Odes* (*Shijing*) at the beginning of this section is a metaphorical illustration of the male and female principles awaiting conjunction to generate the cosmos (see the notes to section 11 above). The turtle and the snake of the Dark Warrior also depict the joining of Yin and Yang as the origin of life: the Dark Warrior is the emblem of Water, the first agent in the "cosmogonic" sequence of the five agents.

The conjunction of Yin and Yang in the world reiterates the joining of Qian and Kun that gives birth to the cosmos. Without bestowing its essence upon the Earth, Heaven could not achieve its potential to generate, and without being fecundated by Heaven, the Earth could not realize its gift of bringing to life. This is the model for the union of the male and female principles illustrated in the *Cantong qi*.

Therefore the ingredients of the Elixir—whether they are material, immaterial, or symbolic—should guarantee the conjunction of Qian and Kun, availing themselves of the intermediation of a third principle represented by the central agent Soil. If the ingredients cannot accomplish this conjunction, no rite, prayer, deity, or immortal could be of help.

1–4. "Guan guan *go the ospreys, . . . for our prince a good mate she.*" This quatrain is quoted from the "*Guan* go the ospreys" poem in the *Book of Odes* (*Shijing*). The first verse of the quatrain is also quoted in section 11 above (see the note to 11:4).

7. *The Dark Warrior's turtle and snake.* The *Cantong qi* is one of the texts that intend the Dark Warrior as a dual emblem made of a turtle and a snake. According to the traditional interpretation, "dark" refers to the obscurity of the North, and "warrior" to the scaly carapace of the turtle, which is similar to a soldier's armor.

11. *Suppose that a house is shared by two women.* Compare *Book of Changes*, "Commentary on the Judgement" on the hexagram Kui ䷥ (no. 38): "Two women live together, but their minds are not directed to common concerns" (see Wilhelm, 574).

13–14. *And that Su Qin, the mediator, and Zhang Yi, the interceder.* Su Qin and Zhang Yi were fourth-century BCE representatives of the so-called School of the Strategists (*zongheng jia*), whose members excelled in rhetoric and eloquence. Su Qin and Zhang Yi are attributed, respectively, with the formulation of the theories of the "vertical" (*zong*, North-South) and the "horizontal" (*heng*, East-West) alliances among states; hence their emblematic role of "intermediaries" between polar principles evoked in the present passage. *Tongyan* ("mediator") might also be translated as "messenger." *Hemei* ("interceder") literally means the "go-between" between future spouses. In later alchemical literature, this is one of several terms that denote the agent Soil as the central "mediator" between Yin (True Mercury) and Yang (True Lead).

21–24. *With ingredients of unlike kinds . . . your guiding thread is lost.* Compare 35:9–10: "Things of the same kind follow each other; if they are at odds, they cannot form the Treasure."

25–28. *Then even if the Yellow Emperor tends to the furnace . . . and Master Huainan adjusts the compounding.* On the Yellow Emperor and on Liu An (Huainan zi, the Master of Huainan) see above the notes to 42:4 and 42:5. The Great One (Taiyi) is the supreme God and one of the deities who revealed the early scriptures on the elixirs. The Eight Sirs (Bagong) were employed at the court of Liu An, and are known as the authors of an early text on the aqueous solutions of minerals.

29. *Even if you set up space for a sumptuous altar.* Compare the similar verse in 26:15: "Amassing soil you set up space for an altar."

32. *And you pay obeisance holding the records.* "Records" refers to the Taoist certificates of transmission and/or ordination, or to similar documents that attest the identity and attainment of a priest or an adept.

BOOK 3

75. The saints and the worthies of old

Sections 75–81 consist of the "Epilogue" ("Luanci"), the first of three separate compositions that form Book 3 of the *Cantong qi*. Sections 75–76 contain the introduction to the "Epilogue."

The present section describes the inner state of "the saints and the worthies of old" in agreement with the alchemical perspective of Book 3. Having attained the One Breath, they compounded the Elixir and transcended the world.

3. *They refined the Nine Tripods.* If this verse is understood literally, it is as odd in English as it is in Chinese. Apparently, it should refer to the Nine Elixirs (*jiudan*), or Elixirs of the Nine Tripods (*jiuding dan*), an early, exemplary set of Waidan compounds. Several commentators, however, have explained the term Nine Tripods as the nine cycles of transmutation of the Elixir.

4. *Then altered their traces and sunk away in hiding.* "Hiding" oneself and disappearing is one of the arts of transformation mentioned in several Taoist texts. Other passages of the *Cantong qi* suggest, though, that this expression refers to the saintly man who conceals his sainthood and lives in retirement. See, in particular, 27:13 ("withdraw, stay concealed, and wait for your time") and 48:10 ("hide yourself and remain secluded").

6. *And spread their virtue through the three luminaries.* The term "three luminaries" usually refers to the Sun, the Moon, and the Northern Dipper. In the *Cantong qi*, it designates the ears, the eyes, and the mouth, and the respective functions of hearing, seeing, and speaking (see section 18).

9–10. *Having removed every evil, they preserved pure Breath for a long time.* On the word *zheng*, here translated as "pure," see the note to 59:12.

76. Wei Boyang and the *Cantong qi*

The saintly men of antiquity wrote works on the Elixir, but concealed their teachings under symbols and metaphors, allusions and secret names. Those who received their works recognized their importance, but did not comprehend their meaning. As a result, they neglected their tasks in order to devote themselves to erroneous methods. Concerned for those who in the future might commit the same mistake, Wei Boyang has written his *Cantong qi* to present the true doctrine of the Elixir. In the next five sections (77–81), he appends an "Epilogue" to provide a way of direct access to his work.

7. *But exposed only the branches.* This is, in fact, what Wei Boyang also did with his *Cantong qi*: "Concisely I will report its guidelines, and let the branches display its luxuriance" (38:17–18).

12. *Stored them in caskets for the whole of their life.* The sense of this verse is that those practitioners stored the texts away and did not benefit from them.

27. *Its count of the mils and ounces.* The *Cantong qi* provides the measures of the ingredients and defines the respective proportions. See, for example, 39:5–6: "Tend to the furnace to determine the scruples and ounces: five parts of Water are more than enough."

32. *And, with attention, comprehend it.* Note the use of the word *yi*, here translated as "attention," but also meaning "intention." In Neidan, this word—symbolically associated with Soil, the central agent—defines the faculty of Spirit that allows the whole alchemical process to unfold and come to achievement.

77. The order of Heaven

Despite its immensity and complexity, the cosmos functions by following regular patterns in the heavens and on the earth. These patterns mirror one another: any alteration in the celestial phenomena would be either a cause or a consequence of irregularities in the events that occur on earth, and vice versa. For example, if the River's Drum constellation faced the wrong sector of space, it would forewarn of an imminent war; if the shadow of the sundial did not follow its expected course, it would signal a disruption in the order of Heaven. The king should accept responsibility for those anomalies, acknowledge his faults to the Celestial Ruler, and amend his ways. When "barriers and locks" protect the kingdom, no harmful and noxious influences can ever enter.

The ascent and descent of Yin and Yang in the cosmos follow constant cycles marked by the earthly branches *zi* 子 and *wu* 午, which respectively represent the North and the South in the domain of space, and winter and summer (or midnight and noon) in the domain of time (see sections 64 and 73). Moreover, the Yang Breath becomes dominant at *yin* 寅 (the third lunar month), and the Yin Breath becomes dominant at *shen* 申 (the ninth lunar month; see section 51). Being effective in representing the apparent movement of the Dipper at the center of Heaven, which establishes the sequence of cyclical change in the cosmos, these and other emblems serve as guidelines to define the corresponding correct activities in the human realm.

1. *"Among models and images, none is greater than Heaven and Earth."* This sentence is quoted from the "Appended Sayings" of the *Book of Changes*, A.11 (see Wilhelm, 319). Compare also this passage of the "Appended Sayings": "When in early antiquity Bao Xi (i.e., Fu Xi) ruled the world, he looked upward and contemplated the images in Heaven, he looked downward and contemplated the models on the Earth" (B.2; see Wilhelm, 328).

2. *And the Dark Ditch measures tens of thousands of miles.* Dark Ditch (*xuangou*) is a name of the Milky Way.

3–4. *If River's Drum faces Stellar Sequence, it will alarm and upset us all.* The River's Drum constellation is also known as Heaven's Drum (*tiangu*). Stellar Sequence (*xingji*) is the first of the twelve sectors of the ecliptic (Major, *Heaven and Earth in Early Han Thought*, 94).

17–18. *Complying with the Dipper and Rising Glimmer, and holding to Scale, they set the prime sequence.* "Dipper" here refers to the so-called "ladle" (*biao*) of the Northern Dipper, i.e., the last three of its seven stars. Rising Glimmer (*shaoyao*, also known as Glimmering Radiance, *yaoguang*) and Scale (*heng*) are the seventh and the fifth stars of the Dipper, respectively.

78. Compounding the Elixir

After those found in sections 39–40 and 62, this section gives another poetical description of the compounding of the Elixir. Lead (the White Tiger, True Yang) first liquefies, so that Mercury (the "green liquid," True Yin) can join it and become one with it (see the corresponding description in section 62). In a different, but equivalent imagery, the Vermilion Sparrow (Fire, Yang) spreads its wings and soars into air, but stumbles upon a "thin net" (Water, Yin), is captured, and is sentenced to die in the boiling pot. However sorrowful its destiny may appear, this is the rule for compounding the Elixir: Water must overcome Fire so that both may join with Soil. The doctrinal principles at the basis of this account are the subject of the next section.

1. *So that its heat may go up to Mount Zeng.* The *zeng* is a pot used for steaming food. It is used here as a metaphor of the tripod or the crucible.

2. *A blazing fire is placed below.* An almost identical verse is found in 40:5: "A blazing fire grows below."

3–4. *The White Tiger leads the song ahead, the green liquid joins after.* Compare 62:7 and 62:11: "The Golden Flower is the first to sing . . . The Yang (i.e., the Flowing Pearl of Great Yang) is next to join it." In these verses, the Golden Flower (True Lead) corresponds to the White Tiger, and the Flowing Pearl of Great Yang (True Mercury) corresponds to the "green liquid." (*Cang* is one of several words that denote different hues of green or blue-green; here it refers to True Mercury, associated with Wood and the green color in the system of the five agents.)

11. *As it enters the boiling pot turned on its head.* *Tanghuo* is the name of the "boiling pot" used for capital punishments.

20. *The dog's teeth form a lattice.* This verse refers to the blisters and bulges found on the "body" of the Elixir, whose irregular and unequal forms are compared to the teeth of a dog.

22. *Like stalactites issued forth from* langgan. This verse has a dual sense. In the first sense, *langgan* 琅玕 is a name of a precious stone (see the note to 62:10) and a synonym of the Elixir, whose excrescences are similar to stalactites. In the second sense, *langgan* is a homophone of *langgan* 闌干 "crosswise, diagonal," and the verse should be intended as meaning "like stalactites protruding and extending crosswise."

79. The Three Fives return to the One

This section explicates the principles at the basis of the alchemical method allusively described in the previous section. Although its language and imagery differ in part from those used in Books 1 and 2 of the *Cantong qi*, it can be understood in light of other passages of the text, especially sections 32 and 41.

The main emblems are the Green Dragon, the White Tiger, and the Vermilion Sparrow. The respective images used in this section are the following:

(1) The Green Dragon is True Mercury. It is represented by Wood, East, and spring in the system of the five agents; by Room (*fang*, the fourth lunar lodge in the Green Dragon sector of heaven); by Zhen ☳ (corresponding to the East in the postcelestial arrangement of the eight trigrams); by *mao* 卯 (the earthly branch associated with the second lunar month, the month of the spring equinox); and by number 6 (the "accomplishment number" of Water, which generates Wood).

(2) The White Tiger is True Lead. It is represented by Metal, West, and autumn in the system of the five agents; by Pleiades (*mao*, the fourth lodge in the White Tiger sector of heaven); by Dui ☱ (corresponding to the West in the postcelestial arrangement of the eight trigrams); by *you* 酉 (the earthly branch associated with the eighth lunar month, the month of the autumn equinox); and by number 7 (the "accomplishment number" of Fire, which conquers Metal).

(3) The Vermilion Sparrow is Fire. It is represented by the South in the system of the five agents; by Extension (*zhang*, the fifth lunar lodge in the Vermilion Sparrow sector of heaven); by Li ☲ (corresponding to the South in the postcelestial arrangement of the eight trigrams); by *wu* 午 (the earthly branch associated with the South); and by number 2 (the "generation number" of Fire).

When Water (Kan ☵, containing Metal, or True Lead) conquers Fire (Li ☲, containing Wood, or True Mercury), the Elixir is attained: Metal (the inner line of Kan) is liberated from its temporary residence in Water, and Qian ☰ is reestablished. For this reason, several commentators have suggested that "the three" (Wood, Metal, and Fire) actually "come to have audience" with Water, because Water holds the key for compounding the Elixir at this stage of the process. Eventually, though, Water in turn will be conquered by Soil (see section 32), and the natures of Water and Fire will merge and become one.

At first there are only Yin and Yang (Water and Fire). When they give birth to the five agents, there are the "three fives," namely, Water and Metal (respectively corresponding to 1 and 4), Fire and Wood (2 and 3), and Soil (5). (*) When the five agents join one another, they return to the state of Unity, represented by the union of *wu* and *ji* (the male and female aspects of the One, here called "the two places").

The four colors mentioned in the final part of this section have been understood in different ways. Several commentators, nevertheless, have taken white and yellow to denote two stages in the compounding of the Elixir: white is the color of True Lead (see the note to 22:3–4), and yellow is the color of the germ of the Elixir—the Yellow Sprout (*huangya*, see section 22) or the Yellow Carriage (*huangyu*, see section 39). Black and red are the colors of native lead and the Reverted Elixir, respectively, which mark the beginning and the end ("without" and "within") of the alchemical process.

(*) On these numerical correspondences, see the notes to section 72. According to another interpretation, "three fives" here means "three times five" and stands for 15, the sum of the numbers associated with the Green Dragon (6), the White Tiger (7), and the Vermilion Sparrow (2).

15. *Compound it according to the rules given above.* According to a different interpretation, *shang* (rendered as "above") here means "the past," and the verse refers to the rules established by the masters of former times.

80. "It is made of its own"

Compounding the Elixir may appear to be complex. If the alchemical work is modeled on the joining of Qian and Kun, however, the required procedure is identical to the processes that occur in nature (see section 35).

3. *Like the breaths of mountains and lakes that share steam.* Ze, usually meaning "marshes," is translated here as "lake" in accordance with the use of this word in the *Book of Changes*, where the lake is an image of the trigram Dui ☱. For the present verse of the *Cantong qi*, compare these passages in the *Book of Changes*, "Explanation of the Trigrams": "Heaven (☰) and Earth (☷) establish the positions; Mountain (☶) and

Lake (☱) spread their breaths onto each other; Thunder (☳) and Wind (☴) arouse one another; Water (☵) and Fire (☲) do not combat each other" (sec. 3; see Wilhelm, 265); and "Therefore Water and Fire complement one another, Thunder and Wind do not interfere with each other, Mountain and Lake spread their breaths onto each other" (sec. 5; see Wilhelm, 272).

81. The Way of Heaven renders no favors

As presented in the *Cantong qi*, the Way of the Golden Elixir is an integral doctrine that takes account of all the essential principles and guides to their realization. This doctrine is unchangeable and everlasting, and is transmitted to all those who are ready to receive it.

15–16. *The Way of Heaven renders no favors: it is always transmitted to those who are worthy.* Compare *Daode jing*: "The Way of Heaven has no sympathies: it constantly stays with the good man" (sec. 79).

82. Song of the Tripod

This section contains the "Song of the Tripod" ("Dingqi ge"), the second of the three compositions that form Book 3 of the *Cantong qi*.

The first two quatrains (verses 1–8) refer to the tripod, and even at a literal level can be read in at least two different ways. In the first reading, the tripod has a circumference of one foot and five inches ("3 and 5" means three times five; one Chinese foot contains ten inches) and a thickness of one inch and one tenth. The mouth is twelve inches wide ("4 and 8" means four plus eight), and its "lips" are two inches thick. The height is one foot and two inches. In the second reading, these numbers refer to the two halves of the tripod. The upper half has a circumference of one foot and five inches and a thickness of one inch and one tenth; the lower half has a circumference of three feet and two inches ("4 and 8" means four times eight inches) and a thickness of two inches.

Beyond these different literal readings, the numbers mentioned in these verses have several symbolic associations and pertain to three sets of emblems. The first and second verses refer to the five agents, whose key numbers are 1, 3, and 5; the third and fourth verses refer to the eight trigrams, whose key numbers are 2, 4, and 8; and the fifth and sixth verses refer to the duodecimal cycles. In detail:

(1) The numbers of the circumference, 3 and 5, allude to the Three Fives and therefore refer to the five agents. (The model of this configuration is the *Hetu*, or *Chart of the Yellow River*; see fig. 1.) The verse "an inch and one part" (*cun yi fen* 寸一分), which in a literal sense describes the thickness of the tripod, can be read as meaning "in its inch [of thickness] (*cun* 寸), there is the One (*yi* 一) divided (*fen* 分) [into the Two]."

(2) The numbers of the mouth, 4 and 8, allude to the four main and the four intermediate directions of space and therefore refer to the eight trigrams. (The model of this configuration is the *Luoshu*, or *Writ of the Luo River*; see fig. 2.) The two inches of the lips allude to the "two principles" (*liangyi*), i.e., Yin and Yang, which border on one another.

(3) The numbers of the height, 1 and 2, refer to the twelve earthly branches and the twelve "sovereign hexagrams" (*bigua*; see table 11), which are evenly divided between Yin and Yang and are used to represent the stages of the "fire times" (*huohou*). The verse "evenly thick and thin" refers to the phases of increase ("thickness") and decrease ("thinness") of the heating.

The verse "its belly on the third day sits beneath the descending warmth" alludes to the monthly lunar cycle: on the third day of that cycle, the luminous, "warm" Yang principle begins its ascent (see 13:1 and 49:13).

The next two quatrains (verses 9–16) refer to the "fire times" for compounding the Elixir. The Yin principle is Water, the Yang principle is Fire. In Waidan, this alludes to the Yang fire of the stove placed underneath the Yin water contained in the vessel. In Neidan, Fire is the heart and corresponds to the trigram Li ☲; Water is the kidneys and corresponds to the trigram Kan ☵. Fire by nature rises upward, carrying with it the True Mercury contained within the heart (True Yin, the inner line of Li ☲). Water on the contrary flows downward, carrying with it the True Lead contained within the kidneys (True Yang, the inner line of Kan ☵). True Yin and True Yang therefore are separated from one another. With the "inversion" (*diandao*) that occurs by means of the Neidan practice, the Yang Fire is moved below and the Yin Water is moved above. In this way, Fire continues to rise upward and Water continues to flow downward, but now the True Yin and the True Yang contained within Li ☲ and Kan ☵ can meet and join with one another.

Repeated heating cycles make it possible to compound the Elixir. The beginning ("head") and end ("tail") of each cycle respectively pertain to Yang and Yin and are represented by the branches *zi* 子 and *wu* 午. At these times, a strong fire is used for refining the Elixir (fire is "fierce" at both of these stages because *zi* is the "tail" of Yin and the "head" of Yang, while *wu* is the "tail" of Yang and the "head" of Yin). The two intermediate stages of the cycle (which in Neidan are referred to "ablutions," *muyu*) correspond to states of balance between Yin and Yang, and are represented by the branches *mao* 卯 and *you* 酉. At these times, a gentle fire is used to "warmly nourish" the Elixir. The strong fire is used for seventy days starting from the winter solstice (*zi* 子) and for thirty days during the month of the summer solstice (*wu* 午); the gentle fire is used in the remaining 260 days, making altogether the 360 days of the twelve lunar months. (See the notes to verses 11–12.)

The next four quatrains (verses 17–32) refer to the nourishment and the growth of the Elixir, which continue to rely on Fire. The Elixir is made of True Mercury and True Lead. "The whiteness of the Yin Fire" alludes to True Mercury (Yin, white) found within Li ☲ (Fire, red). "The lead of the Yellow Sprout" alludes to the True Lead found within Kan ☵ ("yellow sprout" denotes the first stage in the formation of True Lead, or the Elixir). Here Fire is associated with both ingredients: True Mercury is the Yin Fire, True Lead is the Yang Fire. Since Fire is associated with number 7, this passage mentions the "two sevens." (In another interpretation, 2 is the number of Yin Fire, and 7 is the number of Yang Fire; these are respectively the "generation number" and the "accomplishment number" of Fire in the system of the five agents; see table 4.)

In Waidan, the Elixir consists of the essences of the primary ingredients, which rise upward within the tripod and coagulate under the lid (or the upper half of the vessel). In Neidan, the Elixir analogously is generated in the lower Cinnabar Field, and rises in the course of its growth to the upper Cinnabar Field, located in the region of the brain. Here the "Song of the Tripod" uses imagery and language that would later become typical of Neidan, but were already used in the context of the earlier meditation practices on the inner deities: the Elixir is denoted as an "infant," and the upper Cinnabar

Field is called the Mystery, a name reminiscent of Mysterious Barrier (*xuanguan*) and Mysterious Palace (*xuangong*), which denote this locus of the human body. Regardless of whether the whole "Song of the Tripod" is read with reference to Waidan or Neidan, however, the main point is that the Elixir grows until its ingredients are brought back to their original state of purity and unity, and this happens by following an ascensional process.

The last seven quatrains and the final two verses (verses 33–58) conclude the poem by admonishing on the attention required to perform the practice, on its arduousness, and on its secrecy. When the Elixir is achieved, one becomes a True Man. The "Song of the Tripod" depicts this state using classic Taoist imagery: the adepts ascends to Heaven to have audience with the supreme deities, and his name is entered in the "records of the Immortals."

7. *Its belly on the third day.* In this verse, *qi* 齊 (usually meaning "to regulate, equalize") stands for *qi* 臍 ("navel"), and the compound *fuqi* 腹 齊 denotes the belly. According to another interpretation, *qi* 齊 here maintains its ordinary meaning ("to regulate, equalize"), and the verse means "its belly equalizes the three," namely Original Breath (*yuanqi*), Original Essence (*yuanjing*), and Original Spirit (*yuanshen*). In a third interpretation, the verse alludes to the lower Cinnabar Field, which is sometimes said to be located three inches below the navel.

11–12. *Fierce are the head and the tail, gentle in between.* Compare verses 40:7–8, which also refer to the fire placed underneath the vessel: "At first make it gentle so that it may be adjusted, at the end make it fierce and let it spread out." As was noted in the Introduction, § 4, the present passage of the "Song of the Tripod" does not match the method of the "fire times" based on the solar cycle described in section 51.

20. *To support and assist man.* According to several commentaries, "man" in this verse refers to the True Man (*zhenren*) or to Spirit (*shen*).

33–36. *At the end of each cycle . . . let there be no lapse.* Compare 40:11–12: "It will rotate through twelve nodes, and when the nodes are complete, it will again need your care."

41. *Moisten one knife-point.* On the term *daogui* see the note to 40:18.

46. *Should seek out its root.* Compare *Daode jing*, 16: "Things are abounding and overflowing, but each of them goes back to its root."

57–58. *Your name will be inscribed in the Heavenly Charts, and you will be called a True Man.* Compare 27:13–14: "Your work concluded, you ascend on high to obtain the Register and receive the Chart."

83. The Five Categories

The last of the three compositions found in Book 3 (sections 83–88) is entitled "The Five Categories" ("Wu xianglei") or, in certain redactions of the *Cantong qi*, "Filling Lacunae" ("Busai yituo"). It was supposedly written by Wei Boyang to address issues not treated elsewhere in his work.

The present section explains why this composition was added to the *Cantong qi*. Its putative author, Wei Boyang, first states that this part of his work complements Books 1 and 2, and that its import matches the previous portions. He adds, then, that this additional part fully brings to light the ties of his work with the *Book of Changes*.

The chart at the end of the section shows: (a) In the two central columns, the names of the five agents and the respective "generation numbers" (see table 4). (b) In the leftmost and the rightmost columns, the names of the ten celestial stems, which are associated in pairs with the five agents (see table 12). (c) In the two other columns, pairs of Yang (on the left) and Yin (on the right) entities or notions, some of which are directly related to the corresponding agent (e.g., "martial fire" and "civil fire" correspond to the agent Fire). (*)

(*) For certain issues raised by the presence of this chart in the *Cantong qi*, see the textual note on section 83.

10. *My words bridge and complement one another.* The subject of this verse ("my words") is not explicitly stated, but the sense is clear: there is a complete correspondence and identity between the previous parts of the *Cantong qi* and the present, additional composition.

13–15. *Hence once again I put this in writing, and call it "The Five Categories"; with this, the qualities and nature of the great* Book of Changes *are completed.* The final verse in this irregular stanza is inspired by the passage of the "Appended Sayings" quoted at the end of the chart: "The five positions match one another — Each of them finds its equal." After these words, the "Appended Sayings" continues with these words: "This completes the changes and transformations" (A.8; see Wilhelm, 310). See also the note to 84:1–2.

CHART. In the third line of the chart, the compound word *yaowu* 藥物, meaning "ingredients," is split into *yao* 藥 and *wu* 物. The former word is associated with *wu* 戊 (Yang), and the latter word with *ji* 己 (Yin). As this expedient cannot be reproduced in English, *yao* and *wu* have been translated as "Yang ingredient" and "Yin ingredient," respectively.

The sentences "The five positions match one another — Each of them finds its equal" are quoted from the "Appended Sayings": "The numbers of Heaven are five, and the numbers of Earth are also five. The five positions match one another, and each of them finds its equal" (A.8; see Wilhelm, 310). The numbers of Heaven are 1, 3, 5, 7, and 9. The numbers of Earth are 2, 4, 6, 8, and 10. The "five positions" are those of the five agents: North, South, East, West, and Center.

84. The three ways of the *Cantong qi*

The *Cantong qi* unifies the doctrines of the *Book of Changes*, the teachings of Taoism (again referred to here by the names of the Yellow Emperor and Laozi) on "non-doing," and the practice of alchemy. These three ways are separate branches stemming from the same root; having one source, they can be merged into a single path. Wei Boyang derived his teachings from that source; his words, therefore, are truthful and reliable.

1–2. *The qualities and nature of the great* Book of Changes *all follow their measures.* These words refer to the possibility, offered by the *Book of Changes*, of representing nature and qualities of all objects and phenomena in the cosmos by means of emblems. Those emblems assign a value and a function to each object and phenomenon both individually and as a part of a whole. The *Cantong qi* adopts those emblems as a means to comprehend multiplicity and change and their relation to Unity and constancy.

85. The timeless instant between end and beginning

The eleventh month of the lunar calendar, represented by the hexagram Fu ䷗ (Return), is the time in which the Yang principle is reborn after its obscuration. It corresponds to the winter solstice, to the instant between the end of a month and the beginning of the next month (see sections 10 and 48), and to the earthly branch *zi* 子, placed at due North (the Center of the cosmos) between the end of one

cycle—the day, the month, the year, or even longer time sequences—
and the beginning of the next cycle (see table 14). In the eternity of
this instant outside the flow of time, the ruler's task is to provide
support: he forbids common activities and remains secluded. Only
from the perspective of this timeless point is it possible to understand
the meanings and functions of Qian, Kun, Kan, and Li, and to communicate them to others through non-doing.

3–4. *As he attends to the Yang, and forbids travel and trade, the ruler
stays in deep seclusion.* Compare the "Image" on the hexagram Fu ䷗ (no.
24) in the *Book of Changes*: "Thunder within the Earth: Return. Thus the
kings of antiquity closed the passes at the time of solstice. Merchants and
strangers did not go about, and the ruler did not travel through the
provinces" (see Wilhelm, 98).

5. *Complying with the ordinances in accord with the time.* Compare 14:9:
"In issuing commands comply with the seasonal ordinances."

6. *He closes his mouth and does not use it for talking.* Compare 58:11–12:
"Dui ☱ (i.e., the mouth) is closed and not used for talking: you follow the
boundless with inaudible words."

8. *And the Great Mystery has no form or appearance.* Compare *Daode
jing*: "The Great Image has no form" (sec. 41).

9. *None can behold its emptiness and silence.* For "silence" as one of the
qualities of the Dao see the *Daode jing*: "Silent! Still! It stands alone and
never alters" (sec. 25).

10. *As it disappears within its own walls.* Compare 31:5–6: "Hidden
within its inner and outer walls, sinking into the depths of cavernous
Emptiness . . ."

86. Wei Boyang and the *Cantong qi*

At the end of his work, Wei Boyang finally introduces himself in this
and the next two sections. Having renounced the ordinary ways of
humanity, he retired on a mountain to lead a solitary life, and composed the *Cantong qi* on the basis of the *Book of Changes*. (*)

(*) The mention of Wei Boyang's place of origin in this section requires a
brief comment. While Kuaiji is Wei Boyang's traditional birthplace, other
redactions of the *Cantong qi* read either Luguo, in present-day Shandong,

or Kuaiguo, in present-day central Henan. The former name deserves notice, as it seems to preserve a trace of earlier traditions that attributed the authorship of the *Cantong qi* to Xu Congshi (see the Introduction, § 2).

1. *A lowly man born in Kuaiji.* On Kuaiji see the Introduction, p. [Referenced content is missing.], note [Referenced content is missing.].

3. *I cherish plainness and simplicity.* For the expression "plainness and simplicity" (*pusu*) see the *Zhuangzi*: "In quiescence you will be a saint, in movement a king. Resting in non-doing, you will be honored; in plainness and simplicity, your beauty will be such that no one in the world may vie with you" (13.458; see Watson, 143).

7. *Upholding calm and tranquility.* For the expression "calm and tranquility" (*tiandan*) see *Daode jing*, 31: "Calm and tranquility are the best"; and *Zhuangzi*: "Calm and tranquility, silence, emptiness, non-doing—these are the level of Heaven and Earth, the substance of the Way and its Virtue" (15.538; see Watson, 168).

9–10. *Unhurried, dwelling at ease, I wrote this book.* Compare *Zhuangzi*: "The saint, unhurried, embodies change and so comes to his end" (20.694; see Watson, 218). — These verses, moreover, hint to a parallel between Laozi who, in his deified aspect, composed the *Scripture of the Yellow Court* (*Huangting jing*) and Wei Boyang, the immortal who composed the *Cantong qi*. The opening verses of the *Yellow Court* say: "In the purple aurora of the Highest Clarity, in front of the Sovereign of the Void, the Lord of Jade Dawn of the Most High Great Dao, *dwelling at ease* in the Stamen-Pearl Palace, wrote seven-word verses . . ." (*Huangting neijing jing*, sec. 1).

87. The three ways stem from one source

Wei Boyang now describes the three main subjects of the *Cantong qi*, adding more details. Cosmology (verses 5–8) bears on the "outward," in order to adjust and adapt to change. Taoism (verses 9–12) concerns the "inward," in order to cultivate one's inner nature. Alchemy (verses 13–22) provides the method, in order to realize the conjunction of Qian and Kun, or Yin and Yang. Wei Boyang traced the common origin of these three ways, and joined them into one.

4. *The Four Seas are in harmony and at peace.* "Four Seas" (*sihai*) is a common designation of the whole world.

5. *Use them outwardly as a calendar.* Compare 2:7–8: "Abide in the Center to control the outside; the numbers are found in the system of the pitch-pipes and the calendar." As it does in that passage, here too the *Cantong qi* mentions the calendar as the ideal application of the cosmological principles in the "outward" world: it allows the ruler to model his government in agreement with the changes that occur in Heaven.

11. *"Hold the fullness of Virtue."* This sentence is quoted from *Daode jing*, 55: "Holding the fullness of Virtue is being similar to an infant."

12. *And you will go back to the root and return to the origin.* For the term *guigen* ("going back to the root") compare *Daode jing*, 16: "Things are abounding and overflowing, but each of them goes back to its root. Going back to the root is called being quiescent."

15. *Embracing Unity without neglect.* For the term *baoyi* ("embracing Unity") compare *Daode jing*, 10: "In carrying and maintaining your Yin soul (*po*) and in embracing Unity, can you not separate from them?"; and *Daode jing*, 22: "Thus the saint embraces Unity and is a mold for the world."

16. *"You will be able to maintain yourself for long."* This sentence is an almost literal quotation from *Daode jing*, 44: "Know what is sufficient and you will not be disgraced, know where to stop and you will not be in danger — you will be able to last for long"; and *Daode jing*, 59: "If no one knows his limit, he can possess the kingdom; if he possesses the Mother of the kingdom, he will be able to last for long."

19–20. *Dispose of realgar, discard eight minerals!* Realgar in this verse is designated as "Wudu," its well-known, classical place of production in present-day Gansu. On the eight minerals see the note to 32:3–4.

25. *"They come forth together but have different names."* This sentence is an almost literal quotation from *Daode jing*, 1: "These two come forth together but have different names."

30. *As solid as stone to be seen.* For the expression *luoluo*, compare *Daode jing*, 39: "Do not desire what is as cherished as jade, but what is as solid as stone."

35. *"Its words are few," but its intent is great.* Compare *Book of Changes*, "Appended Sayings": "The words of good-natured men are few" (B.9; see Wilhelm, 355). Note that the term "good-natured men" (*jiren*) is found below in the next section, verse 88:15.

88. Wei Boyang's final words

To end his work, Wei Boyang concludes the self-portrait that had begun in section 86. He visited the dangerous boundaries of the known world, and went further, obtaining transcendence. Like the deities and the immortals of his land, who periodically descend to earth in order to grant teachings to humanity, he returns to our world now and again to reveal his doctrines. This time, he has bestowed his *Cantong qi* upon us. Those who follow its teachings, in this or another form, belong to the same unnamed, perennial doctrine. They lead a stable life, and provide support to one another.

3. *I have wondered and roamed through the Unbounded.* The term *liaokuo*, rendered here as "the Unbounded," is also found in 51:67, where it is an adjective and is translated as "vast and broad."

5. *Transmuting my form, transcending the world. Xian* ("transcending the world") can also be translated as "becoming immortal."

6. *I have entered the depths of the Inaudible.* Compare *Zhuangzi*: "To him there is no north or south—in utter freedom he dissolves himself in the four directions and enters the depths of the unfathomable" (17.601; see Watson, 187).

10. *I bend to the east, the west, and the south.* These words indicate that Wei Boyang comes from the north, the direction symbolic of the origin and of the center of Heaven. See also the passage of the *Zhuangzi* quoted in the note to verse 6 above.

11–12. *In times of adversity like those met by Tang, when flood and drought confront one another.* These verses refer to Tang, or Cheng Tang, the first ruler of the Shang dynasty whose reign began, according to one of the traditional chronologies, in 1558 BCE. The myths recorded in several sources mention only a drought that took place at the beginning of his dynasty and lasted five or more years. A flood is said to have occurred, instead, at the beginning of the previous dynasty, the Yin.

15–16. *The good-natured man braves and endures the turn of events: steady and serene, and ready to live a long life.* These two final verses have also been understood as meaning "The good-natured men support one another: steady and serene, he can live a long life." For the term "good-natured men" (*jiren*) compare the sentence of the "Appended Sayings" of the *Book of Changes* quoted in the note to 87:35 above.

Textual Notes

These notes report some of the main issues in translating individual verses of the *Cantong qi,* the most significant variants introduced by Chen Zhixu in his redaction, and other noteworthy textual features.

3:11

The Sun and the Moon set periods and measures (日月為期度). For *riyue* 日月 ("the Sun and the Moon"), all extant redactions prior to Chen Zhixu have *richen* 日辰: "the markers of time set periods and measures." *Richen* specifically denotes the twelve earthly branches that represent the twelve "double hours" of the day.

14:17–18

Only when the function of Qian and Kun is at work can Heaven and Earth be regulated (乾坤用施行、天地然後治). In all redactions prior to Chen Zhixu, these verses are followed by a verse worded in slightly different ways. The Yin Changsheng redaction, Zhu Xi, and Yu Yan have: "Must one not, then, be cautious?" (可不慎乎). Peng Xiao has: "Could one not, then, be cautious?" (可得不慎乎). The Waidan anonymous redaction has: "Must one not, then, accord with it?" (可不順乎). The additional verse originates in a passage of the *Book of Changes:* "Through words and deeds the noble man causes Heaven and Earth to move. Must one not, then, be cautious?" 言行、君子之所以動天地也、可不慎乎 ("Appended Sayings," A.6; see Wilhelm, 305). See also the following note on 15:2.

15:2

Is renewing the tripod and renovating the ancient (鼎新革故). This verse, which is not found in the extant redactions prior to Chen Zhixu, replaces the verse "Must one not, then, be cautious?", which Chen Zhixu omits from his redaction (see above the textual note to 14:17–18). (Although these verses are found in different sections in the present translation, the *Cantong qi* consists in the first place of a continuous sequence of verses, with no divisions into chapters or sections, but only into three Books.) The verse derives from the "Hexagrams in Sequence" appendix of the *Book of Changes,* where the hexagram The Well (Jing ䷯, no. 48) is followed by Renovation (Ge ☲, no. 49) and then by The Tripod (Ding ☲, no. 50): "The setup (*dao*) of a well must necessarily be renovated [in the course of time]; hence there follows Renovation. Nothing renovates things so much as the tripod; hence there follows The Tripod" 井道不可不革、故受之以革、革物者莫若鼎、故受之以鼎 ("Xugua," 2; see Wilhelm, 635 and 641). The sense of these sentences becomes clearer if one considers that *jing* 井, whose primary meaning is "well," also signifies the "rules, norms, laws" (*fadu* 法度) by which the king conducts government; and that the tripod itself is an emblem of royal power. See also the "Hexagrams in Irregular Order": "Renovation means removal of what is antiquate. The Tripod means taking up the new" 革、去故也、鼎、取新也 ("Zagua"; Wilhelm, ibid.). "Renewing the tripod and renovating the ancient" later became an idiom meaning "removing evil and rectifying one's heart." In addition, its import is close to *geming* 革命, or "changing the [Celestial] Mandate" ("revolution" in present-day Chinese): due to the tripod's emblematic value, "renewing the tripod" also means "changing dynasty" ("... avec cette différance essentielle, cependant, que la révolution est faite en vue de la réalisation d'un idéal social préfiguré, alors que le changement de mandat n'est operé que pour le rétablissment de l'ordre"; Vandermeersch, *Wangdao ou La voie royale*, 2:509).

Neither Chen Zhixu nor other commentators motivate the addition or the omission of this verse. It is unclear whether its political overtones may have led to its omission by the authors of other redactions, or vice versa to its addition by Chen Zhixu (who, it may be reminded, lived under the foreign rule of the Yuan dynasty). Nevertheless, several redactions of the *Cantong qi* after the one by Chen Zhixu contain this verse, including some of those based on the "Ancient Text."

24:10

So that the White lies sheltered within (白裏貞居). *Li* 裏 in this verse is an adverb, analogous in meaning to *nei* 內 ("within"). *Zhenju* 貞居 ("lies sheltered") is attested as a compound meaning "to dwell in hiding" or "in retirement." Several other meanings of *zhen* 貞, however, may apply to the present verse, including "firm," "secure," and "correct."

26:1

This is not the method of passing through the viscera (是非歷臟法). The initial words in this verse lend themselves to three different interpretations, according to whether *shi* 是 is taken to have a nominal value ("what is right") and *fei* 非 to be a negative copula ("is not");

whether *shi* 是 is taken to be a demonstrative ("this") and *fei* 非 to be a
negative copula ("is not"); or whether both words are taken to be verbs
("consider what is right," "consider what is wrong"). Grammatically, all
three readings are plausible, but the sense is remarkably different. Chen
Zhixu opens his notes on this section by saying, "Those who practice self-
cultivation should comprehend what is correct in the great Dao. Unless
Yin and Yang join one another and Kan and Li 'emanate and transform,'
what lies outside are all 'side gates' (*pangmen*) and perverse methods
(*zuodao*)" 做修行人、須明大道之正、倘非陰陽配合、坎離施化、外
則皆為傍門左道. Here Chen Zhixu takes *shi* 是 as a synonym of *zheng*
正 ("right, correct"), and in his reading the verse would mean "What is
right is not the method of passing through the viscera." Zhu Yuanyu
agrees with Chen Zhixu when he says in his commentary: "In order to
know what is right in the great Dao, one should first thoroughly investigate what is wrong in the 'side gates'" 欲知大道之是、當先究旁門之非.

Yu Yan instead suggests that *shi* means "this" and *fei* means "is not."
He writes in his *Shiyi*: "[The verse above] means that *this* Way *is not* the
meditation methods of 'passing through the five viscera.' If *shi fei* ('this is
not') is taken to mean *shishi feifei* ('consider what is right and what is
wrong,' i.e., 'discriminate, use discernment'), this is an error" 謂此道非
歷五臟存思之法也、若以是非兩字作是是非非之義、則誤矣. Yuan
Renlin agrees with Yu Yan and writes in a most explicit way in his commentary: "The word *shi* ('this') refers to what has been said above; the
word *fei* ('is not') connects it to what comes below" 是字一讀、承上文、
非字貫下. In his view, therefore, *shi* ('this') refers to the alchemical
principles described in the previous sections (corresponding to sections
22–25 in the present translation), which are contrasted with the practices
mentioned in the present section.

According to the third interpretation, *shifei* 是非 has a verbal value,
and the first verses in this section mean "Consider what is right and what
is wrong in the method of passing through the viscera . . . in treading the
Dipper and pacing the asterisms . . . in sating yourself with the nine-and-
one in the Way of Yin . . . in ingesting breath till it chirps in your
stomach . . ." This reading, however, is hardly consistent with the purport
of the present section, which rejects in a thorough way several practices
and methods as inadequate for true realization.

26:2

Of inner contemplation and having a point of concentration (內觀有所
思). For *neiguan* 內觀 (lit., "contemplating within"), all extant redactions
prior to Chen Zhixu have *neishi* 內視 ("observing within"). *Neiguan*

("inner contemplation") usually refers to a meditation technique developed from the early Tang period, the main purpose of which is purifying the mind from passions and delusive thoughts. *Neishi* ("inner observation"), instead, is typically associated with earlier practices based on the visualization of the inner deities.

26:7

Of ingesting breath till it chirps in your stomach (食氣鳴腸胃). *Ming* 鳴 is a generic term for sounds produced by animals or objects. Given the absence of a precise referent in the present context, the translation matches the components of the graph, "mouth" and "bird." *Changwei* 腸胃 literally means "intestines and stomach."

27:3

For three years preserve and ingest (伏食三載). Chen Zhixu's redaction is the first one to read *fushi* 伏食 ("preserve and ingest") instead of *fushi* 服食 (a compound made of two words both meaning "ingest"), in the present verse and elsewhere in his text (33:5, 35:1, 61:13, and 87:17).

Based on the explications given by Chen Zhixu and Liu Yiming, the word *fu* 伏 in *fushi* 伏食 combines the notions of "storing," "keeping concealed," and "keeping safe." The translation given above, "preserve," conveys these meanings at least in part. In his commentary to section 33, Chen Zhixu writes: "'Preserve' (*fu* 伏) means preserving the Breath prior to Heaven. 'Ingest' (*shi* 食) means swallowing the Elixir sized as a grain of millet. In later times, someone replaced *fu* 伏 ('preserve') with *fu* 服 ('ingest') because he did not understand the wondrousness of 'preserving.' Therefore an immortal master said: 'To preserve Breath, you do not ingest Breath; to ingest Breath, you must preserve Breath. If you ingest Breath, you do not live a long life; to live a long life, you must preserve Breath.' In this single word, 'preserve,' lies the hinge of the transformation brought about by the function of inversion" (i.e., the inversion from the state posterior to Heaven to the state prior to Heaven) 伏者、伏先天之氣、食者、吞黍米之丹、後人誤作服字、是不知伏之為妙也、故仙師云、伏氣不服氣、服氣須伏氣、服氣不長生、長生須伏氣、只一伏字、逆用化機.

Liu Yiming writes in his commentary to the portion corresponding to section 35: "'Preserve' (*fu* 伏) means to preserve and store (*fucang* 伏藏, a compound that also means "concealing") the Breath prior to Heaven, and not foolishly put it in motion. This is what Mengzi meant when he said: 'I am skillful in nourishing my overflowing Breath.' 'Ingest' (*shi* 食) means to seek the actual by means of the empty; it means 'to ingest' something actual. This is what Mengzi meant when he said: 'This Breath is exceedingly vast and exceedingly strong; if it is nourished by being straight (*zhi* 直, i.e., by the virtue of rectitude) and by sustaining no harm, it fills up all between Heaven and Earth'" 伏者、伏藏先天之氣、而不妄動之意、即孟子所謂我善養吾浩然之氣者是也、食者、以虛求實、腹實之義、即孟子所謂其為氣也、至大至剛、以直養而無害、則塞於天地之間者是也. (The sentences quoted by Liu Yiming are found in *Mengzi*, 11/2A/2; see Legge, *The Works of Mencius*, 189–90.) For Liu Yiming and other Taoist authors, "overflowing Breath" (*haoran zhi qi*) is a name of the One Breath prior to Heaven. Thus *fushi* 伏食 means attending to the cultivation of both the "empty" (Chen Zhixu's "Breath prior to Heaven") and the "actual," or rather, to the operation of the "empty" in the "actual."

29:6

The Way of the Changes is correct and unbiased (易道正不傾). After this verse, the Yin Changsheng redaction adds: "There are 384 *zhu* ("scruples"), and they correspond to the sum of the emblematic lines of the fire times" (銖有三百八十四、亦應火候爻象之計). The Waidan anonymous redaction adds: "There are 384 *zhu*, and they correspond to the sum of the lines" (銖有三百八十四、亦應爻之計). Peng Xiao and Yu Yan add: "There are 384 *zhu*, and they correspond to the number of the hexagrams lines" (銖有三百八十四、亦應卦爻之數). These sentences refer to the ancient Chinese weight system, where one pound (*jin* 斤) consists of 16 ounces (*liang* 兩), and one ounce consists of 24 scruples (*zhu* 銖). The 384 scruples contained in one pound match the number of the individual lines contained in the sixty-four hexagrams of the *Book of Changes* (64x6 = 384).

32:8

The Flowing Pearl is the child of Water (流珠水之子). All extant redactions prior to Chen Zhixu have *mu* 母 ("mother") for *zi* 子 ("child"). While these conflicting readings may seem perplexing, both of them are meaningful in the alchemical imaginal language. In the reading of the earlier redactions, mercury is assimilated to the agent Metal, which in the generation sequence of the five agents gives birth to Water; therefore "the Flowing Pearl is the mother of Water." Chen Zhixu's reading refers, instead, to the standard associations used in alchemy. Here mercury corresponds to the agent Wood, which is generated by Water; therefore "the Flowing Pearl is the child of Water." Zhu Yuanyu, Dong Dening, Liu Yiming, and other later commentators follow Chen Zhixu's reading.

35:5

If you support, by its kind, its being what it is (以類輔自然). The rules of prosody demand that this verse is read as made of two clauses, namely *yi lei* 以類 and *fu ziran* 輔自然; therefore *ziran* 自然 ("being what it is") is an object of the verb *fu* 輔 ("to support"). A translation based on reading the verse as consisting of *yi lei fu* 以類輔 and *ziran* 自然 (for example, "supporting [a thing] by its kind is natural") would not respect the prosodic pattern. For the translation given here, compare this passage of *Daode jing*, 64: "Thus the saint desires not to desire and does not value goods that are hard to obtain; he learns not to learn and returns to what the multitudes pass by. In this way *he supports the ten thousand things in being what they are*, and dares not to act" (. . . 以輔萬物之自然、而不敢為).

36:8

And their attitude lacks firmness (度量失操持). *Duliang* 度量, here translated as "attitude," could also be rendered as "approach, stance," or "procedure, course of action." These different translations derive from the literal meaning of "measure." In the context of a description of alchemical practices, nevertheless, the sense of "measure" remains at least implied. According to some commentators, in fact, *duliang* specifically refers to the weights of the ingredients and the amount of heat, which these practitioners calculate or apply incorrectly.

36:9

They pound the chalcanthite from Shao (擣治韶石膽). For *shao shidan* 韶石膽 ("chalcanthite from Shao"), all redactions prior to Chen Zhixu have *qiang shidan* 羌石膽 ("chalcanthite from Qiang"; in the Yin Changsheng redaction, *cha* 差 is an error for *qiang* 羌). Both Shaozhou 韶州 (a prefecture in present-day Guangdong) and Qiang 羌 (a region included among present-day Qinghai, Gansu, and Sichuan) are known as areas of production of chalcanthite.

36:11

They roast sulphur above camphor wood (硫磺燒豫章). *Yuzhang* 豫章 is the name of an area found in present-day Jiangxi. By extension, it is used here to denote the charcoal of the camphor tree, from whose name, *zhang* 樟, the geographical appellation is said to derive.

36:22

At midway they begin to waver (中道生狐疑). The expression *huyi*, lit., "to doubt like a fox," is said to derive from the timorous attitude of foxes when crossing watercourses. This idiom is found in several early texts, including the *Lisao* (Encountering Sorrow) poem of the *Chuci* (Songs of Chu): "My mind was irresolute and havering (lit., "doubting like a fox"); I wanted to go, yet I could not" (trans. Hawkes, 75).

37:18

On behalf of the world I have composed this book (為世定詩書). The Tang redactions, as well as Peng Xiao's and Zhu Xi's redactions, also have *ding Shi Shu* 定詩書, a sentence understood as meaning "he (i.e., Confucius) composed the *Odes* and the *Documents*." Yu Yan's redaction, instead, has *ding ci shu* 定此書, meaning "I (i.e., Wei Boyang) have composed this book (i.e., the *Cantong qi*)."

The reading "he composed the *Odes* and the *Documents*" (*ding Shi Shu* 定詩書) would refer to Confucius' role in editing the two Classics (one of the set phrases that refer to this role is *shanding Shi Shu* 刪定詩書, lit., "he condensed and established the *Odes* and the *Documents*"). This reading, however, has little meaning in the present context: the editing of the *Odes* and the *Documents* is traditionally attributed to Confucius alone, and not to all the "three sages" mentioned at the beginning of this section. The first stanza, moreover, shows that this section is concerned only with the *Book of Changes*, and not with the *Odes* and the *Documents*.

It appears likely, therefore, that *ding shishu* 定詩書 in the present sentence means "I (i.e., Wei Boyang) have composed a book in verses (i.e., the *Cantong qi*)"; or even that the phrase should simply be read as "I have composed this book," since the compound *shishu* 詩書 is attested as also meaning "a book" (*shuji* 書籍; see *Hanyu dacidian*, 11:148, s.v. *shuji* 書籍, no. 1).

Regardless of which reading or interpretation may be correct or preferred, this sentence contains a play on words that assimilates the roles played by Confucius and Wei Boyang in composing the two classics and the *Cantong qi*, respectively.

Section 39

As noted above, sections 39 and 40 are concerned with the first and the second half of the alchemical method, respectively. On the basis of the rhyme patterns, the present section should end with verse 39:10 ("but Fire, which is 2, is fastened to them"). I have, however, translated the whole first part of the method in section 39, and the second part in section 40.

39:9–10

The other three are thus not used, but Fire, which is 2, is fastened to them (其三遂不入、火二與之俱). Yu Yan has: "Soil therefore is not used, but the two are fastened to it" 其土遂不入、二者與之俱. According to his commentary, the "two" are Metal and Water; by virtue of their numerical value (15, corresponding to the "accomplishment number" 10 and the "generation number" 5 of Soil), Soil is included in the vessel even though it is not represented by a particular ingredient.

In verse 10 ("but Fire, which is 2, is fastened to them"), the Tang redactions and Zhu Xi have *shui er* 水二 for *huo er* 火二. According to the Yin Changsheng commentary, this expression means "Water and the other," i.e. Fire; the sense is that Water and Fire compound the Elixir. According to Zhu Xi's commentary, Water instead of Fire is meant in this verse, because Fire is separately mentioned below in verse 13 as *taiyang* 太陽 ("Great Yang"), and because verse 11 says (in Zhu Xi's redaction) "the two things join to each other" (二物相合受), which Zhu Xi deems to be a clear reference to Yin and Yang joining together to form the Elixir.

40:12

And when the nodes are complete, it will again need your care (節盡更須親). According to another interpretation, the graph *qin* 親 stands for *xin* 新: "and when the nodes are complete, they should start over again." (The usage of *qin* 親 for *xin* 新 is attested in several early sources.)

42:6

And Wang Yang commended the Yellow Sprout (王陽加黃芽). All redactions and editions of the *Cantong qi* that I have seen read "Wang Yang" 王陽, with the exception of the editions of Chen Zhixu's text, all of which definitely read "Yu Yang" 玉陽. The correct reading is certainly

"Wang Yang"; see *Hanshu*, 72.3058–68 (which contains the sentence "Wang Yang was able to make gold" 王陽能作黃金 at the end of the biography), and *Fengsu tongyi*, 2.9. Either the graph 「玉」 was mistakenly used by Chen Zhixu himself, or an error found in the first edition of his work has been transmitted to the later editions.

Section 51

This section contains one of the finest passages of the *Cantong qi* from a literary point of view. The poetic and aesthetic mastery of its author is also reflected in the way he refers to the pitch-pipes and the earthly branches, which are one of the main subjects in these verses. The names of the pitch-pipes are sometimes shortened to one graph (e.g. *cou* 輳 for *taicou* 太蔟, and *xi* 洗 for *guxi* 姑洗), while the names of the earthly branches are often contained within other graphs (e.g. *wei* 未 within *mei* 昧, and *shen* 申 within *shen* 伸). In either case, while the graphs allude to the cosmological emblems, they also retain their ordinary lexical meaning within the poem. Similarly, the names of the hexagrams are meaningful within the verses in which they appear. "Return" (Fu ䷗), for instance, refers to the new ascending phase of Yang that begins after the end of the previous year. For this reason, the hexagrams names have been translated in this section.

Pitch-pipes and earthly branches appear as follows (numbers on the left refer to the corresponding months):

11 The branch *zi* 子 and the pitch-pipe Yellow Bell (*huangzhong* 黃鍾) are mentioned in verse 5

12 The branch *chou* 丑 and the pitch-pipe Great Regulator (*dalü* 大呂) are mentioned in verse 13

1   The branch *yin* 寅 is mentioned in verse 19; the words *da* 大 ("great") in verse 18 and *cou* 輳 ("converge") in verse 19 allude to the pitch-pipe Great Budding (*taicou* 太蔟)

2   The branch *mao* 卯 is mentioned in verse 22; the words *jia* 俠 ("knights") in verse 22 and *lai* 萊 ("[oak] seeds") in verse 23 allude to the pitch-pipe Pinched Bell (*jiazhong* 夾鍾)

3   The word *zhen* 振 ("shaking off") in verse 30 contains the branch *chen* 辰; the word *xian* 洗 ("washes") in verse 29 alludes to the pitch-pipe Maiden Purity (*guxi* 姑洗)

4   The branch *si* 巳 is mentioned in verse 33; the word *zhong* 中 ("center") in verse 34 alludes to the pitch-pipe Median Regulator (*zhonglü* 仲呂)

5 The branch *wu* 午 and the pitch-pipe Luxuriant (*ruibin* 蕤賓) are mentioned in verse 38

6 The word *mei* 昧 ("darkness") in verse 44 contains the branch *wei* 未; the word *qi* 棲 ("lodging") in verse 44 alludes to the pitch-pipe Forest Bell (*linzhong* 林鐘)

7 The word *shen* 伸 ("stretches") in verse 47 contains the branch *shen* 申

8 The middle month of autumn, mentioned in verse 50, is the period of the year associated with the branch *you* 酉 (note also the similar shapes of the graphs *you* 酉 and *mao* 冒)

9 The word *mie* 滅 ("extinguishing") in verse 56 contains the branch *xu* 戌; the word *wang* 亡 ("forgotten") in verse 58 alludes to the pitch-pipe Tireless (*wuyi* 無射; *wu* 無 = *wang* 亡)

10 The word *he* 闠 ("distant, separated") in verse 64 contains the branch *hai* 亥; the word *ying* 應 ("due, suitable") in verse 65 alludes to the pitch-pipe Responsive Bell (*yingzhong* 應鐘)

59:7

In sleep, embrace your Spirit (寢寐神相抱). This translation assumes that *shen xiang bao* 神相抱 is a contraction of *yu shen xiang bao* 與神相抱. Chen Xianwei follows this reading in his commentary. According to other commentators, instead, the elided word is *qi* 氣 ("breath"), and the verse means "Breath and Spirit embrace one another." A translation that implies an allusion to multiple "spirits" or inner deities (e.g., "your spirits embrace one another") might be grammatically admissible, but hardly defensible from a doctrinal point of view since the inner gods are not part of the teachings of the *Cantong qi*.

69:15

"They owe their beginning to this," and are permeated and made good by it (資始統正). All extant redactions prior to Chen Zhixu have *tongzheng* 統政 for *tongzheng* 統正: "and are ruled by it."

70:9–10

Between the month's last day and next month's first, it encroaches, overcasting and upsetting (晦朔薄蝕、掩冒相傾). These verses are translated in agreement with the reading of Chen Zhixu, Liu Yiming, and other commentators. According to this reading, *xiang* 相 in the second verse does not signal reciprocity ("they upset one another"), but rather that the action of "upsetting" affects an object, in this case the Yang principle. In another reading, which is supported by Peng Xiao and other commentators, *xiang* instead does signal reciprocity, and the verses should be translated: "Between the last day of one month and next month's first day, they (i.e., Yin and Yang, or the Sun and the Moon) encroach upon each other, overcasting and upsetting one another." This reading is in agreement with the statement in 41:5–6: "The Sun and the Moon always encroach upon one another on the month's first day and the day of full moon" (日月相薄蝕、常在朔望間; all extant redactions prior to Chen Zhixu have ". . . between the month's last day and next month's first" 常在晦朔間). It is not easy to make a choice between these two readings, but the general theme of this section, and especially the verse "When Yang loses its token . . .", suggest that the first reading may be preferred.

72:9–13

The liver is green and is the father, the lungs are white and are the mother, the kidneys are black and are the son, the heart is red and is the daughter. — The spleen is yellow and is the forefather (肝青為父、肺白為母、腎黑為子、離赤為女、脾黃為祖). Verses 12–13 ("the heart is red and is the daughter — the spleen is yellow and is the forefather") are not found in the Yin Changsheng redaction. They are found before verse 11 ("the kidneys are black and are the son") in Yu Yan's redaction. Verse 12 ("the heart is red and is the daughter") is not found in Peng Xiao's and Zhu Xi's redactions.

In verse 12 ("the heart is red and is the daughter"), Chen Zhixu calls the heart Li 離 ☲ (the trigram that denotes Fire and corresponds to the heart), possibly in order to avoid ambiguities between the heart as an emblem of the five agents and as the center of the human being. Yu Yan has *xin* 心, the common word for "heart."

76:9

They disguised every name (託號諸名). All extant redactions prior to Chen Zhixu have *shi* 石 for *ming* 名: "they disguised every stone," with reference to the ingredients of the Elixir.

Section 83

The chart at the end of this section is included in the present translation as it is found in Chen Zhixu's redaction of the *Cantong qi*. There are good reasons to suggest that it should not be considered part of the text of the *Cantong qi*. The chart introduces notions that are extraneous to the language and the imagery of the *Cantong qi*—in particular, those of "martial fire" (*wuhuo*) and "civil fire" (*wenhuo*). Moreover, silver (*yin*) is not mentioned in the *Cantong qi*, and the placement of "true mercury" and "true lead" respectively on the "Yang" and "Yin" sides of the chart is perplexing. (No edition that I have seen contains variants in this line.) For these and other reasons, it is not surprising that Zhu Xi, Yu Yan, and about a dozen of Ming- and Qing-dynasty commentaries to the standard text of the *Cantong qi* that I have seen do not include the chart. (The only exceptions are Zhang Wenlong's and Xu Wei's commentaries, which faithfully follow Chen Zhixu's text. Note that the chart cannot have a place at all in the "Ancient Text" of the *Cantong qi*, where the title "The Five Categories" is replaced by "The Three Categories.") Finally, it is significant that, although the chart is a noticeable formal feature in Peng Xiao's and Chen Zhixu's texts of the *Cantong qi*, even they do not provide any explanation of it in their own commentaries.

Section 88

Several commentators and scholars have pointed out that this section contains a "cryptogram" that, according to different views, hides the name of Wei Boyang (「魏伯陽」), or the phrase "composed by Wei Boyang" (「魏伯陽造」), or the title "Song of Wei Boyang" (「魏伯陽歌」).

(1) The graphs 「委」 (*wei*, "to forsake," in verse 1) and 「鬼」 (*gui*, "demons," 4) together form the graph 「魏」 (WEI).

(2) The graph 「人」 (*ren*, "humans," in verse 7) and the lower part of the graph 「百」 (*bai*, "one hundred," 8), i.e., 「白」, together form the graph 「伯」 (BO).

(3) The left part of the graph 「隔」 (*ge*, "to confront," in verse 12), i.e., 「阝」, and the right part of the graph 「湯」 (the name of the Shang ruler, Tang, 11), i.e., 「昜」, together form the graph 「陽」 (YANG).

According to another view, the graphs 「人」 (*ren*, "humans," in verse 15) and 「吉」 (*ji*, "good fortune," 15) together form—or, at least, resemble—the graph 「造」 (*zao*, "to make, to compose").

According to a third, later view, the graph 「柯」 (*ke*, "stems," in verse 13) without its "glow" (*rong* 榮, 14), i.e., 「可」, repeated twice and arranged so that one 「可」 "carries" (*sheng* 乘, 15) the other, and the graph 「欠」 (*qian*, which combines the upper and the lower parts of *fu* 負, "to support," 15), together form the graph 「歌」 (*ge*, "song").

Tables and Figures

Table 1

	WOOD	FIRE	SOIL	METAL	WATER
DIRECTIONS	east	south	center	west	north
SEASONS	spring	summer	(midsummer)	autumn	winter
COLORS	green	red	yellow	white	black
EMBLEMATIC ANIMALS	green dragon	vermilion sparrow	yellow dragon	white tiger	snake and turtle
NUMBERS	3, 8	2, 7	5, 10	4, 9	1, 6
YIN-YANG (1)	minor Yang	great Yang	balance	minor Yin	great Yin
YIN-YANG (2)	True Yin	Yang	balance	True Yang	Yin
STEMS	*jia* 甲 *yi* 乙	*bing* 丙 *ding* 丁	*wu* 戊 *ji* 己	*geng* 庚 *xin* 辛	*ren* 壬 *gui* 癸
BRANCHES	*yin* 寅 *mao* 卯	*wu* 午 *si* 巳	*xu* 戌, *chou* 丑 *wei* 未, *chen* 辰	*you* 酉 *shen* 申	*hai* 亥 *zi* 子
PLANETS	Jupiter	Mars	Saturn	Venus	Mercury
RELATIONS	father	daughter	forefather	mother	son
VISCERA	liver	heart	spleen	lungs	kidneys
BODY ORGAN	eyes	tongue	mouth	nose	ears

The five agents (*wuxing* 五行) and their associations.

Table 2

	FIRE	
	South	
	Vermilion Sparrow	
	2	
	cinnabar	
	Original Spirit (*yuanshen* 元神)	

WOOD	SOIL	METAL
East	Center	West
Green Dragon		White Tiger
3	5	4
True Mercury		True Lead
inner nature (*xing* 性)	intention (*yi* 意)	qualities (*qing* 情)

	WATER	
	North	
	Dark Warrior	
	1	
	black lead	
	Original Essence (*yuanjing* 元精)	

Spatial arrangement of the five agents (*wuxing* 五行),
with some of their main associations. In agreement with the
traditional Chinese convention, North is shown
at the bottom, South at the top, East on the left,
and West on the right.

Table 3

	GENERATES	IS GENERATED BY	CONQUERS	IS CONQUERED BY
WATER	Wood	Metal	Fire	Soil
WOOD	Fire	Water	Soil	Metal
FIRE	Soil	Wood	Metal	Water
SOIL	Metal	Fire	Water	Wood
METAL	Water	Soil	Wood	Fire

"Generation" (*xiangsheng* 相生)
and "conquest" (*xiangke* 相剋)
sequences of the five agents (*wuxing* 五行).

Table 4

AGENT	GENERATION NUMBER	ACCOMPLISHMENT NUMBER
WATER	1	6
FIRE	2	7
WOOD	3	8
METAL	4	9
SOIL	5	10

"Generation numbers" (*shengshu* 生數)
and "accomplishment numbers" (*chengshu* 成數)
of the five agents.

Table 5

☰	☱	☲	☳	☴	☵	☶	☷
乾	兌	離	震	巽	坎	艮	坤
QIAN	DUI	LI	ZHEN	XUN	KAN	GEN	KUN
heaven	lake	fire	thunder	wind	water	mountain	earth
father	youngest daughter	second daughter	eldest son	eldest daughter	second son	youngest son	mother
south	southeast	east	northeast	southwest	west	northwest	north
northwest	west	south	east	southeast	north	northeast	southwest

The eight trigrams (*bagua* 八卦) and their main
associations. From top to bottom: elements in nature, family
relations, and directions in the cosmological
configurations "prior to Heaven" (*xiantian* 先天)
and "posterior to Heaven" (*houtian* 後天).

Table 6

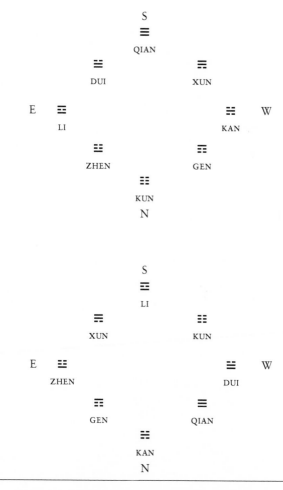

Spatial arrangements of the eight trigrams (*bagua* 八卦)
in the cosmological configurations "prior to Heaven"
(*xiantian* 先天, top) and "posterior to Heaven"
(*houtian* 後天, bottom).

Table 7

	DAYTIME			NIGHTTIME
1	Zhun 屯	䷂	䷃	Meng 蒙
2	Xu 需	䷄	䷅	Song 訟
3	Shi 師	䷆	䷇	Bi 比
4	Xiaoxu 小畜	䷈	䷉	Lü 履
5	Tai 泰	䷊	䷋	Pi 否
6	Tongren 同人	䷌	䷍	Dayou 大有
7	Qian 謙	䷎	䷏	Yu 豫
8	Sui 隨	䷐	䷑	Gu 蠱
9	Lin 臨	䷒	䷓	Guan 觀
10	Shike 噬嗑	䷔	䷕	Bi 賁
11	Bo 剝	䷖	䷗	Fu 複
12	Wuwang 無妄	䷘	䷙	Dachu 大畜
13	Yi 頤	䷚	䷛	Daguo 大過
14	Xian 咸	䷞	䷟	Heng 恆
15	Dun 遯	䷠	䷡	Dazhuang 大壯
16	Jin 晉	䷢	䷣	Mingyi 明夷
17	Jiaren 家人	䷤	䷥	Kui 睽
18	Juan 蹇	䷦	䷧	Jie 解
19	Sun 損	䷨	䷩	Yi 益
20	Guai 夬	䷪	䷫	Gou 姤
21	Cui 萃	䷬	䷭	Sheng 升
22	Kun 困	䷮	䷯	Jing 井
23	Ge 革	䷰	䷱	Ding 鼎
24	Zhen 震	䷲	䷳	Gen 艮
25	Jian 漸	䷴	䷵	Guimei 歸妹
26	Feng 豐	䷶	䷷	Lü 旅
27	Xun 巽	䷸	䷹	Dui 兌
28	Huan 渙	䷺	䷻	Jie 節
29	Zhongfu 中孚	䷼	䷽	Xiaoguo 小過
30	Jiji 既濟	䷾	䷿	Weiji 未濟

Sequence of the sixty hexagrams
during the thirty days of the month.

Table 8

	QIAN	KUN	ZHEN	SUN	KAN	LI	GEN	DUI
6th	壬戌 renxu	癸酉 guiyou	庚戌 gengxu	辛卯 xinmao	戊子 wuzi	己巳 jisi	丙寅 bingyin	丁未 dingwei
5th	壬申 renshen	癸亥 guihai	庚申 gengshen	辛巳 xinsi	戊戌 wuxu	己未 jiwei	丙子 bingzi	丁酉 dingyou
4th	壬午 renwu	癸丑 guichou	庚午 gengwu	辛未 xinwei	戊申 wushen	己酉 jiyou	丙戌 bingxu	丁亥 dinghai
3rd	甲辰 jiachen	乙卯 yimao	庚辰 gengchen	辛酉 xinyou	戊午 wuwu	己亥 jihai	丙申 bingshen	丁丑 dingchou
2nd	甲寅 jiayin	乙巳 yisi	庚寅 gengyin	辛亥 xinhai	戊辰 wuchen	己丑 jichou	丙午 bingwu	丁卯 dingmao
1st	甲子 jiazi	乙未 yiwei	庚子 gengzi	辛丑 xinchou	戊寅 wuyin	己卯 jimao	丙辰 bingchen	丁巳 dingsi

Celestial stems (*tiangan* 天干) and earthly branches (*dizhi* 地支)
associated with the six lines of the "eight pure hexagrams"
(*ba chungua* 八純卦). These associations are used
in verses 45:1–2 of the *Cantong qi*
("Zhun ䷂ uses *zi* and *shen*, Meng ䷃ employs *yin* and *xu*").

NOTE. Each hexagram is formed by an "inner" (lower) trigram and an "outer" (upper) trigram. In the "eight pure hexagrams," the two component trigrams are identical, and each of their lines is associated with one celestial stem and one earthly branch, as shown in this table. In the *Cantong qi* verses quoted above, the branches that represent each hexagram are those associated with the first line of its "inner" trigram and the first line of its "outer" trigram, which correspond to the first and the fourth lines of the respective "pure hexagrams." In particular, Zhun ䷂ is formed by Zhen ☳ and Kan ☵, and Meng ䷃ is formed by Kan ☵ and Gen ☶. With regard to Zhun ䷂, the branches associated with the first line of its inner trigram Zhen ☳ (corresponding to the first line of the hexagram Zhen ䷲) and with the first line of its outer trigram Kan ☵ (corresponding to the fourth line of the hexagram Kan ䷜) are *zi* 子 and *shen* 申, respectively. With regard to Meng ䷃, the branches associated with the first line of its inner trigram Kan ☵ (corresponding to the first line of the hexagram Kan ䷜) and with the first line of its outer trigram Gen ☶ (corresponding to the fourth line of the hexagram Gen ䷳) are *yin* 寅 and *xu* 戌, respectively.

Table 9

HEXAGRAMS			CELESTIAL STEMS	
Qian	乾	☰	*jia, ren*	甲, 壬
Kun	坤	☷	*yi, gui*	乙, 癸
Gen	艮	☶	*bing*	丙
Dui	兌	☱	*ding*	丁
Kan	坎	☵	*wu*	戊
Li	離	☲	*ji*	己
Zhen	震	☳	*geng*	庚
Xun	巽	☴	*xin*	辛

Correspondences between hexagrams and celestial stems
in Jing Fang's 京方 (77–37 BCE) *bagua najia* 八卦納甲
(Matching Stems of the Eight Trigrams) device.

Table 10

NODE	DAY	PHASE	TRIGRAM			STEM AND DIRECTION		
(1–5)	3	beginning of waxing (*shuo* 朔)	Zhen	震	☳	*geng*	庚	W
(6–10)	8	first quarter (*shangxian* 上弦)	Dui	兌	☱	*ding*	丁	S
(11–15)	15	full moon (*wang* 望)	Qian	乾	☰	*jia*	甲	E
(16–20)	16	beginning of waning (*jiwang* 既望)	Xun	巽	☴	*xin*	辛	W
(21–25)	23	last quarter (*xiaxian* 下弦)	Gen	艮	☶	*bing*	丙	S
(26–30)	30	end of cycle (*hui* 晦)	Kun	坤	☷	*yi*	乙	E

The *yueti najia* 月體納甲 (Matching Stems of the Moons) device
as developed by Yu Fan 虞翻 (164–233)
and applied in the *Cantong qi*.

Table 11

復	臨	泰	大壯	夬	乾	姤	遯	否	觀	剝	坤
FU	LIN	TAI	DAZHUANG	GUAI	QIAN	GOU	DUN	PI	GUAN	BO	KUN
子	丑	寅	卯	辰	巳	午	未	申	酉	戌	亥
zi	chou	yin	mao	chen	si	wu	wei	shen	you	xu	hai
黃鐘	大呂	太蔟	夾鐘	姑洗	仲呂	蕤賓	林鐘	夷則	南呂	無射	應鐘
huangzhong	dalü	taicou	jiazhong	guxi	zhonglü	ruibin	linzhong	yize	nanlü	wuyi	yingzhong
11	12	1	2	3	4	5	6	7	8	9	10
23–1	1–3	3–5	5–7	7–9	9–11	11–13	13–15	15–17	17–19	19–21	21–23

The twelve "sovereign hexagrams" (*bigua* 辟卦)
and their relation to other duodenary series:
earthly branches (*dizhi* 地支), bells and pitch-pipes
(*zhonglü* 鍾律), months of the year,
and "double hours" (*shi* 時).

Table 12

STEMS			AGENTS	DIRECTIONS	COLORS	VISCERA	NUMBERS
1	*jia*	甲					
			WOOD	east	green	liver	3, 8
2	*yi*	乙					
3	*bing*	丙					
			FIRE	south	red	heart	2, 7
4	*ding*	丁					
5	*wu*	戊					
			SOIL	center	yellow	spleen	5
6	*ji*	己					
7	*geng*	庚					
			METAL	west	white	lungs	4, 9
8	*xin*	辛					
9	*ren*	壬					
			WATER	north	black	kidneys	1, 6
10	*gui*	癸					

The ten celestial stems (*tiangan* 天干)
and their associations.

Table 13

	BRANCHES		AGENTS	DIRECTIONS	HOURS	NUMBERS
1	*zi*	子	WATER	N	23–1	1, 6
2	*chou*	丑	SOIL	NNE 3/4 E	1–3	5, 10
3	*yin*	寅	WOOD	ENE 3/4 N	3–5	3, 8
4	*mao*	卯	WOOD	E	5–7	3, 8
5	*chen*	辰	SOIL	ESE 3/4 S	7–9	5, 10
6	*si*	巳	FIRE	SSE 3/4 E	9–11	2, 7
7	*wu*	午	FIRE	S	11–13	2, 7
8	*wei*	未	SOIL	SSW 3/4 W	13–15	5, 10
9	*shen*	申	METAL	WSW 3/4 S	15–17	4, 9
10	*you*	酉	METAL	W	17–19	4, 9
11	*xu*	戌	SOIL	WNW 3/4 N	19–21	5, 10
12	*hai*	亥	WATER	NNW 3/4 W	21–23	1, 6

The twelve earthly branches (*dizhi* 地支)
and their associations.

Table 14

S
wu 午
FIRE

E
mao 卯
WOOD

W
you 酉
METAL

N
zi 子
WATER

Spatial arrangement of the four cardinal
earthly branches (*dizhi* 地支).

Table 15

1 jiazi	甲子	13 bingzi	丙子	25 wuzi	戊子	37 gengzi	庚子	49 renzi	壬子
2 yichou	乙丑	14 dingchou	丁丑	26 jichou	己丑	38 xinchou	辛丑	50 guichou	癸丑
3 bingyin	丙寅	15 wuyin	戊寅	27 gengyin	庚寅	39 renyin	壬寅	51 jiayin	甲寅
4 dingmao	丁卯	16 jimao	己卯	28 xinmao	辛卯	40 guimao	癸卯	52 yimao	乙卯
5 wuchen	戊辰	17 gengchen	庚辰	29 renchen	壬辰	41 jiachen	甲辰	53 bingchen	丙辰
6 jisi	己巳	18 xinsi	辛巳	30 guisi	癸巳	42 yisi	乙巳	54 dingsi	丁巳
7 gengwu	庚午	19 renwu	壬午	31 jiawu	甲午	43 bingwu	丙午	55 wuwu	戊午
8 xinwei	辛未	20 guiwei	癸未	32 yiwei	乙未	44 dingwei	丁未	56 jiwei	己未
9 renshen	壬申	21 jiashen	甲申	33 bingshen	丙申	45 wushen	戊申	57 gengshen	庚申
10 guiyou	癸酉	22 yiyou	乙酉	34 dingyou	丁酉	46 jiyou	己酉	58 xinyou	辛酉
11 jiaxu	甲戌	23 bingxu	丙戌	35 wuxu	戊戌	47 gengxu	庚戌	59 renxu	壬戌
12 yihai	乙亥	24 dinghai	丁亥	36 jihai	己亥	48 xinhai	辛亥	60 guihai	癸亥

Sexagesimal cycle of the celestial stems (*tiangan* 天干)
and the earthly branches (*dizhi* 地支).

Table 16

EAST

	1	jiao	角	Horn
	2	kang	亢	Neck
	3	di	氐	Root
	4	fang	房	Room
	5	xin	心	Heart
	6	wei	尾	Tail
	7	ji	箕	Winnowing Basket

NORTH

	8	dou	斗	Dipper
	9	niu (qianniu)	牛 (牽牛)	Ox (or Ox Leader)
	10	nü (shunnü)	女 (須女)	Maid (or Serving Maid)
	11	xu	虛	Emptiness
	12	wei	危	Rooftop
	13	shi (yingshi)	室 (營室)	Encampment
	14	bi	壁	Wall

WEST

	15	kui	奎	Stride
	16	lou	婁	Bond
	17	wei	胃	Stomach
	18	mao	昴	Pleiades
	19	bi	畢	Net
	20	zi	觜	Turtle Beak
	21	shen	參	Alignment

SOUTH

	22	jing	井	Well
	23	gui (yugui)	鬼 (輿鬼)	Spirit (or Spirit Bearer)
	24	liu	柳	Willow
	25	xing (qixing)	星 (七星)	[Seven] Stars
	26	zhang	張	Extension
	27	yi	翼	Wings
	28	zhen	軫	Chariot Platform

The twenty-eight lunar lodges (*xiu* 宿). Translations based on
Major, *Heaven and Earth in Early Han Thought*, 127.

Figure 1

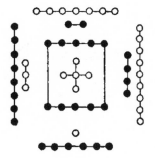

Hetu 河圖 (Chart of the Yellow River).

Figure 2

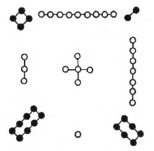

Luoshu 洛書 (Writ of the Luo River).

Figure 3

"Kan and Li are the inner and the outer walls" (1.3)

Kan ☵ and Li ☲ represented as two joined semicircles.

Figure 4

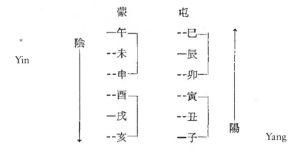

The twelve lines of the first pair of hexagrams
(Zhun ䷂ on the right, Meng ䷃ on the left)
and their associations with the twelve earthly branches.

Appendixes

Two Biographies of Wei Boyang

Biography in the Shenxian zhuan

As we saw in the Introduction (§ 2), Peng Xiao claims that his account of Wei Boyang's life is based on the *Shenxian zhuan* (Biographies of the Divine Immortals), a work traditionally attributed to Ge Hong (283–343). The first full record of the *Shenxian zhuan* biography, which is also deemed to be the most reliable one, is found in the *Taiping guangji* (Extended Collection of Records of the Taiping xingguo Reign Period), dating from 978. This version is translated below.

Wei Boyang was a native of Wu.[1] He was the son of a high-ranking family, but by nature was devoted to the arts of the Dao. Later he retired on a mountain with three disciples in order to compound the divine Elixir. Knowing that his disciples were not thoroughly committed in their hearts, when the Elixir was ready he said in order to test them: "The Elixir is ready, but it ought first to be tested on our dog. If the dog rises to Heaven, we may take it ourselves. If the dog dies, we should not take it." He gave the Elixir to the dog, and the dog immediately fell dead.

Boyang told his disciples: "I am afraid that the Medicine was not ready. It has caused death upon ingestion, so it seems not to be in harmony with the Numinous Light (*shenming*). If we ingest the Medicine, I fear we will share the fate of our dog. What shall we do?" The disciples asked: "Master, would you take it yourself?" Boyang replied: "I have turned my shoulders to the worldly ways and have forsaken my home in order to retire on this mountain. I would be ashamed to return without having found the Dao. Whether I die or not, I must take it." Thereupon he ingested the Elixir. No sooner was it in his mouth, he died instantly.

---

[1] Present-day Jiangsu, and parts of Anhui and Zhejiang.

On seeing this, one of the disciples said: "The purpose of making the Elixir is to live a long life. If we ingest it and die, what sense does it make?" Another disciple said: "Our Master was not an ordinary person. If he ingested it and died, he must have done it with a purpose." So he took the Elixir, ingested it, and died. The other two disciples said to one another: "We have made the Elixir in order to attain a long life. If we ingest it and die, what is the purpose? By not taking this Medicine, we can still spend a few more decades in this world." So they left the mountain without ingesting the Elixir, with the intention of arranging a funeral for Boyang and their dead fellow disciple.

After the two disciples left, Boyang came to life again. He took the Elixir that he had compounded and poured some of it into the mouths of the dead disciple and the white dog. Both of them also came to life again. Boyang and his disciple, whose surname was Yu, went further into the mountains as immortals. On the way they met a wood-cutter, and handed him a letter of thanks for the other two disciples. When they read it, they were filled with regret.

Boyang wrote the *Cantong qi* and the *Wuxing xianglei* (The Categories of the Five Agents), altogether in three chapters (*juan*). His work talks about the *Book of Changes*, but in fact utilizes its lines and images to discuss the principles of compounding the Elixir. Knowing nothing about the divine Elixir, the worldly scholars have written several commentaries on it based on Yin and Yang. They have truly missed its meaning. (*Taiping guangji*, 2.11–12)

Biography by Peng Xiao

Although Peng Xiao cites *the Shenxian zhuan* as his authority, his account is remarkably different from the one translated above:

According to the *Shenxian zhuan*, the True Man Wei Boyang was a native of Shangyu in Kuaiji. His family had inherited official appointments for generations, but the Master did not serve in office. He cultivated the truth in secret and silence, and nourished his mind in Empty Non-being. He was widely versed in both prose and poetry, and was competent in the "weft" and the prognostication texts (*weihou*).[2] Calm and tranquil, he guarded simplicity and

___
[2] The term *weihou* denotes the Han-dynasty esoteric texts commonly

followed nothing but the Dao. He always looked upon ceremonial garments as things of no value.

We do not know the name of the master who transmitted it to him, but he received the *Guwen longhu jing* (Ancient Text of the Scripture of the Dragon and Tiger). Having fully grasped its subtle meaning, he wrote the *Cantong qi* in three parts (*pian*) in agreement with the *Book of Changes*. It is said, moreover, that since he had not thoroughly treated the fine points, he also wrote the portion entitled "Filling Lacunae" ("Busai yituo"), which elaborates on the mysteries of the scriptures on the Elixir. His accounts repeatedly use metaphors and analogies, hiding the apparent under unusual words.

Wei Boyang secretly disclosed his book to Xu Congshi, a native of Qingzhou, who wrote a commentary on it keeping his name hidden.[3] At the time of Emperor Huan of the Later Han (r. 146–167), the Master again transmitted it to Chunyu Shutong. Since then, it has circulated in the world. (*Zhouyi cantong qi fenzhang tong zhenyi*, Preface, 1a-b)

The fictional nature of this account has been noted for a long time. Nevertheless, several elements in Peng Xiao's account are significant: the indication of Shangyu as the area of origin of both Wei Boyang and Chunyu Shutong; Wei Boyang's expertise in the esoteric "weft texts"; the close relation between the *Cantong qi* and the *Longhu jing*; the subdivision of the *Cantong qi* into three parts, all of which—according to Peng Xiao—were written by Wei Boyang; the hint that the composition process took place in more than one stage; the reputed date of the text, which would fall around the mid-second century; and the attribution of an early commentary to Xu Congshi.

---

known as "apocrypha." This term is found in the preface to the "Biographies of the Masters of Methods" in the *History of the Later Han Dynasty* (*Hou Hanshu*), 82A.2703, where it refers to the apocrypha attached to seven Classics (*Changes, Documents, Odes, Rites, Music, Spring and Autumns*, and *Filial Piety*) and to another text belonging to the same corpus, the *Shangshu zhonghou* (Prognostications Based on the *Book of Documents*). See Ngo Van Xuyet, *Divination, magie et politique dans la Chine ancienne*, p. 74. The relation between the *Cantong qi* and the apocrypha has been examined above, pp. 17 ff.

[3] Since Peng Xiao has stated in the previous paragraph that Wei Boyang "wrote the *Cantong qi* in three parts," i.e., the entire text of the scripture, Xu Congshi's commentary was, in Peng Xiao's view, an independent work, and not one incorporated into the present *Cantong qi*.

Chinese Text

This translation of the *Cantong qi* is based on the text found in Chen Zhixu's *Zhouyi cantong qi zhujie* 周易參同契注解 (Commentary and Explication of the *Cantong qi*), composed in ca. 1330. I have used the earliest extant edition, published by the Jinling shufang 金陵書坊 (Nanjing Print Shop) in 1484. This edition appears to be extant in a single exemplar, which is kept at the Shanghai Library (Shanghai Tushuguan).

Chen Zhixu divides the text of the *Cantong qi* into thirty-five chapters (*zhang* 章). These divisions are not reported in the present translation, which is divided into sections according to the criteria mentioned above (p. 67).

The Shanghai exemplar of Chen Zhixu's work lacks the portion corresponding to the second half of Chapter XXXIV and the whole Chapter XXXV (in the present translation, the portion going from verse 83:16 to the end of section 88). For the missing portion, I have used a Japanese manuscript dating from the Edo period (1603–1868) kept at the Cabinet Library (Naikaku Bunko) in Tokyo. This manuscript is almost certainly a copy of the "Yifu" 伊府 edition of Chen Zhixu's text, which was published in 1552 and belongs to the same textual lineage as the Jinling shufang edition.

The *Gujin tushu jicheng* 古今圖書集成 edition (first published in 1726) also belongs to the same lineage but includes a large number of errors and is unreliable as a witness of Chen Zhixu's text. The other main textual branch of Chen Zhixu's redaction was originated by the *Jindan zhengli daquan* 金丹正理大全 (first published in 1538). This edition, which contains several errors and readings drawn from other redactions of the *Cantong qi*, is in turn at the basis of the editions found in the *Siku quanshu* 四庫全書 (1782) and the *Daozang jiyao* 道藏輯要 (ca. 1800, expanded in 1906).

I have corrected about three dozen errors found in the Jinling shufang edition. With only four exceptions, these errors are demonstrated by one or more of the following types of evidence: citation of the same word or verse in the commentary; disregard of rhyme patterns; reading of the Edo manuscript; and context of the verse.[1] The four exceptions are readings for which no evidence is available, but are very unlikely to be correct. These are the 夭 : 天 variant in 26:21; the 王 : 玉 variant in 42:6; the 萌 : 明 variant in 49:14; and the 釜 : 金 variant in 74:37. In these cases, I have adopted the readings found in other redactions of the *Cantong qi* and (except for the variant in 42:6, which appears to be Chen Zhixu's own error) in the other editions of Chen Zhixu's work that I have seen.

My emendations are listed below. Each line shows the section and verse numbers; the emended sentence; the variant in the Jinling shufang edition; and, where available, the evidence for the emendation.

2:1	覆冒陰陽之道	冒 : 育	冒 Edo ms.
10:13	蝀勤莫不由	蝀 : 螻	蝀 comm.
13:12	屈折低下降	折 : 拆	折 Edo ms.
17:2	存亡之緒	亡 : 已	亡 Edo ms.; 亡 comm.
17:9	執法刺譏	刺 : 剌	刺 required by context
22:10	北方河車	車 : 東	車 Edo ms.; 車 comm.
24:12	混而相拘	拘 : 居	拘 Edo ms.; 拘 comm.
26:21	遂以夭命死	夭 : 天	
33:8	守界定規矩	定 : 之	定 Edo ms.; 定 comm.
34:4	解釋成太玄	玄 : 盧	玄 Edo ms.; 玄 req. by rhyme
34:8	終始自相因	終始 : 始終	終始 comm.
37:1	若夫至聖	若 : 若若	若 Edo ms.
37:5	文王帝之宗	王 : om.	王 Edo ms.
37:18	為世定詩書	詩 : 時	詩 Edo ms.
38:28	幽明本共居	共 : 若	共 Edo ms.; 共 comm.
38:6	陶冶有法度	冶 : 治	冶 Edo ms.; 冶 comm.
39:12	變化狀若神	狀 : 壯	狀 required by context
40:16	赫然成還丹	赫 : 赤	赫赤 comm.
42:6	王陽加黃芽	王 : 玉	[See the Textual Notes, p. 240]
42:8	不肖毋與俱	毋 : 母	毋 Edo ms.
47:13	四時順宜	順 : 傾	順 Edo ms.

[1] I have emended the Jinling shufang text exclusively on the basis of context in these cases: 刺 : 剌 (17:9); 狀 : 壯 (39:12); 糾 : 斜 (74:8); 擣 : 大 (74:27); and 檗 : 蘗 (80:7).

49:4	嘔輪吐萌	萌：明	
49:6	發散精光	精：清	精 comm.
49:12	陰以八通	八：入	八 Edo ms.
64:16	烏雀畏鸇	鸇：顫	鸇 comm.
72:6	列為龍虎	列：則	列 comm.
74:8	蟠紏相扶	紏：斜	紏 required by context
74:27	八公擣鍊	擣：大	擣 required by context
74:37	亦猶和膠補釜	釜：金	
76:12	餫櫝終身	櫝：匱	匵 Edo ms.
77:17	循斗而招搖兮	搖：謠	搖 comm.
80:6	火滅化為土	土：上	土 Edo ms.
80:7	若櫱染為黃兮	櫱：蘗	櫱 required by context
82:12	中間文	間：問	間 comm.

The 折：拆 and the 刺：刾 errors in 13:12 and 17:9 are also found in several editions of the other redactions that I have seen. In verse 24:12, the error is probably due to the accidental repetition of the homophonous word *ju* 居, which is found in the same position two verses before (24:10:「白裏貞居」). In verse 40:16, the compound word *hechi* 赫赤 used by Chen Zhixu in his commentary is likely to be a gloss on *he* 赫, rather than *chi* 赤.

Finally, I have replaced several variant graphs with the corresponding standard forms.

The text reproduced in the following pages is based on the Jinling shufang edition, edited according to the criteria outlined above.

周易參同契

上篇

【第一節】

乾坤者易之門戶、眾卦之父母、坎離匡郭、運轂正軸、 5 牝牡四卦、
以為橐籥。

【第二節】

覆冒陰陽之道、猶工御者、準繩墨、執銜轡、 5 正規矩、隨軌轍、處
中以制外、數在律曆紀。

【第三節】

月節有五六、經緯奉日使、兼并為六十、剛柔有表裏、 5 朔旦屯直
事、至暮蒙當受、晝夜各一卦、用之依次序、既未至晦爽、 10 終則復
更始、日月為期度、動靜有早晚、春夏據內體、從子到辰巳、 15 秋冬
當外用、自午訖戌亥、賞罰應春秋、昏明順寒暑、爻辭有仁義、 20 隨
時發喜怒、如是應四時、五行得其理。

【第四節】

天地設位、而易行乎其中矣、 天地者乾坤之象也、設位者列陰陽配合
之位也、 5 易謂坎離、坎離者乾坤二用、二用無爻位、周流行六虛、
往來既不定、 10 上下亦無常。

【第五節】

幽潛淪匿、變化於中、包囊萬物、為道紀綱、 5 以無制有、器用者
空、故推消息、坎離沒亡。

【第六節】

言不苟造、論不虛生、引驗見效、校度神明、 5 推類結字、原理為
證。

【第七節】

坎戊月精、離己日光、日月為易、剛柔相當、 5 土旺四季、羅絡始
終、青赤黑白、各居一方、皆裏中宮、 10 戊己之功。

【第八節】

易者象也、懸象著明、莫大乎日月、窮神以知化、 5 陽往則陰來、輻
輳而輪轉、出入更卷舒。

【第九節】

易有三百八十四爻、據爻摘符、符謂六十四卦。

【第十節】

晦至朔旦、震來受符、當斯之際、天地媾其精、 5 日月相撢持、雄陽
播玄施、雌陰化黃包、混沌相交接、權輿樹根基、 10 經營養鄞鄂、凝
神以成軀、眾夫蹈以出、蠕動莫不由。

【第十一節】

於是仲尼讚鴻濛、乾坤德洞虛、稽古當元皇、關雎建始初、 5 冠婚氣
相紐、元年乃芽滋、聖人不虛生、上觀顯天符、天符有進退、 10 屈伸
以應時。

【第十二節】

故易統天心、復卦建始萌、長子繼父體、因母立兆基、 5 消息應鍾
律、昇降據斗樞。

【第十三節】

三日出為爽、震庚受西方、八日兌受丁、上弦平如繩、 5 十五乾體
就、盛滿甲東方、蟾蜍與兔魄、日月氣雙明、蟾蜍視卦節、 10 兔者吐
生光、七八道已訖、屈折低下降、十六轉受統、巽辛見平明、 15 艮直
於丙南、下弦二十三、坤乙三十日、東北喪其朋、節盡相禪與、 20 繼
體復生龍、壬癸配甲乙、乾坤括始終、七八數十五、九六亦相應、 25
四者合三十、陽氣索滅藏。

【第十四節】

八卦布列曜、運移不失中、元精眇難覩、推度效符證、 5 居則觀其
象、準擬其形容、立表以為範、占候定吉凶、發號順時令、 10 勿失爻
動時、上察河圖文、下序地形流、中稽於人心、參合考三才、 15 動則
循卦節、靜則因象辭、乾坤用施行、天地然後治。

【第十五節】

御政之首、鼎新革故、管括微密、開舒布寶、 5 要道魁柄、統化綱
紐、爻象內動、吉凶外起、五緯錯順、 10 應時感動、四七乖戾、誃離
俯仰、文昌統錄、詰責台輔、 15 百官有司、各典所部。

【第十六節】

日合五行精、月受六律紀、五六三十度、度竟復更始。

【第十七節】

原始要終、存亡之緒、或君驕佚、亢滿違道、 5 或臣邪佞、行不順
軌、弦望盈縮、乖變凶咎、執法刺譏、 10 詰過貽主、辰極受正、優游
任下、明堂布政、國無害道。

【第十八節】

內以養己、安靜虛無、原本隱明、內照形軀、 5 閉塞其兌、築固靈
株、三光陸沈、溫養子珠、視之不見、 10 近而易求。

【第十九節】

黃中漸通理、潤澤達肌膚、初正則終脩、幹立末可持、 5 一者以掩蔽、世人莫知之。

【第二十節】

上德無為、不以察求、下德為之、其用不休。

【第二十一節】

上閉則稱有、下閉則稱無、無者以奉上、上有神德居、 5 此兩孔穴法、金氣亦相胥。

【第二十二節】

知白守黑、神明自來、白者金精、黑者水基、 5 水者道樞、其數名一、陰陽之始、玄含黃芽、五金之主、 10 北方河車、故鉛外黑、內懷金華、被褐懷玉、外為狂夫。

【第二十三節】

金為水母、母隱子胎、水為金子、子藏母胞。

【第二十四節】

真人至妙、若有若無、髣髴太淵、乍沈乍浮、 5 退而分布、各守境隅、採之類白、造之則朱、鍊為表衛、 10 白裏貞居、方圓徑寸、混而相拘、先天地生、巍巍尊高。

【第二十五節】

旁有垣闕、狀似蓬壺、環帀關閉、四通踟躕、 5 守禦密固、閼絕奸邪、曲閣相通、以戒不虞、可以無思、 10 難以愁勞、神氣滿室、莫之能留、守之者昌、失之者亡、 15 動靜休息、常與人俱。

【第二十六節】

是非歷臟法、內觀有所思、履行步斗宿、六甲以日辰、 5 陰道厭九
一、濁亂弄元胞、食氣鳴腸胃、吐正吸外邪、晝夜不臥寐、 10 晦朔未
嘗休、身體日疲倦、恍惚狀若癡、百脈鼎沸馳、不得清澄居、 15 累土
立壇宇、朝暮敬祭祀、鬼物見形象、夢寐感慨之、心歡意悅喜、 20 自
謂必延期、遽以夭命死、腐露其形骸、舉措輒有違、悖逆失樞機、 25
諸術甚眾多、千條有萬餘、前卻違黃老、曲折戾九都、明者省厥旨、
30 曠然知所由。

【第二十七節】

勤而行之、夙夜不休、伏食三載、輕舉遠遊、 5 跨火不焦、入水不
濡、能存能亡、長樂無憂、道成德就、 10 潛伏俟時、太一乃召、移居
中洲、功滿上昇、膺籙受圖。

【第二十八節】

火記不虛作、演易以明之、偃月法鼎爐、白虎為熬樞、 5 汞日為流
珠、青龍與之俱、舉東以合西、魂魄自相拘。

【第二十九節】

上弦兌數八、下弦艮亦八、兩弦合其精、乾坤體乃成、 5 二八應一
斤、易道正不傾。

【第三十節】

金入於猛火、色不奪精光、自開闢以來、日月不虧明、 5 金不失其
重、日月形如常。

【第三十一節】

金本從月生、朔旦日受符、金返歸其母、月晦日相包、 5 隱藏其匡
郭、沈淪於洞虛、金復其故性、威光鼎乃熺。

【第三十二節】

子午數合三、戊己號稱五、三五既和諧、八石正綱紀、 5 呼吸相含
育、伭思為夫婦、黃土金之父、流珠水之子、水以土為鬼、 10 土鎮水
不起、朱雀為火精、執平調勝負、水盛火消滅、俱死歸厚土、 15 三性
既合會、本性共宗祖。

【第三十三節】

巨勝尚延年、還丹可入口、金性不敗朽、故為萬物寶、 5 術士伏食
之、壽命得長久、土遊於四季、守界定規矩、金砂入五內、 10 霧散若
風雨、薰蒸達四肢、顏色悦澤好、髮白皆變黑、齒落生舊所、 15 老翁
復丁壯、耆嫗成姹女、改形免世厄、號之曰真人。

【第三十四節】

胡粉投火中、色壞還為鉛、冰雪得溫湯、解釋成太玄、 5 金以砂為
主、稟和於水銀、變化由其真、終始自相因。

【第三十五節】

欲作伏食仙、宜以同類者、植禾當以穀、覆雞用其卵、 5 以類輔自
然、物成易陶冶、魚目豈為珠、蓬蒿不成檟、類同者相從、 10 事乖不
成寶、燕雀不生鳳、狐兔不乳馬、水流不炎上、火動不潤下。

【第三十六節】

世間多學士、高妙負良材、邂逅不遭遇、耗火亡資財、 5 據按依文
説、妄以意為之、端緒無因緣、度量失操持、擣治羗石膽、 10 雲母及
礬磁、硫磺燒豫章、泥汞相鍊治、鼓下五石銅、以之為輔樞、 15 雜性
不同類、安肯合體居、千舉必萬敗、欲黠反成癡、僥倖訖不遇、 20 至
人獨知之、稚年至白首、中道生狐疑、背道守迷路、出正入邪蹊、 25
管窺不廣見、難以揆方來。

【第三十七節】

若夫至聖、不過伏羲、始畫八卦、效法天地、 5 文王帝之宗、結體演
爻辭、夫子庶聖雄、十翼以輔之、三君天所挺、 10 迭興更御時、優劣
有步驟、功德不相殊、制作有所踵、推度審分銖、 15 有形易忖量、無
兆難慮謀、作事令可法、為世定詩書、素無前識資、 20 因師覺悟之、
皓若褰帷帳、瞋目登高臺。

【第三十八節】

火記六百篇、所趣等不迷、文字鄭重説、世人不熟思、 5 尋度其源
流、幽明本共居、竊為賢者談、曷敢輕為書、若遂結舌瘖、 10 絕道獲
罪誅、寫情著竹帛、又恐泄天符、猶豫增歎息、俯仰綴斯愚、 15 陶冶
有法度、未可悉陳敷、略述其綱紀、枝條見扶疏。

【第三十九節】

以金為隄防、水入乃優游、金計有十五、水數亦如之、 5 臨爐定銖
兩、五分水有餘、二者以為真、金重如本初、其三遂不入、 10 火二與
之俱、三物相合受、變化狀若神、下有太陽氣、伏蒸須臾間、 15 先液
而後凝、號曰黃輿焉、歲月將欲訖、毀性傷壽年、形體如灰土、 20 狀
若明窗塵。

【第四十節】

擣治并合之、持入赤色門、固塞其際會、務令致完堅、 5 炎火張於
下、晝夜聲正勤、始文使可修、終竟武乃陳、候視加謹慎、 10 審察調
寒溫、周旋十二節、節盡更須親、氣索命將絕、休死亡魄魂、 15 色轉
更為紫、赫然成還丹、粉提以一丸、刀圭最為神。

【第四十一節】

推演五行數、較約而不繁、舉水以激火、奄然滅光明、 5 日月相薄
蝕、常在朔望間、水盛坎侵陽、火衰離晝昏、陰陽相飲食、 10 交感道
自然、名者以定情、字者以性言、金來歸性初、乃得稱還丹。

【第四十二節】

吾不敢虛說、倣傚聖人文、古記題龍虎、黃帝美金華、5 淮南鍊秋
石、王陽加黃芽、賢者能持行、不肖毋與俱、古今道猶一、10 對談吐
所謀、學者加勉力、留念深思惟、至要言甚露、昭昭不我欺。

中篇

【第四十三節】

乾剛坤柔、配合相包、陽稟陰受、雄雌相須、5 須以造化、精氣乃
舒、坎離冠首、光耀垂敷、玄冥難測、10 不可畫圖、聖人揆度、參序
元基、四者混沌、逕入虛無、15 六十卦周、張布為輿、龍馬就駕、明
君御時、和則隨從、20 路平不邪、邪道險阻、傾危國家。

【第四十四節】

君子居其室、出其言善、則千里之外應之、謂萬乘之主、5 處九重之
室、發號出令、順陰陽節、藏器俟時、勿違卦月。

【第四十五節】

屯以子申、蒙用寅戌、餘六十卦、各自有日、5 聊陳兩象、未能究
悉、立義設刑、當仁施德、逆之者凶、10 順之者吉、按歷法令、至誠
專密、謹候日辰、審察消息、15 纖芥不正、悔吝為賊。

【第四十六節】

二至改度、乖錯委曲、隆冬大暑、盛夏霜雪、5 二分縱橫、不應漏
刻、水旱相伐、風雨不節、蝗蟲涌沸、10 羣異旁出、天見其怪、山崩
地裂。

【第四十七節】

孝子用心、感動皇極、近出己口、遠流殊域、5 或以招禍、或以致
福、或興太平、或造兵革、四者之來、10 由乎胸臆、動靜有常、奉其

繩墨、四時順宜、與氣相得、 15 剛柔斷矣、不相涉入、五行守界、不妄盈縮、易行周流、 20 屈伸反覆。

【第四十八節】

晦朔之間、合符行中、混沌鴻濛、牝牡相從、 5 滋液潤澤、施化流通、天地神明、不可度量、利用安身、 10 隱形而藏。

【第四十九節】

始於東北、箕斗之鄉、旋而右轉、嘔輪吐萌、 5 潛潭見象、發散精光、昴畢之上、震出為徵、陽氣造端、 10 初九潛龍、陽以三立、陰以八通、三日震動、八日兌行、 15 九二見龍、和平有明、三五德就、乾體乃成、九三夕惕、 20 虧折神符、盛衰漸革、終還其初、巽繼其統、固際操持、 25 九四或躍、進退道危、艮主止進、不得踰時、二十三日、 30 典守弦期、九五飛龍、天位加喜、六五坤承、結括終始、 35 韞養眾子、世為類母、上九亢龍、戰德于野、用九翩翩、 40 為道規矩、陽數已訖、訖則復起、推情合性、轉而相與。

【第五十節】

循環璇璣、昇降上下、周流六爻、難可察覩、 5 故無常位、為易宗祖。

【第五十一節】

朔旦為復、陽氣始通、出入無疾、立表微剛、 5 黃鍾建子、兆乃滋彰、播施柔暖、黎蒸得常、臨爐施條、 10 開路正光、光耀漸進、日以益長、丑之大呂、結正低昂、 15 仰以成泰、剛柔並隆、陰陽交接、小往大來、輻輳於寅、 20 運而趨時、漸歷大壯、俠列卯門、榆莢墮落、還歸本根、 25 刑德相負、晝夜始分、夬陰以退、陽昇而前、洗濯羽翮、 30 振索宿塵、乾健盛明、廣被四鄰、陽終於巳、中而相干、 35 姤始紀序、履霜最先、井底寒泉、午為蕤賓、賓伏於陰、 40 陰為主人、遯去世位、收斂其精、懷德俟時、棲遲昧冥、 45 否塞不通、萌者不生、陰伸陽屈、沒陽姓名、觀其權量、 50 察仲秋情、任畜微稚、老枯復榮、薺麥芽蘗、因冒以生、 55 剝爛肢體、消滅其形、化氣既竭、

亡失至神、道窮則返、60 歸乎坤元、恒順地理、承天布宣、玄幽遠
眇、隔閡相連、65 應度育種、陰陽之元、寥廓恍惚、莫知其端、先迷
失軌、70 後為主君。

【第五十二節】

無平不陂、道之自然、變易更盛、消息相因、5 終坤復始、如循連
環、帝王承御、千載常存。

【第五十三節】

將欲養性、延命卻期、審思後末、當慮其先、5 人所稟軀、體本一
無、元精雲布、因氣託初、陰陽為度、10 魂魄所居、陽神日魂、陰神
月魄、魂之與魄、互為室宅。

【第五十四節】

性主處內、立置鄞鄂、情主營外、築垣城郭、5 城郭完全、人物乃
安、爰斯之時、情合乾坤。

【第五十五節】

乾動而直、氣布精流、坤靜而翕、為道舍廬、5 剛施而退、柔化以
滋、九還七返、八歸六居、男白女赤、10 金火相拘、則水定火、五行
之初、上善若水、清而無瑕、15 道之形象、真一難圖、變而分布、各
自獨居。

【第五十六節】

類如雞子、白黑相符、縱橫一寸、以為始初、5 四肢五臟、筋骨乃
俱、彌歷十月、脫出其胞、骨弱可卷、10 肉滑若鉛。

【第五十七節】

陽燧以取火、非日不生光、方諸非星月、安能得水漿、5 二氣玄且
遠、感化尚相通、何況近存身、切在於心胸、陰陽配日月、10 水火為
效徵。

【第五十八節】

耳目口三寶、閉塞勿發通、真人潛深淵、浮游守規中、 5 旋曲以視
聽、開闔皆合同、為己之樞轄、動靜不竭窮、離氣內營衛、 10 坎乃不
用聰、兌合不以談、希言順鴻濛。

【第五十九節】

三者既關鍵、緩體處空房、委志歸虛無、無念以為常、 5 證難以推
移、心專不縱橫、寢寐神相抱、覺悟候存亡、顏色浸以潤、 10 骨節益
堅強、排卻衆陰邪、然後立正陽。

【第六十節】

修之不輟休、庶氣雲雨行、淫淫若春澤、液液象解冰、 5 從頭流達
足、究竟復上昇、往來洞無極、怫怫被容中、反者道之驗、 10 弱者德
之柄、耕耘宿汙穢、細微得調暢、濁者清之路、昏久則昭明。

【第六十一節】

世人好小術、不審道淺深、棄正從邪徑、欲速闕不通、 5 猶盲不任
杖、聾者聽商宮、沒水捕雉兔、登山索魚龍、植麥欲穫黍、 10 運規以
求方、竭力勞精神、終年無見功、欲知伏食法、事約而不繁。

【第六十二節】

太陽流珠、常欲去人、卒得金華、轉而相因、 5 化為白液、凝而至
堅、金華先唱、有頃之間、解化為水、 10 馬齒琅玕、陽乃往和、情性
自然、迫促時陰、拘畜禁門、 15 慈母育養、孝子報恩、嚴父施令、教
敕子孫。

【第六十三節】

五行錯旺、相據以生、火性銷金、金伐木榮、 5 三五與一、天地至
精、可以口訣、難以書傳。

【第六十四節】

子當右轉、午乃東旋、卯酉界隔、主客二名、 5 龍呼於虎、虎吸龍精、兩相飲食、俱相貪便、遂相銜嚥、 10 咀嚼相吞、熒惑守西、太白經天、殺氣所臨、何有不傾、 15 貍犬守鼠、鳥雀畏鸇、各得其功、何敢有聲。

【第六十五節】

不得其理、難以妄言、竭殫家產、妻子飢貧、 5 自古及今、好者億人、訖不諧遇、希有能成、廣求名藥、 10 與道乖殊。

【第六十六節】

如審遭逢、覩其端緒、以類相況、揆物終始、 5 五行相剋、更為父母、母含滋液、父主稟與、凝精流形、 10 金石不朽、審專不泄、得為成道。

【第六十七節】

立竿見影、呼谷傳響、豈不靈哉、天地至象、 5 若以野葛一寸、巴豆一兩、入喉輒僵、不得俯仰、當此之時、 10 周文揲蓍、孔子占象、扁鵲操鍼、巫咸扣鼓、安能令甦、復起馳走。

【第六十八節】

河上姹女、靈而最神、得火則飛、不見埃塵、 5 鬼隱龍匿、莫知所存、將欲制之、黃芽為根。

【第六十九節】

物無陰陽、違天背元、牝雞自卵、其雛不全、 5 夫何故乎、配合未連、三五不交、剛柔離分、施化之精、 10 天地自然、火動炎上、水流潤下、非有師導、使其然也、 15 資始統正、不可復改、觀夫雌雄、交媾之時、剛柔相結、 20 而不可解、得其節符、非有工巧、以制御之、男生而伏、 25 女偃其軀、裹乎胞胎、受氣元初、非徒生時、著而見

之、 30 及其死也、亦復效之、此非父母、教令其然、本在交媾、 35
定置始先。

【第七十節】

坎男為月、離女為日、日以施德、月以舒光、 5 月受日化、體不虧
傷、陽失其契、陰侵其明、晦朔薄蝕、 10 掩冒相傾、陽消其形、陰凌
災生、男女相胥、含吐以滋、 15 雌雄錯雜、以類相求。

【第七十一節】

金化為水、水性周章、火化為土、水不得行、 5 男動外施、女靜內
藏、溢度過節、為女所拘、魄以鈐魂、 10 不得淫奢、不寒不暑、進退
合時、各得其和、俱吐證符。

【第七十二節】

丹砂木精、得金乃并、金水合處、木火為侶、 5 四者混沌、列為龍
虎、龍陽數奇、虎陰數偶、肝青為父、 10 肺白為母、腎黑為子、離赤
為女、脾黃為祖、子五行始、 15 三物一家、都歸戊己。

【第七十三節】

剛柔迭興、更歷分部、龍西虎東、建緯卯酉、 5 刑德並會、相見歡
喜、刑主伏殺、德主生起、二月榆落、 10 魁臨於卯、八月麥生、天罡
據酉、子南午北、互為綱紀、 15 一九之數、終而復始、含元虛危、播
精於子。

【第七十四節】

關關雎鳩、在河之洲、窈窕淑女、君子好逑、 5 雄不獨處、雌不孤
居、玄武龜蛇、蟠糾相扶、以明牝牡、 10 竟當相須、假使二女共室、
顏色甚姝、蘇秦通言、張儀合媒、 15 發辯利舌、奮舒美辭、推心調
諧、合為夫妻、弊髮腐齒、 20 終不相知、若藥物非種、名類不同、分
劑參差、失其綱紀、 25 雖黃帝臨爐、太一執火、八公擣鍊、淮南調
合、立宇崇壇、 30 玉為階陛、麟脯鳳脂、把籍長跪、禱祝神祇、請哀

諸鬼、 35 沐浴齋戒、冀有所望、亦猶和膠補釜、以硇塗瘡、去冷加冰、 40 除熱用湯、飛龜舞蛇、愈見乖張。

下篇

【第七十五節】

惟昔聖賢、懷玄抱真、伏鍊九鼎、化迹隱淪、 5 含精養神、通德三光、津液腠理、筋骨緻堅、衆邪辟除、 10 正氣長存、累積長久、變形而仙。

【第七十六節】

憂憫後生、好道之倫、隨傍風采、指畫古文、 5 著為圖籍、開示後昆、露見枝條、隱藏本根、託號諸名、 10 覆謬衆文、學者得之、輣櫝終身、子繼父業、孫踵祖先、 15 傳世迷惑、竟無見聞、遂使宦者不仕、農夫失耘、商人棄貨、 20 志士家貧、吾甚傷之、定錄此文、字約易思、事省不繁、 25 披列其條、核實可觀、分兩有數、因而相循、故為亂辭、 30 孔竅其門、智者審思、用意參焉。

【第七十七節】

法象莫大乎天地兮、玄溝數萬里、河鼓臨星紀兮、人民皆驚駭、 5 晷影妄前卻兮、九年被凶咎、皇上覽視之兮、王者退自改、關鍵有低昂兮、 10 害氣遂奔走、江淮之枯竭兮、水流注於海、天地之雌雄兮、徘徊子與午、 15 寅申陰陽祖兮、出入復終始、循斗而招搖兮、執衡定元紀。

【第七十八節】

昇熬於甑山兮、炎火張設下、白虎導唱前兮、蒼液和於後、 5 朱雀翱翔戲兮、飛揚色五彩、遭遇羅網施兮、壓之不得舉、嗷嗷聲甚悲兮、 10 嬰兒之慕母、顛倒就湯鑊兮、摧折傷毛羽、漏刻未過半兮、魚鱗狎鬣起、 15 五色象炫燿兮、變化無常主、滴滴鼎沸馳兮、暴涌不休止、接連重疊累兮、 20 犬牙相錯距、形似仲冬冰兮、琅玕吐鍾乳、崔嵬而雜廁兮、交積相支拄。

【第七十九節】

陰陽得其配兮、淡薄而相守、青龍處房六兮、春華震東卯、 5 白虎在
昴七兮、秋芒兌西酉、朱雀在張二兮、正陽離南午、三者俱來朝兮、
10 家屬為親侶、本之但二物兮、末而為三五、三五并與一兮、都集歸
二所、 15 治之如上科兮、日數亦取甫、先白而後黃兮、赤黑達表裏、
名曰第一鼎兮、 20 食如大黍米。

【第八十節】

自然之所為兮、非有邪偽道、山澤氣相蒸兮、興雲而為雨、 5 泥竭遂
成塵兮、火滅化為土、若蘗染為黃兮、似藍成綠組、皮革煮成膠兮、
10 麴蘗化為酒、同類易施工兮、非種難為巧。

【第八十一節】

惟斯之妙術兮、審諦不誑語、傳於億世後兮、昭然自可考、 5 煥若星
經漢兮、昺如水宗海、思之務令熟兮、反覆視上下、千周燦彬彬兮、
10 萬遍將可覩、神明或告人兮、心靈乍自悟、探端索其緒兮、必得其
門戶、 15 天道無適莫兮、常傳於賢者。

【第八十二節】

圓三五、寸一分、口四八、兩寸脣、 5 長尺二、厚薄均、腹齊三、坐
垂溫、陰在上、 10 陽下奔、首尾武、中間文、始七十、終三旬、 15
二百六、善調勻、陰火白、黃芽鉛、兩七聚、 20 輔翼人、瞻理腦、定
昇玄、子處中、得安存、 25 來去遊、不出門、漸成大、情性純、卻歸
一、 30 還本原、善愛敬、如君臣、至一周、甚辛勤、 35 密防護、莫
迷昏、途路遠、復幽玄、若達此、 40 會乾坤、刀圭霑、淨魄魂、得長
生、居仙村、 45 樂道者、尋其根、審五行、定銖分、諦思之、 50 不
須論、深藏守、莫傳文、御白鶴、駕龍鱗、 55 遊太虛、謁仙君、錄天
圖、號真人。

【第八十三節】

參同契者、敷陳梗概、不能純一、泛濫而説、 5 纖微未備、闕略髣
髴、今更撰錄、補塞遺脱、潤色幽深、 10 鉤援相逮、旨意等齊、所趣
不悖、故復作此、命五相類、 15 則大易之情性盡矣。

乙浮右	丁文火	己物	辛世銀	癸真鉛	五位相得
三木	二火	五土	四金	一水	
甲沈左	丙武火	戊藥	庚世金	壬真汞	而各有合

【第八十四節】

大易情性、各如其度、黃老用究、較而可御、 5 爐火之事、真有所
據、三道由一、俱出徑路、枝莖華葉、 10 果實垂布、正在根株、不失
其素、誠心所言、審而不誤。

【第八十五節】

象彼仲冬節、竹木皆摧傷、佐陽詰賈旅、人君深自藏、 5 象時順節
令、閉口不用談、天道甚浩廣、太玄無形容、虛寂不可覩、 10 匡郭以
消亡、謬誤失事緒、言還自敗傷、別序斯四象、以曉後生盲。

【第八十六節】

會稽鄙夫、幽谷朽生、挾懷樸素、不樂權榮、 5 棲遲僻陋、忽略利
名、執守恬淡、希時安寧、晏然閑居、 10 乃撰斯文、歌敍大易、三聖
遺言、察其旨趣、一統共倫。

【第八十七節】

務在順理、宣燿精神、神化流通、四海和平、 5 表以為曆、萬世可
循、序以御政、行之不煩、引內養性、 10 黃老自然、含德之厚、歸根
返元、近在我心、不離己身、 15 抱一毋舍、可以長存、配以伏食、雄
雌設陳、挺除武都、 20 八石棄捐、審用成物、世俗所珍、羅列三條、
枝莖相連、 25 同出異名、皆由一門、非徒累句、諧偶斯文、殆有其
真、 30 礫硌可觀、使予敷偽、卻被贅愆、命參同契、微覽其端、 35
辭寡意大、後嗣宜遵。

【第八十八節】

委時去害、依託丘山、循遊寥廓、與鬼為鄰、₅化形而仙、淪寂無
聲、百世而下、遨遊人間、敷陳羽翮、₁₀東西南傾、湯遭厄際、水旱
隔并、柯葉萎黃、失其華榮、₁₅吉人相乘負、安穩可長生。

Index of Main Subjects

References are to section numbers. The capitalization of certain words is different in the translation.

1 (*yi* 一), 22
3 and 5 (*sanwu* 三五), *see* Three Fives
6 (*liu* 六), 7 (*qi* 七), 8 (*ba* 八), and 9 (*jiu* 九), 55

abyss (*yuan* 淵), 24, 58
altar (*yan* 壇), 26, 74
alum (*fan* 礬), 36
Armil (*ji* 璣), 50
artisan (*gong* 工), 2
Assistant (*fu* 輔), 15
August Ultimate (*huangji* 皇極), 47
autumn (*qiu* 秋), 3, 51, 79; *see also* four seasons
Autumn Stone (*qiushi* 秋石), 42

badou 巴豆 (croton seeds), 67
Being (*you* 有), *see* Non-being and Being
"being of the same kind" (*tonglei* 同類), 35, 36, 80
bellows and nozzles (*tuoyue* 橐籥), 1
bells and pitch-pipes (*zhonglü* 鍾律), 12; *see also* pitch-pipes
Bian Que 扁鵲, 67
bing 丙 (celestial stem), 13
bit and bridle (*xianpei* 銜轡), 2; *see also* chariot
black (*hei* 黑), 7, 22, 56, 72, 79
Bo ☶, 51
Book of Changes (Yi[jing] 易[經]), 9, 28, 29, 83, 84, 86; *see also* Judgements; Sequence; Statements on the Lines; Ten Wings
brain (*nao* 腦), 82
Breath, or breaths (*qi* 氣), 13, 21, 39, 40, 47, 51, 57, 58, 60, 64, 69, 75, 77, 80; ingestion of, 26; *see also* Essence and Breath; Spirit and Breath; Yang Breath

Glossary of Chinese Characters

Bagong 八公

baji 八極 (eight directions)

bajie 八節 (eight "nodal days")

Bao Xi 包犠

Baopu zi 抱朴子 (Book of the Master Who Embraces Spontaneous Nature)

baoyi 抱一 ("embracing Unity")

bi 畢 ("Net")

biao 杓 (or 標) ("Ladle," of the Northern Dipper)

bigua 辟卦 ("sovereign hexagrams")

bing 柄 ("Handle," of the Northern Dipper)

bishu 祕書 ("secret writings")

bugang 步罡 ("pacing the celestial net")

"Busai yituo" 補塞遺脱 ("Filling Lacunae")

cang 蒼 (hue of green)

Cantong qi 參同契 (The Seal of the Unity of the Three)

Cantong qi Lüli zhi 參同契律曆志 (? "Monograph on the Pitch-pipes and the Calendar according to the *Cantong qi*")

Cantong zhizhi 參同直指 (Straightforward Directions on the *Cantong qi*)

Caodong 曹洞

Chen Xianwei 陳顯微 (?–after 1254)

Chen Zhixu 陳致虛 (1290–ca. 1368)

Cheng Tang 成湯

chengshu 成數 ("accomplishment numbers")

chi 齒 (tooth)

chiqi 赤氣 ("red breath")

Chizi 赤子 (Red Child)

Chu Huagu 儲華谷 (i.e., Chu Yong)

Chu Yong 儲泳 (fl. ca. 1230)

Chuci 楚辭 (Songs of Chu)

chunyang 純陽 (Pure Yang)

Chunyu Shutong 淳于叔通

Chunyu Zhen 淳于斟 (i.e., Chunyu Shutong)

congshi 從事 ("retainer")

Danhu jing 丹壺經 (Scripture of the Cinnabar Pot; or Scripture of the Elixir's Pot)

dansha 丹砂 ("cinnabar sand")

dantian 丹田 (Cinnabar Field)

dao 刀 ("blade, spatula")

Daode jing 道德經 (Book of the Way and Its Virtue)

daogui 刀圭 ("knife-point")

daren 大人 ("great man")

dashu 大暑 ("Great Heat")

daxue 大雪 ("Great Snow")

diandao 顛倒 ("inversion")

"Dingqi ge" 鼎器歌 ("Song of the Tripod")

dizhi 地支 (earthly branches)

Dong Dening 董德寧 (fl. 1787–88)

dongxu 洞虛 ("cavernous emptiness")

Du Yicheng 杜一誠 (fl. 1517)

du 度 (spans of space)

duliang 度量 ("attitude")

dumai 督脈 (Control vessel)

erba 二八 ("two eights," lit., "two times 8")

fa 罰 ("punishment")

fanfu 反覆 ("to go back and forth," "to go to and fro")

fang 房 ("Room")

fangshi 方士 ("master of the methods")

fen 分 ("inch")

Fengdu 酆都

Fenghui 豐惠

fenzhu 分銖 ("inches and scruples")

fu 符 ("symbolon, tally, token")

fu 輔 (Assistant)

Fu Xi 伏羲

fushi 伏食 (""preserving and ingesting"")

gangji 綱紀 ("guiding thread")

gangniu 綱紐 ("strings")

Ge Hong 葛洪 (283–243)

guan 灌 ("to irrigate")

guan 觀 ("contemplation")

guang 光 ("radiance")

guangui 官鬼 ("demon")

gui 圭 (the "two Soils")

gui 鬼 ("demon")

guigen 歸根 ("going back to the root")

guiju 規矩 ("compass and square," "rules")

Guwen cantong qi 古文參同契 (Ancient Text of the *Cantong qi*)

Guwen longhu jing 古文龍虎經 (Ancient Text of the Scripture of the Dragon and Tiger)

Guwen longhu jing 古文龍虎經 (Ancient Text of the Scripture of the Dragon and Tiger)

Han Wei congshu 漢魏叢書 (Collected Works of the Han and the Wei Dynasties)

hantu 含吐 ("inhale and exhale"; "nurture"; "harmonize")

heche 河車 (River Chariot)

hemei 合媒 ("interceder")

heng 橫 ("horizontal")

heng 衡 (Scale)

heshang chanü 河上姹女 (Lovely Maid of the River)

Hetu 河圖 (Chart of the Yellow River)

"Hongfan" 洪範 ("Great Plan")

hongmeng 鴻濛 ("boundless")

hongri 汞日 ("Mercurial Sun")

hou 候 ("periods")

hou 後 ("after")

houmo 後末 "end")

houtian 後天 ("posterior to Heaven," "postcelestial")

hua 化 ("to transform"; "to generate")

Huainan zi 淮南子 (Master of Huainan)

Huan, Emperor 桓帝 (r. 146–167)

huandan 還丹 (Reverted Elixir)

huangji 皇極 ("August Ultimate")

huangjing 黃精 ("yellow essence")

Huangting jing 黃庭經 (Scripture of the Yellow Court)

huangya 黃芽 (Yellow Sprout)

huangyu 黃輿 (Yellow Carriage)

huangzhong 黃中 (Yellow Center)

huaqi 化氣 ("transmuting Breath")

hufen 胡粉 (white lead, ceruse)

Huiche zi 慧車子

huiguang neizhao 迴光內照 ("circulating the light to illuminate within")

hun 魂 (celestial soul)

huohou 火候 ("fire times")

huoji 火記 ("records of fire")

huyi 狐疑 (lit., "to doubt like a fox")

ji 璣 (Armil)

Jiang Yan 江淹 (444–505)

Jiangnan 江南

jie 節 ("node" or "sector")

jiejie 解結 ("untie the knots")

jieqi 節氣 ("nodal breaths")

jin 斤 (pound)

jin 金 (Metal; Gold)

Jinbi jing 金碧經 (Scripture on Gold and Jade)

Jindan jinbi qiantong jue 金丹金碧潛通訣 (Instructions on Gold and Jade for Piercing the Unseen by the Golden Elixir) *jindan zhi dao* 金丹之道 (Way of the Golden Elixir)

Jing Fang 京方 (77–37 BCE)

jing 精 (essence)

jing 經 ("warp")

"Jing" 經 ("Canon")

jinhua 金華 (Golden Flower)

jinjing 金精 ("essence of Metal")

jinli 金醴 (Golden Nectar)

jinmen 禁門 ("Forbidden gates")

jinsha 金砂 ("Golden Sand," or "Metal Sand")

jinye 金液 (Golden Liquor)

jiren 吉人 ("good-natured men")

jiudan 九丹 (Nine Elixirs)

jiuding dan 九鼎丹 (Elixirs of the Nine Tripods)

jiudu 九都 ("nine capitals")

jiufu 九府 (Nine Palaces)

jiuqian yishen 九淺一深 ("nine shallow and one deep")

jiuzhong 九重 ("nine layers")

ke 刻 ("notches")

Kuaiguo 鄶國

Kuaiji 會稽

kuangguo 匡郭 ("inner and outer walls")

kui 魁 ("Head," of the Northern Dipper)

langgan 琅玕 (a precious stone)

langgan 闌干 ("crosswise, diagonal")

"Laojun ge" 老君歌 ("Song of Lord Lao")

Laozi zhongjing 老子中經 (Central Scripture of Laozi)

lei 類 ("kind, category")

Li Dingzuo 李鼎祚 (Tang dynasty)

Li Guangdi 李光地 (1642–1718)

Li Shixu 黎世序 (1773–1824)

li 禮 ("rites")

liang 兩 (ounce)

liangyi 兩儀 ("two principles")

liaokuo 寥廓 ("vast and broad," "the Unbounded")

libiao 立表 (gnomon)

Ling, Emperor 靈帝 (r. 168–189)

Longhu jing 龍虎經 (Scripture of the Dragon and Tiger)

Lingbao 靈寶 (Numinous Treasure)

liquan 醴泉 (Fount of Nectar)

Lisao 離騷 (Encountering Sorrow)

Liu An 劉安 (179?–122)

liu jia 六甲 (six *jia*)

Liu Yan 劉演 (Six Dynasties?)

Liu Yiming 劉一明 (1734–1821)

Liu Zhigu 劉知古 (fl. ca. 750)

liuxing 流形 ("flowing into the form")

liuzhu 流珠 (Flowing Pearl)

lizang 歷臟 ("passing through the viscera")

Longhu jing 龍虎經 (Scripture of the Dragon and Tiger)

Lu Xixing 陸西星 (1520–1601 or 1606)

lü 律 (pitch-pipes)

"Luanci" 亂辭 ("Epilogue")

luchen 陸沈 ("sinking into the ground")

Luguo 魯國

lüli 律曆 ("pitch-pipes and calendar")

luoluo 礫硌 ("solid as stone")

Luoshu 洛書 (Writ of the Luo River)

mao 昴 (Pleiades)

ming 命 ("existence"; "vital force")

mingtang 明堂 (Hall of Light)

Minshan jing 岷山經 (Scripture of Mount Min)

muyu 沐浴 ("ablutions")

najia 納甲 (Matching Stems)

nei 內 ("inner")

neishi 內視 ("inner observation")

neizhao 內照 ("to illuminate within")

ni 擬 ("observe")

ning 凝 ("coagulation")

niwan 泥丸 (Muddy Pellet)

Pan Gu 盤古

Peng Haogu 彭好古 (fl. 1586–99)

Peng Xiao 彭曉 (?–955)

Penghu 蓬壺
Penglai 蓬萊
pian 篇 (a piece of writing)
ping 平 ("level")
po 魄 (earthly soul)
pusu 樸素 ("plainness and
   simplicity")
qi 器 ("instrument")
qi 契 ("token, pledge seal";
   "contract")
qi 期 (terms of time)
qi 氣 (Breath)
Qian zuodu 乾鑿度 (Opening the Way
   to the Understanding of Qian ☰)
Qin Gao 琴高
qing 情 (individual "qualities"; temperament, feelings, emotions, etc.)
qinglong 青龍 ("green dragon")
Qingzhou 青州
Qiu Zhao'ao 仇兆鰲 (1638–1713)
qiushi 秋石 (Autumn Stone)
qushen 屈伸 ("bend and stretch")
quzhe 曲折 ("winding courses,"
   "crouchings and bendings")
ren 仁 (humanity)
renmai 任脈 (Function vessel)
renwu 人物 ("people," "people and
   things")
richen 日辰 ("markers of time")
ru 儒 ("scholars")
Ruan Dengbing 阮登炳 (fl. 1284)
"San xianglei" 三相類 ("The Three
   Categories")
sanbao 三寶 ("three treasures")
santai 三台 (Three Terraces)
sanwu 三五 ("3 and 5," "three fives")
saoti 騷體 (a prosodic style)
sha 砂 ("sand")
shang 上 ("above")
shang 賞 ("reward")
shangde 上德 ("superior virtue")
Shangqing 上清 (Highest Clarity)
Shangshu zhonghou 尚書中候 (Prognostications Based on the *Book of
   Documents*)
Shangyu 上虞
shaoyang 少陽 ("minor Yang")
shaoyao 招搖 (Rising Glimmer)
shaoyin 少陰 ("minor Yin")
shaqi 殺氣 ("life-taking breath")
shen 審 ("to examine")
shen 神 (Spirit)
shen 身 ("living being")
shengqi 生氣 ("life-giving breath")
shengshu 生數 ("generation
   numbers")
shenming 神明 (Numinous Light)
Shenxian zhuan 神仙傳 (Biographies
   of the Divine Immortals)
shi 施 ("giving forth")
shi 時 ("double hours")
shi'er xiaoxi 十二消息 (Twelve-stage
   Ebb and Flow)
Shitou Xiqian 石頭希遷 (700–91)
Shiyi 釋疑 (Explication of Doubtful
   Points)
"Shiyi" 十翼 (Ten Wings; or Ten Appendixes)
shou guizhong 守規中 ("keeping to
   the compass")
shoufu 受符 ("receive the tally")
shu 術 ("art")
shuangjiang 霜降 (Descent of Frost)
shuiqi 水氣 (Breath of Water)
shuiyin 水銀 (quicksilver, lit., "water
   silver")
shuji 樞機 ("pivot, mainspring, vital
   point")
"Shuogua" 説卦 (Explanation of the
   Trigrams)
Shuowen jiezi 説文解字 (Elucidations
   on the Signs and Explications of
   the Graphs)
shushu 數術 ("arts of the numbers")
sifu 四輔 (Four Assistants)
sihai 四海 ("Four Seas")
silin 四鄰 ("four neighborhoods")
siming 司命 (Controller of Destinies)

siqi 四七, "four [times] seven"

sitong 四通 ("everywhere")

sui 隨 ("to follow")

suiyue 歲月 ("years and months")

tai 台 (Terrace)

taibai 太白 (Great White)

Taiping guangji 太平廣記 (Extended Collection of Records of the Taiping xingguo Reign Period)

Taiqing 太清 (Great Clarity)

taixuan 太玄 (Great Mystery)

taiyang 太陽 ("great Yang")

taiyin 太陰 ("great Yin")

tanghuo 湯鑊 ("boiling pot")

Tao Hongjing 陶弘景 (456–536)

ti 體 ("body"; "substantive basis")

tiandan 恬淡 ("calm and tranquility")

tiandi 天帝 (Celestial Emperor)

tianfu 天符 ("tally of Heaven")

tiangan 天干 (celestial stems)

tiangang 天罡 (Celestial Net)

tiangu 天鼓 (Heaven's Drum)

tianxin 天心 (Heart of Heaven)

tonglei 同類 ("to be of the same kind")

tongli 通理 ("to comprehend the principle(s)", "to spread through the veining")

tongyan 通言 ("mediator")

"Tuan" 彖 (Judgements)

"Tuanzhuan" 彖傳 (Commentary on the Judgements)

tugu naxin 吐古納新 ("exhaling the old and inhaling the new [breath]")

tuidu 推度 ("inferring the rules")

tupo 兔魄 ("hare")

Wang Fu 汪紱 (1692–1759)

Wang Jiachun 王家春 (fl. 1591?)

Wang Jie 王吉 (Han dynasty)

Wang Wenlu 王文祿 (1503–86)

wanwu 萬物 ("ten thousand things")

Wei Boyang 魏伯陽

Wei Boyang neijing 魏伯陽內經 (Inner Scripture of Wei Boyang)

wei zhi 為之 ("doing")

wei 緯 ("horizontal")

weihou 緯候 ("weft" and prognostication texts)

weishu 緯書 ("weft texts," apocrypha)

wenchang 文昌 (Literary Glory)

wenhuo 文火 ("civil fire")

"Wenyan zhuan" 文言傳 (Commentary on the Words of the Text)

Wu 吳

Wu Xian 巫咸

Wu xianglei 五相類 (The Five Categories)

Wudu 武都

wuhuo 武火 ("martial fire")

wuwei 無為 ("non-doing")

wuxing 五行 (five agents)

Wuxing xianglei 五行相類 (The Categories of the Five Agents)

wuyou 無憂 ("undistraught, without grief")

wuzang 五臟 (five viscera)

Wuzhen pian 悟真篇 (Awakening to Reality)

xiade 下德 ("inferior virtue")

xian 仙 ("to become immortal," "to transcend"))

xian 先 ("before")

xianchang 先唱 ("to be the first to sing," "to take the lead")

xiang 象 ("image," "symbolic form")

xiangke 相剋 ("conquest" sequence)

xiangsheng 相生 ("generation" sequence)

"Xiangzhuan" 象傳 (Commentary on the Images)

xiantian 先天 ("prior to Heaven," "precelestial")

xiantian yiqi 先天一氣 (One Breath prior to Heaven)

xiaoshu 小術 ("minor arts")

xiaoxue 小雪 ("Great Heat")

"Xici" 繫辭 (Appended Sayings)

xiehou 邂逅 ("unexpected

Zhouyi cantong qi 周易參同契 (The Seal of the Unity of the Three, in Accordance with the *Book of Changes*)

Zhouyi cantong qi dingqi ge mingjing tu 周易參同契鼎器歌明鏡圖 (The "Song of the Tripod" and the "Chart of the Bright Mirror" of the *Cantong qi*)

Zhouyi cantong qi fahui 周易參同契發揮 (Elucidation of the *Cantong qi*)

Zhouyi cantong qi fenzhang tong zhenyi 周易參同契分章通真義 (True Meaning of the *Cantong qi*, with a Subdivision into Sections)

Zhouyi cantong qi jie 周易參同契解 (Explication of the *Cantong qi*)

Zhouyi cantong qi kaoyi 周易參同契考異 (Investigation of Discrepan-cies in the *Cantong qi*)

Zhouyi cantong qi zhu 周易參同契注 (Commentary to the *Cantong qi*)

Zhouyi cantong qi zhujie 周易參同契注解 (Commentary and Explica-tion of the *Cantong qi*)

Zhouyi jijie 周易集解 (Collected Ex-plications of the *Book of Changes*)

zhu 銖 ("scruple")

"Zhu" 注 ("Commentary")

Zhu Xi 朱熹 (1130–1200)

Zhu Yuanyu 朱元育 (fl. 1657–69)

zhun 準 ("level")

zhunni 準擬 ("abide by, conform to")

zhusha 朱砂 ("vermilion sand")

"Zixu qihou" 自敍啟後 ("Author's Postface: My Bequest")

zong 縱 ("vertical")

zongheng jia 縱橫家 (School of the Strategists)

Works Quoted

Sources

Baopu zi neipian 抱朴子內篇 [Inner Chapters of the Book of the Master Who Embraces Spontaneous Nature]. Ge Hong 葛洪, ca. 317, revised ca. 330. Ed. by Wang Ming 王明, *Baopu zi neipian jiaoshi* 抱朴子內篇校釋 (second revised edition, Beijing: Zhonghua shuju, 1985).

Cantong zhizhi 參同直指 [Straightforward Directions on the *Cantong qi*], Liu Yiming 劉一明, 1799. In *Daoshu shi'er zhong* 道書十二種 (Twelve Books on the Dao). Jiangdong shuju 江東書局 ed., 1913. Repr. Taipei: Xinwenfeng chubanshe, 1975.

Chuci 楚辭 [Songs of Chu]. Fourth to first centuries BCE. Sibu beiyao 四部備要 ed.

Chunqiu 春秋 [Springs and Autumns]. Ca. fifth century BCE. Text in *Chunqiu Zuozhuan zhuzi suoyin* 春秋左轉逐字索引 (*A Concordance to the Chunqiu Zuozhuan*). Hong Kong: Shangwu yinshuguan, 1995.

Daode jing 道德經 [Book of the Way and its Virtue]. Fourth to third centuries BCE (?). Ed. by Zhu Qianzhi 朱謙之, *Laozi jiaoshi* 老子校釋 (Beijing: Zhonghua shuju, 1984).

Dongxuan lingbao zhenling weiye tu 洞玄靈寶真靈位業圖 [Chart of the Ranks and Functions of the Perfected Numinous Beings of the Numinous Treasure of the Cavern Mystery]. Tao Hongjing 陶弘景 (456–536); edited by Lüqiu Fangyuan 閭丘方遠 (?–902). CT 167.

Fengsu tongyi 風俗通義 [Comprehensive Meaning of Customs and Mores]. Ying Shao 應劭, ca. 200. Text in *Fengsu tongyi zhuzi suoyin* 風俗通義逐字索引 (*A Concordance to the Fengsutongyi*). Hong Kong: Shangwu yinshuguan, 1996.

Guanzi 管子 [Book of Guan Zhong]. Prob. fifth to first centuries BCE. Text in *Guanzi zhuzi suoyin* 管子逐字索引 (*A Concordance to the Guanzi*). Hong Kong: Shangwu yinshuguan, 2001.

Guben Zhouyi cantong qi jizhu 古本周易參同契集注 [Collected Commentaries on the Ancient Version of the *Cantong qi*]. Qiu Zhao'ao 仇兆鰲, 1704. Hecheng zhai 合成齋 ed., 1873. Repr. in the series *Guben qigong jingdian congshu* 古本气功经典丛书 (Beijing: Zhongyi guji chubanshe, 1990).

Hanshu 漢書 [History of the Former Han Dynasty]. Ban Gu 班固 et al., ca. 90 CE. Zhonghua shuju ed. (Beijing, 1962).

Hou Hanshu 後漢書 [History of the Later Han Dynasty]. Fan Ye 范曄 et al., 445. Zhonghua shuju ed. (Beijing, 1965).

Huainan zi 淮南子 [Book of the Master of Huainan]. Liu An 劉安, ca. 139 BCE. Ed. by He Ning 何寧, *Huainan zi jishi* 淮南子集釋 (Beijing: Zhonghua shuju, 1998).

Huangdi neijing, Suwen 黃帝內經素問 [Inner Book of the Yellow Emperor: The Plain Questions]. Originally ca. third-second century BCE. Sibu congkan 四部叢刊 ed.

Huangting neijing jing 黃庭內景經 [Scripture of the Inner Effulgences of the Yellow Court]. Late fourth century. In *Yunji qiqian* 雲笈七籤 (Seven Lots from the Bookcase of the Clouds), Daozang ed., 11–12.27b.

Isho shūsei 緯書集成 [Complete Collection of Weft Texts]. Ed. by Yasui Kōzan 安居香山 and Nakamura Shōhachi 中村璋八. Tokyo: Meitoku shuppansha, 1971–88.

Jiang Wentong jihui zhu 江文通集彙注 [Collected Works of Jiang Yan, with Annotations]. Beijing: Zhonghua Shuju, 1984.

Jingdian shiwen 經典釋文 [Lexicon of Classical Texts]. Lu Deming 陸德明, early seventh century. Baojing tang ed., 1791.

Laozi zhongjing 老子中經 [Central Scripture of Laozi]. Third or fourth century. Daozang, CT 1168.

Liezi 列子 [Book of Master Lie Yukou]. Originally ca. fourth century BCE, received text ca. fourth century CE. Ed. by Yang Bojun 楊伯峻, *Liezi jishi* 列子集釋 (Beijing: Zhonghua shuju, 1979).

Lishi zhenxian tidao tongjian 歷世真仙體道通鑑 [Comprehensive Mirror of True Immortals Who Embodied the Dao through the Ages]. Zhao Daoyi 趙道一, ca. 1294. Daozang, CT 296.

Lunyu 論語 [Confucian Analects]. Fifth to third centuries BCE. Text in *Lunyu yinde* 論語引得 (*A Concordance to the Analects of Confucius*). Peking: Harvard-Yenching Institute, 1940.

Mengzi 孟子 [Book of Master Meng Ko]. Fourth century BCE. Text in *Mengzi yinde* 孟子引得 (*A Concordance to Meng Tzu*). Peking: Harvard-Yenching Institute, 1941.

Riyue xuanshu lun 日月玄樞論 [Essay on the Mysterious Pivot of the Sun and the Moon]. Liu Zhigu 劉知古, ca. 750. In *Daoshu* 道樞 [Pivot of the Dao](Daozang, CT 1017), 26.1a-6b.

Shiji 史記 [Records of the Historian]. Sima Qian 司馬遷, ca 90 BCE. Zhonghua shuju ed. (Beijing, 1985).

Shijing 詩經 [Book of Odes]. Ca. tenth to sixth centuries BCE. Text in *Maoshi yinde* 毛詩引得 (*A Concordance to Shih ching*). Peking: Harvard-Yenching Institute, 1934.

Shujing 書經 [Book of Documents]. Ca. ninth to fourth centuries BCE. Text in *Shisan jing zhushu* 十三經註疏, ed. of 1815.

Shuowen jiezi 説文解字 [Elucidations on the Signs and Explications of the Graphs]. Xu Shen 許慎, 100 CE. Ed. of 1873. Repr. Beijing: Zhonghua shuju, 1972.

Taiping guangji 太平廣記 [Extended Collection of Records of the Taiping xingguo Reign Period]. Li Fang 李昉 et al., 984. Renmin wenxue chubanshe ed. (Beijing, 1959).

Xiaojing 孝經 [Book of Filial Piety]. Probably fourth/third century BCE. Text in *Xiaojing yinde* 孝經引得 (*A Concordance to Hsiao ching*). Peking: Harvard-Yenching Institute, 1950.

Yanshi jiaxun 顏氏家訓 [Family Instructions for the Yan Clan]. Yan Zhitui 顏之推, ca. 589. Sibu congkan 四部叢刊 ed.

Yijing 易經 [Book of Changes]. Original portions ca. ninth century BCE, commentaries and appendixes ca. 350 to 250 BCE. Text in *Zhouyi yinde* 周易引得 (*A Concordance to Yi Ching*). Peking: Harvard-Yenching Institute, 1935.

Yili 儀禮 [Book of Ceremonials]. Originally fifth century BCE (?), present version ca. third/second centuries BCE. Text in *Shisan jing zhushu* 十三經註疏, ed. of 1815.

Zhengao 真誥 [True Revelations]. Tao Hongjing 陶弘景 (456–536). Daozang, CT 1016.

Zhouyi cantong qi fahui 周易參同契發揮 [Elucidation of the *Cantong qi*]. Yu Yan 俞琰, 1284. Daozang ed., CT 1005.

Zhouyi cantong qi fenzhang tong zhenyi 周易參同契分章通真義 [True Meaning of the *Cantong qi*, with a Subdivision into Sections]. Peng Xiao 彭曉, 947. Daozang ed., CT 1002.

Zhouyi cantong qi [kaoyi] 周易參同契考異 [Investigation of Discrepancies in the *Cantong qi*]. Zhu Xi 朱熹, 1197. Daozang ed., CT 1001.

Zhouyi cantong qi shiyi 周易參同契釋疑 [Explication of Doubtful Points in the *Cantong qi*]. Yu Yan, 1284. Daozang ed., CT 1006.

Zhouyi cantong qi zhu 周易參同契注 [Commentary to the *Cantong qi*]. Anonymous, ca. 700. Daozang, CT 1004.

Zhouyi cantong qi zhujie 周易參同契注解 [Commentary and Explication of the *Cantong qi*]. Chen Zhixu 陳致虛, ca. 1330. Jinling shufang 金陵書坊 ed., 1484.

Zhouyi jijie 周易集解 [Collected Explications of the *Book of Changes*]. Li Dingzuo 李鼎祚, Tang dynasty. Congshu jicheng ed.

Zhuangzi 莊子 [Book of Master Zhuang Zhou]. Original portions fourth century BCE, completed in the second century BCE. Ed. by Guo Qingfan 郭慶藩, *Zhuangzi jishi* 莊子集釋 (Beijing: Zhonghua shuju, 1961).

Studies, Translations, and Reference Works

Bertschinger, Richard. *The Secret of Everlasting Life: The First Translation of the Ancient Chinese Text of Immortality*. Shaftesbury, Dorset: Element, 1994.

Chavannes, Édouard. *Les Mémoires historiques de Se-ma Ts'ien*. 5 vols. Paris: Leroux, 1895–1905. Reprint, with an additional sixth volume edited and completed by Paul Demiéville, Max Kaltenmark, and Timoteus Pokora, Paris: Adrien Maisonneuve, 1969.

Chen Guofu 陳國符. "*Zhouyi cantong qi*" 周易參同契. In *Daozang yuanliu xukao* 道藏源流續考 [Further studies on the origins and development of the Taoist Canon], 352–55. Taipei: Mingwen shuju, 1983.

Despeux, Catherine. *Taoïsme et corps humain: Le Xiuzhen tu*. Paris: Guy Trédaniel, 1994.

DeWoskin, Kenneth. *Doctors, Diviners, and Magicians of Ancient China: Biographies of Fang-shih*. New York: Columbia University Press, 1983.

Fang Xu 方煦. "*Zhouyi cantong qi* jiangjie" 周易參同契講解 [An explication of the *Zhouyi cantong qi*]. In Zhejiang sheng qigong kexue yanjiuhui 浙江省氣功科學研究會 and Qigong zazhi bianjibu 「氣功」雜誌編輯部, eds., *Zhongguo qigong si da jingdian jiangjie* 中國氣功四大經典講解 [Explications of four great scriptures of Chinese Qigong], 111–218. Hangzhou: Zhejiang guji chubanshe, 1988.

Fukui Kōjun 福井康順. "A Study of *Chou-i Ts'an-t'ung-ch'i*." *Acta Asiatica* 27 (1974): 19–32.

Graham, A.C. *The Book of Lieh-tzu*. London: John Murray, 1960.

Hanyu dacidian 漢語大詞典 [Great dictionary of the Chinese language]. Ed. by Luo Zhufeng 羅竹風. 13 vols. Shanghai: Cishu chubanshe, 1986–93.

Hawkes, David. *The Songs of the South: An Anthology of Ancient Chinese Poems by Qu Yuan and Other Poets*. Harmondsworth: Penguin Books, 1985.

Kaltenmark, Max. *Le Lie-sien tchouan* 列仙傳 *(Biographies légendaires des Immortels taoïstes de l'antiquité)*. Pékin: Université de Paris, Publications du Centre d'Études Sinologiques de Pékin, 1953.

Larre, Claude. *Le Traité VII du Houai nan tseu: Les esprits légers et subtils animateurs de l'essence*. Taipei, Paris, and Hong Kong: Institut Ricci, 1982.

Le Blanc, Charles, and Mathieu, Rémi, eds. *Huainan zi*. Paris: Gallimard, 2003. [*Philosophes taoïstes*, vol. 2.]

Legge, James. *Confucian Analects, The Great Learning, and The Doctrine of the Mean*. Second revised edition. Oxford: Clarendon Press, 1893. [*The Chinese Classics*, vol. 1.]

Legge, James. *The Sacred Books of China*. Vol. 3. Oxford: Clarendon Press, 1899. [*The Sacred Books of the East*, 3.]

Legge, James. *The Works of Mencius.* Second revised edition. Oxford: Clarendon Press, 1895. [*The Chinese Classics*, vol. 2.]

Major, John. *Heaven and Earth in Early Han Thought: Chapters Three, Four and Five of the Huainanzi.* Albany: State University of New York Press, 1993.

Meng Naichang 孟乃昌. *Zhouyi cantong qi kaobian* 「周易參同契」考辯 [An inquiry into the *Zhouyi cantong qi*]. Shanghai: Shanghai guji chubanshe, 1993.

Ngo Van Xuyet. *Divination, magie et politique dans la Chine ancienne: Essai suivi de la traduction des "Biographies des Magiciens" tirées de l'"Histoire des Han postérieurs."* Paris: Presses Universitaires de France, 1976.

Pregadio, Fabrizio. "Early Daoist Meditation and the Origins of Inner Alchemy." In Benjamin Penny, ed., *Daoism in History: Essays in Honour of Liu Ts'un-yan*, 121–58. London: Routledge, 2006.

Pregadio, Fabrizio. *Great Clarity: Daoism and Alchemy in Early Medieval China.* Stanford: Stanford University Press, 2006.

Rickett, W. Allyn. *Guanzi: Political, Economic, and Philosophical Essays from Early China.* 2 vols. Princeton: Princeton University Press, 1985, 1998.

Robinet, Isabelle. *Taoist Meditation: The Mao-shan Tradition of Great Purity.* State University of New York Press.

Schipper, Kristofer M., and Franciscus Verellen, eds. *The Taoist Canon: A Historical Companion to the Daozang.* 3 vols. Chicago: Chicago University Press, 2004.

Seidel, Anna. "Imperial Treasures and Taoist Sacraments: Taoist Roots in the Apocrypha." In *Tantric and Taoist Studies in Honour of Rolf A. Stein*, ed. by Michel Strickmann, 2:291–371. Brussels: Institute Belge des Hautes Études Chinoises, 1983.

Seidel, Anna. *La divinisation de Lao Tseu dans le taoïsme des Han.* Paris: École Française d'Extrême-Orient, 1969.

Shaughnessy, Edward L. "I ching (Chou i)." In *Early Chinese Texts: A Bibliographical Guide*, ed. by Michael Loewe, 216–28. Society for the Study of Early China and Institute of East Asian Studies, University of California, 1993.

Sivin, Nathan. "The Theoretical Background of Elixir Alchemy." In Joseph Needham, *Science and Civilisation in China*, vol. V: *Chemistry and Chemical Technology*, part 4: *Spagyrical Discovery and Invention: Apparatus, Theories and Gifts*, 210–305. Cambridge: Cambridge University Press, 1980.

Suzuki Yoshijirō 鈴木由次郎. *Shūeki sandōkei* 周易參同契 [*Zhouyi cantong qi*]. Tokyo: Meitoku shuppansha, 1977.

Teng Ssu-yü. *Family Instructions for the Yan Clan.* Leiden: E.J. Brill, 1968.

Vandermeersch, Léon. *Wangdao ou la Voie Royale: Recherches sur l'esprit des institutions de la Chine archaïque*. 2 vols. Paris: École Française d'Extrême-Orient, 1977–80.

Waley, Arthur. "Notes on Chinese Alchemy." *Bulletin of the School of Oriental Studies* 6 (1930–32): 1–24.

Waley, Arthur. *The Book of Songs*. London: George Allen and Unwin, 1937.

Wang Ming 王明. "*Zhouyi cantong qi* kaozheng" 「周易参同契」考证 [An examination of the *Zhouyi cantong qi*]. In *Daojia he daojiao sixiang yanjiu* 道家和道教思想研究 [Studies on Taoist thought], 241–92. Beijing: Zhongguo shehui kexue chubanshe, 1984.

Ware, James. *Alchemy, Medicine and Religion in the China of A.D. 320: The Nei P'ien of Ko Hung (Pao-p'u tzu)*. Cambridge, MA: MIT Press, 1966.

Watson, Burton. *The Complete Works of Chuang Tzu*. New York: Columbia University Press, 1968.

Wilhelm, Richard. *The I-ching or Book of Changes*. New York: Bollingen, 1950.

Wu Enpu 乌恩浦. "*Zhouyi cantong qi*" 周易参同契. In *Qigong jingdian yizhu* 气功经典译注 [Annotations on Qigong scriptures], 166–263. Changchun shi: Jilin wenshi chubanshe, 1992.

Wu Lu-ch'iang, and Tenney L. Davis. "An Ancient Chinese Treatise on Alchemy Entitled *Ts'an T'ung Ch'i*." *Isis* 18 (1932): 210–89.

Yang Xiaolei 杨效雷. "*Zhouyi cantong qi* yanjiu" 「周易参同契」研究 [A study of the *Zhouyi cantong qi*]. In Huang Minglan 黄明兰 et al., *He Luo wenming lunwenji* 河洛文明论文集 [Collected papers on the "Civilization of the He and Luo Rivers"], 552–83. Zhengzhou: Zhongzhou guji chubanshe, 1993.

Zhou Shiyi [周士一]. *The Kinship of the Three*. Foreword by Joseph Needham. Changsha: Hunan jiaoyu chubanshe, 1988.

Golden Elixir Press

www.goldenelixir.com

Cultivating the Tao: Taoism and Internal Alchemy, by Liu Yiming (1734-1821)
Divided into 26 short chapters, this book provides a comprehensive overview of the basic principles of Taoism and an introduction to Taoist Internal Alchemy, or Neidan, written by one of the most important masters of this tradition. Read more.

Foundations of Internal Alchemy: The Taoist Practice of Neidan, by Wang Mu
A clear description of the Taoist practice of Internal Alchemy, or Neidan, based on the system of the *Wuzhen pian* (Awakening to Reality) and enriched by about two hundred quotations from original Taoist texts.

Awakening to Reality: The "Regulated Verses" of the Wuzhen pian, a Taoist Classic of Internal Alchemy, by Fabrizio Pregadio
The *Wuzhen pian* (Awakening to Reality) is one of the most important and best-known Taoist alchemical texts. Written in the 11th century, it describes in a poetical form several facets of Neidan, or Internal Alchemy.

Commentary on the Mirror for Compounding the Medicine: A Fourteenth-Century Work on Taoist Internal Alchemy, by Wang Jie (?-ca. 1380)
Dating from the 10th century, the *Ruyao jing* (Mirror for Compounding the Medicine) describes Internal Alchemy in 20 short poems of four verses. This book contains the first complete translation of the text and of the commentary by Wang Jie (14th century).

The World Upside Down: Essays on Taoist Internal Alchemy, by Isabelle Robinet
Four essays translated for the first time into English. Their subjects are: (1) The alchemical principle of "inversion"; (2) The devices used by the alchemists to "manifest the authentic and absolute Tao"; (3) The role of numbers in Taoism and in Internal Alchemy; and (4) The meanings of the terms External Elixir and Internal Elixir.

Made in the USA
San Bernardino, CA
19 April 2017